The New Corporate Facts of Life

Rethink Your Business to
Transform Today's Challenges Into
Tomorrow's Profits

DIANA RIVENBURGH

American Management Association

New York • Atlanta • Brussels • Chicago • Mexico City • San Francisco
Shanghai • Tokyo • Toronto • Washington, D.C.

Bulk discounts available. For details visit:
www.amacombooks.org/go/specialsales
Or contact special sales:
Phone: 800-250-5308
E-mail: specialsls@amanet.org
View all the AMACOM titles at: www.amacombooks.org
American Management Association: www.amanet.org

Library of Congress Cataloging-in-Publication Data

Rivenburgh, Diana.
  The new corporate facts of life : rethink your business to transform today's challenges into tomorrow's profits / Diana Rivenburgh. — First Edition.
    pages cm
  Includes bibliographical references and index.
  ISBN-13: 978-0-8144-3304-1
  ISBN-10: 0-8144-3304-9
  1. Leadership. 2. Strategic planning. 3. Organizational change. I. Title.
  HD57.7.R58 2013
  658.4—dc23

2013018270

About AMA
American Management Association (www.amanet.org) is a world leader in talent development, advancing the skills of individuals to drive business success. Our mission is to support the goals of individuals and organizations through a complete range of products and services, including classroom and virtual seminars, webcasts, webinars, podcasts, conferences, corporate and government solutions, business books and research. AMA's approach to improving performance combines experiential learning—learning through doing—with opportunities for ongoing professional growth at every step of one's career journey.

Printing number

10 9 8 7 6 5 4 3 2 1

To Paul:
For always believing in me.

To my nieces and nephews:
May this book inspire you to make a difference in this world.

Contents

Acknowledgments

WRITING A BOOK like *The New Corporate Facts of Life* takes a great deal of time and effort, not to mention extensive research and in-depth conversations with a wide range of people. Some of these people deserve special recognition and my enduring gratitude for contributing their time, talents, knowledge, and perspectives. Their generosity has enriched my life more than I can say.

First, I must acknowledge Paul Schempp for convincing me to go from talking about writing a book to actually writing one. Thank you, Paul, for your support, love, and unwavering faith in me every step of the way.

My literary and publishing team deserves high praise and gratitude for believing in me, and for giving me their honest feedback and unbridled encouragement. I'm immensely grateful to my literary agent, Michael Snell, for taking this journey with me, not just as my agent, but as collaborator, editor, muse, humorist, and friend. As I planted the seeds, Michael watered and tended them, and pulled out no small number of weeds. Many dedicated and talented people on the AMACOM publishing team skillfully shepherded the manuscript through the editorial, design, and production process. I'm especially thankful for the keen eye and expertise of AMACOM's Senior Acquisitions Editor, Bob Nirkind, who saw value in my book proposal and thoughtfully improved the manuscript through more than a few iterations. My thanks also go to marketing consultant Betty Rauch, who helped me find the heart of this book and bring it into the light of day.

Many leaders spent time talking with me, sharing experiences and inviting me into their organizations to learn more. Among those who deserve special thanks: Kurt Kuehn, Scott Wicker, Ross McCullough, Michael Johnson, Patrice André, Paul Nieminen, Dean Foust, Karen Kreager, Michael Hance, and David Gurnsey from UPS; John Brock, Pamela Kimmet and Fred Roselli at Coca-Cola Enterprises; Preben Haaning, Diane Cox and the senior leadership team at Novo Nordisk's U.S. operations in North Carolina; John Gardner at Novelis; Mogens Smed, Tracy Baker, Laura Lee Bocade, Alicia Farrington, Kate Elliot, Liane MacNeil, and Mike Greer from DIRTT; John Wells and Jim Hartzfeld and the inspirational legacy of Ray Anderson at Interface; Steve and Marie Nygren of Serenbe; Paul Snyder and Maury Zimring of InterContinental Hotels Group; John Lyell Clarke III at Clarke; President G.P. "Bud" Peterson, Val Peterson, Marcia Kinstler, Michael Chang, and Cindy Jackson from Georgia Institute of Technology; President Elizabeth Kiss and Susan Kidd of Agnes Scott College; William Strang of TOTO Americas; James Farrar and Rachel Parikh of SAP; Lindsay Levin of Leaders Quest; Terry Stinson and the sustainability leadership team at the Mandarin Oriental Hotel Group; and Ken Cornelius and Alison Taylor of Siemens.

My appreciation also extends to the many people who have conducted and published valuable research, made introductions, and shared their expertise and advice, especially, Peter Senge of MIT and the Society for Organizational Learning; Jorge Fernandez with the Metro Atlanta Chamber of Commerce; Suzanne Burnes with Sustainable Atlanta; Anthony Cortese of Second Nature; John Horton of Syllogy Healthcare Analytics; Nicole Lipkin, author of *What Keeps Leaders Up at Night*; William Seidman of Cerebyte and author of *The Star Factor*; Alexandra Hemrick, author, artist, and researcher; Martin Delahoussaye; James Thebaut, award-winning documentary film producer and founder of The Chronicles Group; Stephen Brereton, Canadian Consul General; Annabelle Malins, British Consul-General; David Adelman, U.S. Ambassador to Singapore; and Thomas Thomas of the Singapore Compact.

I would also like to thank my clients for welcoming me into their organizations, and for their willingness to embrace new perspectives, engage diverse groups of stakeholders, and display the leadership needed to prosper through responsible, innovative practices.

My thanks also go to the faculty and participants of the University of Cambridge and the Prince of Wales's Business and Sustainability Programme, especially Karen-Flanders Reid, leader for the Atlanta summit; Matt Arnold with J.P. Morgan Chase; Jonathon Porritt of Forum for the Future; Professor Tom Gladwin with the University of Michigan; Polly Courtice of the University of Cambridge; Kirsty Jenkinson with the World Resources Institute; Michael Kobori of Levi Strauss & Co.; Eric Ostern with Unilever; Aimee Christensen of Christensen Global Strategies; Peter Evans with GE Energy; Linda Fisher with DuPont; Jeff Seabright, John Reid and Liz Gorski from The Coca-Cola Company; Robert Franklin of Morehouse College; Reggie Walker, Lillian Borsa, and Ciaran Morris with PricewaterhouseCoopers LLP; Rawson Haverty of Haverty's Furniture; Denise Quarles with the City of Atlanta; Susan Davis with Improve International; Walter Kraus of Weston Foods; Alfred Blackmar of Aflac; Mahadev Raman of Arup; Jason Teter with Lafarge; and Peter Thompson of Boeing.

I benefitted greatly for the help of outstanding professors and thought leaders at Case Western Reserve University, who have done more than they may realize to shape my work and my life, especially Harlow Cohen, David Cooperrider, Ron Fry, Chris Laszlo, Richard Boyatzis, and Ante Glavas. My gratitude extends to my learning partners, and brilliant friends, who have stood by me through the CWRU journey and beyond, especially: Jacqueline Wong, Davina Brown, Robyne Blood, Marco Bertola, Deborah Levine, Laura Peterson, Vania Bueno, and Diana Durek.

Finally, I would like to thank my family, friends, and loved ones for their support, patience, and social therapy while I've been busy "living the dream."

An Unending Journey

Two roads diverged in a wood, and,
I took the one less traveled by,
And that has made all the difference.

—Robert Frost

WHEN I STARTED to write the Introduction to this book, I sat at my desk, thinking about how I had come to this amazing point in my career. You see, I have dreamed about writing a book ever since I was a child. I thought for a long time about the right way to introduce myself and explain why I spent several years of my life researching and writing the book you hold in your hand. What should I tell you about myself and my work? Why have I tackled such a weighty topic as the irresistible forces fundamentally changing the business landscape? Why have I chosen a career helping leaders shift their perspectives and organizations change their cultures to a shared-value model? Why do I feel compelled to share this journey?

It all started when I found myself at a legendary fork in the road. You know the one. Down the left lane lies the comfortable route you had planned to take all along. To the right stretches an unknown and slightly scary road less traveled.

I arrived at my crossroads on a perfectly sunny, late summer morning in 2001. I was sitting at my desk in my office in Stamford, Connecticut,

1

busily working at my job as a vice president for the technology research and consulting firm Gartner. I loved that job. When Gartner had hired me to launch its organization development function, I felt as if I had finally reached the destination for which all my passion and education had prepared me. Nothing excited me more than helping an organization grow and thrive. Then my world suddenly tilted off its axis. A colleague rushed into my office to tell me that two planes had crashed into the Twin Towers at the World Trade Center in New York City. I stopped what I was doing, got on the Internet, and stared at my monitor, transfixed by the horror unfolding before my eyes.

I couldn't get to my home on Long Island because the New York City metro area had completely shut down. But that's not what worried me at that moment. What scared me to death was the fate of my brother-in-law, Jimmy, a New York City firefighter. It took an eternity for me to get through the jammed phone lines to reach my sister Carolyn. I cried with relief when she told me Jimmy was safe. He wasn't scheduled to work that day. Tragically, however, every member of his squad working that day perished along with hundreds of other rescue workers when the towers collapsed.

That event stopped me in my tracks. In the days and weeks that followed, I did what I always do when the world seems to rumble beneath my feet. I took stock of my life. All my training, all my experience, and all the work I did to bank a big paycheck now paled in comparison with the shock waves created by the collapse of those two buildings. I had always longed to start my own firm. And I wanted to make a difference, a big difference. When I thought of the thousands who had died or suffered terrible losses on September 11, I realized that something unexpected could end your dreams at any moment. A month later, I left Gartner to launch my own consulting firm, with the expressed mission to help business leaders build better enterprises in this scary new post-9/11 world.

In the first few years on my new path, my colleagues and I provided organization development services, helping clients create better strategies, manage change more skillfully, build higher-performing cultures, and develop stronger leaders. The work gave me great pleasure. I worked with a lot of interesting clients and ethical leaders. I got involved in and led challenging projects. I earned a good living. Yet some deep inner voice kept telling me I could do more. It kept asking hard questions: "What does your work *mean*? Will what you do make any real difference to the quality of people's lives? Can meaningful work and profitability go hand in hand? What abiding passion will keep you hopping out of bed each morning, eager to get to work?" It made my head hurt. So maybe, I concluded, I should stop using my head and start following my heart.

In an effort to find answers to those nagging questions, I enrolled in graduate school while still running my business. I selected Case Western Reserve University (CWRU) because it boasted one of the best organizational behavior departments in the world, with rock star professors who groomed students not just to earn a degree but to make a difference in the world. That's when I began learning more about the huge forces that are dramatically changing businesses, communities, universities, and governments around the globe. And that's when I began to see a new, emerging business model built on the premise that businesses, not governments, could most effectively harness the forces of change to find innovative solutions to society's greatest problems and increase their profitability while doing so. I came to call these forces *The New Corporate Facts of Life*: disruptive innovation, economic instability, societal upheaval, stakeholder power, environmental degradation, globalization, and population shifts. Throughout this book you'll learn how these forces impact your organization, and you'll discover how you can turn these challenges into profitable opportunities. Leaders who grasp the power of The New Corporate Facts of Life use those realities to renew energy, enthusiasm, and engagement throughout their companies. They also enjoy the tangible benefits of greater customer loyalty, a more compelling brand image, market-dominating products and services, and a more impressive bottom line.

I felt myself standing at another fork in the road. Down one path I saw business as usual, with its single-minded and shortsighted obsession with today's bottom line. Down the other, I detected a more expansive, long-term, shared-value approach to business where forward-looking companies could make more money by doing more good in the world.

At CWRU, I learned a lot from David Cooperrider[1] and Ron Fry, two of the founders of the program, who had led a 2004 United Nations summit called Business as an Agent of World Benefit. At that event, hundreds of corporate CEOs and nongovernment organization (NGO) leaders discussed innovative solutions to the world's most challenging issues—solutions that would benefit both societies and businesses. During a class taught by Chris Laszlo,[2] I learned how sustainable growth had become a vital driver of innovation for the twenty-first century. Corporate giants such as Walmart, Nike, and Unilever were sending shock waves throughout their global supply chains, insisting that vendors adopt practices that respect people, community values, and the environment. Small and medium-sized firms—among them the carpet manufacturer Interface, the apparel company Patagonia, and the office furniture maker Herman Miller—were changing the game with disruptive innovations and even showing the global giants how to operate differently. Small social enterprises such as Grameen Bank in Bangladesh were bringing creative microfinance models and commerce to people in emerging nations. I learned that half the world's population lived on less than $2.50 a day, and I gained an appreciation for the ways a company's actions helped or harmed stakeholders all along the value chain. My worldview shifted totally and unalterably. I could no longer look at a water bottle, lipstick tube, or carpet the same way again. I found this all so inspiring that, as part of a leadership course taught by Richard Boyatzis,[3] I wrote a paper about the competencies leaders will need to propel their companies into a better and more profitable twenty-first century.

I eagerly began incorporating all that I was learning into my work with clients. The new ideas fit snugly with what I had been doing all along, helping companies with leadership, culture, and strategy issues. Now, however, I added an increasing emphasis on how these issues have become inexorably intertwined with the irresistible social, environmental, and economic forces buffeting all markets and talent pools. Heed these forces, and you can thrive. Ignore them, and you may well join all the other dinosaurs and dodo birds in an early grave.

I thought I was following my passion back in pre-9/11. But that passion could not rival the one now burning in my heart. Finally, I had found some answers to those pesky questions, and each answer brought up even more nettlesome questions. I knew then that I had found my true path. My work grew more and more meaningful and fulfilling as I found new ways to help organizations turn modern-day problems into strategic opportunities for greater profit, innovation, and leadership. This shared value model began to permeate everything my company did, igniting passion, raising awareness, and shifting the perspectives of countless clients along the way.

This path naturally led to the perfect topic for the book I longed to write. Before I fired up my computer, however, I began looking closely at the practices of hundreds of organizations, both large and small and engaged in every imaginable industry around the globe. As I explored these organizations, I met many smart, dedicated people, including John Brock, CEO of Coca-Cola Enterprises; Kurt Kuehn, CFO of UPS; and G.P. "Bud" Peterson, President of Georgia Institute of Technology—each of them leading change and building incredible organizations. Early on, I discovered James Farrar, VP of Sustainability for SAP, through his popular blog and arranged to meet with him at the technology giant's corporate headquarters in Waldorf, Germany. I learned much from James about how sustainability went far beyond greening the data centers to ignite innovation and global change.

Every time I needed to find a thought leader, an expert, an executive, or a government leader, someone would make an introduction or that person would appear. During a tour of a Georgia Power energy plant, I met a woman who asked me to help her design a sustainability vision summit for city managers in a client's community. At a reception during a United Nations water conference, I got to know James Thebaut, an award-winning documentary producer of the film series *Running Dry*. Jim became a friend and mentor, educating me over the next few years about the world's water crisis. At one point, he asked me to contribute to a white paper for the U.S. Army Corps of Engineers titled "Coping with Drought and Water Scarcity."[4]

The further my research and interviews took me, the more clearly I saw a before-and-after picture of business success. The before rules of self-centered corporate strategy would no longer lead to success. The after rules, following an enduring new business model compelled by The New Corporate Facts of Life, would prevail. In the pages ahead, I will not only sketch these powerful forces and reveal their impact on your business, I will offer practical tools you can use to harness those forces for greater innovation, engagement, and leadership, at the same time boosting your bottom line.

As I keep discovering more and more about the heart and soul of my business, the more I keep listening to that persistent inner voice that also brings me strength and optimism. I hearken to the words of the English author George Eliot: "It's never too late to be who you might have been." I feel so lucky to do work that helps my clients prosper while implementing strategies that benefit *all* stakeholders, including the unborn generations who will inherit the planet. Each and every one of us can make a major contribution. Imagine a world where each of us does something to further the cause. One person lights a fire in ten other hearts, and those ten, in turn, ignite the flame in ten others. It wouldn't take long to reach a million or even a billion.

I honestly believe we are looking down an historic fork in the road. I hope we all choose the one that will make a positive difference, not just to our company's balance sheet, but to the world we are creating for future generations.

CHAPTER 1

Meet The New Corporate Facts of Life

It is not the strongest of the species that survives;
nor the most intelligent that survives. It is the one
that is most adaptable to change.

—CHARLES DARWIN

FEW LOGOS ENJOY as much global recognition as the Nike Swoosh. You see it on people's clothes and shoes all over the world. But Bill Bowerman and Phil Knight, founders of the iconic Nike brand, never thought of themselves as mere apparel and footwear salesmen. It all started when Bowerman, a nationally recognized track-and-field coach at the University of Oregon, always searching for ways to improve the performance of his athletes, joined forces with one of his former runners to create and market better running shoes. One of the company's early innovations came from Mrs. Bowerman's waffle iron, which inspired a more effective design for the soles of high-performance footgear.

Like many of the companies you'll meet in this book, Nike constantly strives for excellence but cannot avoid its share of serious business problems. Corporations, after all, are only human (or, more accurately, collections of humans). In the late 1990s, Nike came under attack for some of its suppliers' terrible labor practices. The press and the public condemned the unsafe working conditions, forced labor, and child employment involved in the manufacture of some products bearing the Nike

7

Swoosh. When Nike did not swiftly move to address these issues, protesters burned Nike shoes, boycotted Nike products and demanded action. In 1998, the company's earnings dropped by a whopping 69 percent. Swoosh had obviously stepped into a quagmire.

While that experience didn't knock Nike off the track, it dramatically changed the rules of the game. Redefining its entire perspective on supply chain management, Nike moved to clean it up by training and auditing suppliers and choosing to do business only with those who adhere to fair and legal labor practices. But the campaign did not stop there. Nike moved beyond managing risk and rebuilding its brand, and assumed a leadership position, with the overriding goal of redefining every aspect of its business and thereby transforming an entire industry.

While the company aims to find new and better ways to serve its customers' needs to grow and to make money, it does so under an overarching umbrella of sustainable growth through innovation. For instance, it uses its Flyknit technology to make lighter weight and more custom-fitted shoes. But the process accomplishes even more. By weaving the upper portion of a shoe with a single thread, the manufacturing process creates far less waste than conventional methods. Additionally, a waterless dyeing technology conserves a valuable resource by using CO_2 rather than H_2O to dye textiles. On a broader scale, Nike collaborates with NASA, the U.S. Department of State, and the United States Agency for International Development (USAID) to encourage innovations for more socially and environmentally sustainable materials. The company also shares intellectual property for green product design, packaging, and manufacturing with competitors in order to help the entire industry operate more sustainably.

My research into Nike and scores of other forward-looking companies during the past several years has identified seven powerful, interconnected forces that will trigger a catalytic change in the global business landscape:

1. Disruptive innovation

2. Economic instability

3. Societal upheaval

4. Stakeholder power

5. Environmental degradation

6. Globalization

7. Population shifts

These irresistible forces have created what I call The New Corporate Facts of Life (NCFOL). They cannot be ignored. Although the incremental changes of the past did not fundamentally alter the business terrain, and required relatively minor tactical adjustments, the ones emerging from this era of catalytic change demand a major shift in strategic thinking. We stand on a brink of changes every bit as massive as those that shaped the Industrial Revolution and the Information Age.

Like many of the changes brought about by the Industrial Revolution, Henry Ford's automobile provided more than horseless transportation; it launched an era of mass production and modern management techniques. It paved the way for a sprawling infrastructure of roads and fueling stations, and supported a vast array of new industries. And as it reshaped the landscape, a large percentage of the population shifted from an agricultural to an urban lifestyle. Likewise, the Information Age has irreversibly transformed everything we do, from buying and selling goods and services to accessing entertainment, knowledge, and social communication.

The NCFOL are also reshaping our world in powerful and irreversible ways. They demand that business leaders think deeply and ask questions about the future of their companies, such as how do we innovate in a world where our products and services can become obsolete overnight? What investment decisions must we make in the midst of global economic instability? How should we respond to the social upheaval rocking the world? How can we best serve our increasingly powerful stakeholders? What steps can we take to protect the environment from continued degradation and remain profitable? How can we enter emerging markets with the greatest rates of population growth and a burgeoning middle class? How should we operate in this highly interdependent global maket?

The NCFOL do not affect just the global business giants like Siemens; they cascade into every nook and cranny of every little entrepreneurial venture on every street corner in every country on earth. Ignore them at your peril. If you despair that they pose insurmountable problems that only others can solve, they will eventually undermine your future. Redefine them as opportunities, as Nike has done, and you will greatly improve the odds that your organization—be it a business, a government agency, a not-for-profit or community organization, or an educational institution—will thrive. Milton Friedman's well-known observation that "the business of business is business" has rapidly changed to a view that business cannot ignore the world in which it operates. The two are inextricably interconnected. One cannot thrive if the other suffers.

This book will present not only the case for embracing this new reality but also many practical models and tools that will help any organization seize and profit from all the opportunities this new reality creates.

As Figure 1-1 illustrates, you can redefine key aspects of your enterprise by shifting your perspectives, redefining your vision and strategies, and executing your strategies through culture, leadership, engagement, and business model alignment to achieve and maintain dominance in your field.

In the chapters ahead, we will consider how the forces on the left may require rethinking the basic aspects of business on the right. For instance, when you think about your corporate culture, should you make some important changes in the light of disruptive innovation ("Does our current culture promote creative breakthroughs?") and globalization ("Have we created a culture that transcends national boundaries?")? At the end of each chapter, you will find The New Corporate Facts of Life Barometer, which will help you weigh the need for change in your organization. Although not every NCFOL will dramatically affect a given aspect of your business, you should still consider them all. The balance

Figure 1-1. NCFOL Require New Business Directions.

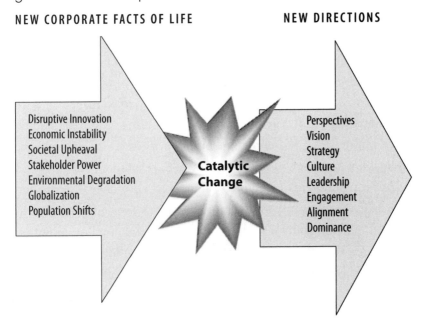

NEW CORPORATE FACTS OF LIFE

Disruptive Innovation
Economic Instability
Societal Upheaval
Stakeholder Power
Environmental Degradation
Globalization
Population Shifts

Catalytic Change

NEW DIRECTIONS

Perspectives
Vision
Strategy
Culture
Leadership
Engagement
Alignment
Dominance

of this chapter will conduct a satellite's-eye tour of The New Corporate Facts of Life and both the challenges and opportunities they pose.

Disruptive Innovation

Disruptive innovation occurs when a new product, service, or business model renders the old way of doing business obsolete. The Internet has disrupted everything from health care to shopping to dating. Telemedicine puts patient records on handheld devices and in the cloud, while smart grids redefine energy use. Personal computers bring instant information, interactive communication, productivity software, and endless entertainment to our desks and laps, while smartphones put it all in the palms of our hands.

The proliferation of cell phones provides an excellent case in point. A 2012 United Nations (UN) study reported that cell phones have been lifting more people out of poverty than any other innovation in history.

The World Bank estimates that by 2012, approximately 75 percent of the world's population enjoyed access to cell phones, with 5 billion of the 6 billion mobile subscribers living in developing countries. Access to mobile communication advances human and economic development in so many ways—from paying bills, finding the lowest-priced products and services, and accessing health-care information, to keeping abreast of local, state, national, and international news, sharing information, joining protests, and pushing for more democratic processes.

Kenya has been leading the mobile wallet revolution since 2007. M-Pesa (*M* for mobile plus *Pesa*, the Swahili word for money) has created a mobile financial system that has transformed the lives and businesses of more than half the country's adult population. Launched as a joint venture between Vodaphone and Kenya's Safaricom, M-Pesa's mobile payment system allows Kenyans to transfer funds, pay bills, and eliminate the need for Masai herders to carry cash after selling their goods at the market. Cell phone technology goes beyond apps and gizmos; it promotes equality. Later in this book we'll see how innovations such as mobile devices contribute to other new corporate facts of life, including societal upheaval, stakeholder power, and globalization.

The 2012 GE Global Innovation Barometer survey of 1,000 global executives predicted that future innovations that address human need would eclipse those that merely generate high profit. The report does not urge company leaders to ignore the bottom line, but it does urge them to peer into the future, where shared-value innovations will increase access to health care, enhance wellness, improve the environment, spur job growth, promote energy security, and elevate education. Companies that seize those opportunities will reap the profits.

Challenges

Technology empires rise and fall quickly. In 2000, Microsoft owned the software universe, Apple languished as a niche player, Google had not yet evolved a business model, and the founder of Facebook had not yet graduated from high school. By 2012, RIM's Blackberry, once a disruptive innovation that married cell phone, Internet, and computer technologies into a handheld device, had lost most of its market share to other smartphones, especially to Apple's iPhone, and its stock had fallen by 93 percent. When digital photography replaced film, Eastman Kodak's business collapsed. Apple's iTunes transformed the music industry, and online travel sites all but eliminated travel agencies.

Opportunities

To keep up with such changes, companies must redefine how they foster innovation. The 2012 GE Global Innovation Barometer revealed that 88 percent of executives believe that the twenty-first-century approach to innovation will differ radically from yesterday's business-as-usual methods. The most forward-looking companies are adopting a new innovation model whereby they form and benefit from strategic alliances, tap into the creativity of individuals and smaller companies, and customize solutions to meet local needs.

Many have gone far beyond conventional corporate responsibility to create affordable solutions to major local problems in emerging economies. They do a world of good that not incidentally improves their bottom line. Unilever, for example, tackled the life-and-death problem of safe drinking water in developing countries and came up with a low-cost, high-quality solution, Pureit, a portable water-purifying device that makes water for drinking for less than half a cent per liter without using a single watt of electricity or existing tap water. Having launched the product in 2004, Unilever estimates that by early 2012 about 35 million people were using Pureit. With a tenfold growth forecast by 2020, Pureit will at that point become a multibillion-dollar business.

Even the least technological companies can create disruptive business models. Starbucks reinvented the coffee shop by turning their locations into ecofriendly gathering spaces with trendy design, Internet access, and their own music collections. Muhammad Yunus, a college professor in Bangladesh, launched global microfinancing through Grameen Bank by first helping local women start businesses funded with only a few dollars each. Zipcar and peer-to-peer car-sharing schemes, such as Spride Share, have disrupted traditional rental car companies by allowing people to rent vehicles by the hour through a network of screened renters.

Disruptive innovations range from the complex (developing a new computer operating system) to the simple (putting wheels on luggage). Although many companies launched during periods of economic prosperity, others sprouted despite adverse economic conditions. Apple, Microsoft, IBM, and Disney all came into the world during recessions.

All companies—not just those in the technology sector—face a daily onslaught of game-changing disruptive innovation. How do you stay on the leading edge of blindingly fast change? Courageous leaders choose to revolutionize the world, not just evolve with it. That means shifting your perspectives and rethinking the very design of your organization.

Economic Instability

Financial uncertainty threatens all countries, industries, and people. Our hyperconnected world links economies around the globe, in which events in even the tiniest countries impact the biggest ones. Industries in Thailand rely on industries in the United States. Small businesses in India depend on the success of global giants based in Germany. When a financial crisis strikes Europe, both private and public sectors must pull together to address the problem. What happens in Athens affects what happens on Wall Street. The business practices that took down Lehman Brothers and threatened the collapse of large institutions like AIG, Ford, and General Motors caused a tsunami-sized ripple affecting homeowners, merchants, and people in every imaginable job, from bricklayers to bankers, in every country from Afghanistan to Zimbabwe. Bailouts in the United States that helped save companies and jobs and thwarted a total economic collapse drove up the U.S. national debt, lowering its credit rating and threatening tax increases. The ripples flooded all the way to China.

In September 2012, Germany's top court voted to ratify and contribute to Europe's 700-billion-euro bailout fund. With that vote, Germany joined the 17-nation Eurozone behind the European Stability Mechanism (ESM) designed to throw a lifeline to Greece, Spain, and other troubled European Union (EU) countries. But German voters balked at that idea, endangering Prime Minister Angela Merkel's hold on government. The international community called for decisive and urgent leadership. Economic experts feared that Italy, the Eurozone's third largest economy, was too big to bail but too big to fail. Meanwhile, Greece's debt woes grew ever larger as Greece and Spain dealt with a 25 percent unemployment rate and France risked losing its wealthiest citizens in the wake of a threatened 75 percent income tax on the rich. The EU economic crisis fanned the flames of the global firestorm ignited by the 2008 financial meltdown.

Challenges

Businesspeople in the United States and other developed nations cry foul when manufacturing moves to China, India, and Bangladesh, yet those who object want affordable giant flat-screen TVs, iPads, and designer clothes. As wages in emerging nations such as China rise, manufacturers seek even cheaper labor elsewhere. However, a company must consider more than labor costs. The cost of transportation, import and export duties, maintaining a secure supply chain, shipping time, and fluctuating currency values also figure into manufacturing strategies. Many manufacturers now realize that it makes more sense to manufacture closer to the customers who buy their products. Companies such as Apple, Coleman, Caterpillar, Ford, GE, Whirlpool, and Toto recently onshored some of their manufacturing. The Boston Consulting Group's 2011 report, "Made in America, Again: Why Manufacturing Will Return to the U.S," predicted that by 2015 many goods destined for North American consumers will bear "Made in the U.S.A" labels.

In addition, many firms have joined the recent trend of moving higher-skilled white-collar jobs to nearby countries where closer time zones help them better serve clients. Tata Consultancy Services Ltd., India's largest software exporter, and midsized competitor MindTree Ltd. have responded to tighter U.S. visa rules by hiring technology professionals in the United States to serve the needs of their clients there. France's Capgemini's global outsourcing operations capitalize on nearshoring by moving marketing, legal review, finance, and human resource services from the United States to Guatemala City and from Paris, Brussels, and London to Kraków, Poland. Capgemini's clients save up to 50 percent on labor costs while gaining access to college-educated staff who speak multiple languages with customer-friendly accents.

Economic instability swings both ways. Booming economic periods usher in their own challenges and opportunities. New businesses prosper and move from ramshackle garages to plush corporate buildings. Companies go global and expand into previously untapped markets. Launching your business in foreign countries may lower your production costs and reach new consumers, but not unless you navigate the landmines of politics, piracy, corruption, and cultural differences.

In boom times, technology companies drove up wages as they bid for high-tech workers, and the housing industry enjoyed skyrocketing home prices as banks extended loans to people who previously could not qualify. Builders erected new communities that needed new infrastructure to overcome the problems associated with jammed roadways, water shortages, and overcrowded schools. All of this proved unsustainable, however, and the bubble burst. People lost their jobs, much of their wealth, and most, if not all, of their retirement funds. As economies thrive, companies must manage growth while also creating contingency plans should new bubbles burst and threaten their very existence.

Opportunities

The period of economic decline that began in 2008 strongly affected consumerism as people bought less, demanded bargains, and searched the Internet for everything from used furniture to prescription drugs. Whole

Foods Markets, an upscale pricey grocer for connoisseurs of organic food, introduced lower-price-point products and built smaller suburban stores to attract more middle-income customers. Walmart, once disdained by many as a poor shopper's paradise, attracted price-conscious customers who never would have set foot in their stores before 2008. People looking for online deals flocked to businesses like Groupon and Pinterest.

Today, many companies strive for ever greater efficiency to keep costs down. Companies such as UPS, Coca-Cola, and Novo Nordisk believe greater efficiencies today will enable them to remain profitable during tomorrow's inevitable difficult times and keep them positioned for long-term growth.

Other companies expand their presence in emerging and second-tier markets by offering low-cost products and services. Medtronic's Healthy Heart for All program brings pacemakers to hundreds of thousands of patients in India. Medtronic, the world's largest medical device manufacturer, set up rural camps with low-cost electrocardiogram (ECG) machines to send wirelessly transmitted ECGs to doctors hundreds of miles away. Relying on existing technology, the company's creative business model allowed it to enter new markets and position itself for expansion throughout the developing world.

Challenging economic times amplify societal challenges. Rising unemployment, increasing income inequities, escalating housing foreclosures, and expanding poverty and desperation plague cities and countries around the globe. A 2009 Boston University Report, "Beyond GDP: The Need for New Measures of Progress," stressed the use of more complete measures of a country's well-being and progress to revise economic measures by, for example, adding so-called community capital indicators for ecological, social, human, and infrastructure progress. Doing so would give policy makers and society more complete data for making decisions by tracking whether a community is plundering its community capital rather than living off its interest.[1] Companies such as Unilever, adidas, and BMW measure more than just economic value. They track resources saved, lives touched, and impacts on the communities they serve.

Societal Upheaval

Corruption, political unrest, poverty, food shortages, terrorism, pollution, unemployment, unfair labor practices, limited education, inadequate health care, and crimes against humanity erode the quality of life for people around the world. An oppressed and struggling population, armed only with smartphones, rises up to demand change. The resultant upheaval affects businesses far beyond that country's borders. Conventional corporate social responsibility, which often received more lip service than serious strategic investment, has become an imperative in today's turbulent world. Business leaders who fail to anticipate and manage societal issues make a big mistake because those issues can take down a company. Rather than ignoring societal upheaval, smart executives look for the opportunities hidden in all the noise of revolution.

In Tunisia, a 26-year-old fruit vendor named Mohamed Bouazizi protested government corruption and abuse and his village's 30 percent unemployment rate by drenching himself in paint thinner and setting himself ablaze in front of the governor's high gate. News of this December 17, 2010, event rapidly spread throughout the Arab world and beyond. Tunisian revolutionaries, employing a new arsenal of social media weapons, drove Zine-el-Abidine, the country's 23-year dictator, into exile and ignited what became known as the Arab Spring, as uprisings spread to Egypt, Bahrain, Yemen, Libya, and Iran. Frustrated people around the world, including disaffected young Americans who flocked to the Occupy movement to protest societal and economic equality, continued to rise up and demand change. In 2011, the self-proclaimed "99%" launched the Occupy Wall Street movement that spread to other cities, where hundreds of thousands protested corporate greed and inequity and the perceived excessive influence of corporations on government. Even people in the richest countries on the planet suffer the effects of homelessness, crime, limited education, racial and gender prejudice, illegal immigration, and teen pregnancy, to name but a few social ills. Businesses cannot ignore such problems. Whether you sell products in the Middle East or Middle America, you operate in the context of a society. If that context becomes hostile or creates dangerous conditions, the effects can cascade all the way to your bottom line.

Challenges

Companies must navigate social, cultural, and political landmines both at home and abroad. When a company fully appreciates both the power and responsibility of its brand, it will address social issues to protect and positively enhance its image. They do not pay lip service to responsibility; they act on it. They police their supply chains for abuse of workers, unethical and illegal practices, and improperly acquired and processed raw materials. They strive for greater traceability of raw materials and transparency of business practices. When it became clear that the sale of illegal minerals from the Congo used in some smartphones and computers finance terrorism, the U.S. Congress passed the 2010 Dodd-Frank Act, which required companies to disclose and crack down on their use of Congolese "conflict minerals." Armed groups have used minerals such as tin, tantalum, gold, and tungsten (used by manufacturers in everything from smartphones to jewelry) to finance horrendous humanitarian atrocities in the Democratic Republic of the Congo (DRC) region. In 2012, the United States Securities and Exchange Commission began requiring companies to disclose their use of conflict minerals originating in the DRC or adjoining countries.

More than 1,100 garment workers died and hundreds more suffered serious injuries in the 2013 collapse of Rana Plaza in Bangladesh. Three weeks later, clothing makers around the world joined together to create a legally binding agreement to improve safety and working conditions for Bangladeshi factories in their supply chains. More than 70 apparel companies signed the agreement, including H & M, Zara, Abercrombie & Fitch, and PVH (parent company of such brands as Tommy Hilfiger and Calvin Klein). The agreement's five-year commitment calls for independent, publicly reported safety inspections and provides financing for factories to improve safety. Several NGOs backed the agreement, including

IndustriALL Global Union and UNI Global Union, which represent workers in 140 countries.

Opportunities

Strategically minded companies can find solutions to social issues that spur business growth and strengthen brand recognition. Water, women, and well-being offered just such an opportunity to Coca-Cola. The company's 5by20 initiative aimed to improve the economic well-being of 5 million women around the world by the year 2020. For instance, the company sets up manual distribution centers, many run by women in nations lacking transportation infrastructure, such as Kenya and Indonesia. Everyone wins. The company successfully enters new markets, and people in the communities gain income from new jobs.

In one case, Rosemary Njeri's distribution business in Kenya expanded from a small enterprise to become the second largest of the 37 centers supported by Coca-Cola in Nairobi. The company trained Rosemary to do required bookkeeping, manage inventory, and apply the necessary technology, and the local Coca-Cola bottling partner provided equipment and signage. Rosemary's business went from two employees to 16, including several members of her family. She has also started a support group of women distributors who meet regularly to discuss and find solutions for the business issues they face. Through efforts such as this, Coca-Cola gains respect for its brand with the message that "every bottle has a story."

Other food and beverage companies fight obesity and increase revenues by offering healthier products. In the United States, the beverage industry voluntarily replaced high-calorie soft drinks with healthier options in schools. Several large corporations within the industry banded together in 2006 to form the Children's Food and Beverage Advertising Initiative to encourage food and beverage companies to advertise healthier food to children. In the first year, McDonald's, Burger King, Kraft, Mars, and eight other companies pledged their commitment.

Partnering with nongovernmental organizations (NGOs)—once the height of business heresy—has enabled many companies to benefit both society and their business. When the Clinton Global Initiative began its AIDS initiative in 2002, only 230,000 people in developing nations were receiving medications. As of 2012, that number had grown to 8 million, due in large part to partnerships with pharmaceutical companies such as Pfizer and GlaxoSmithKline. By moving from a high-margin, low-volume to a high-volume, low-margin strategy, these companies bring lifesaving aid to people around the world while improving their profitability.

Addressing a major catalytic change and striving to discover and fulfill unmet needs goes beyond the old ideas of philanthropy and corporate responsibility. Smart, values-driven companies strive to devise innovative and profitable solutions that will simultaneously benefit people and boost the bottom line. All it takes is a new perspective, one that links a company's strategy to a radically new future.

Stakeholder Power

Since the dawn of the public corporation, business leaders focused primarily on their board members and shareholders as their key stakeholders. Yet doing so can lead to unintended consequences. Devout fans of Ben & Jerry's ice cream who admired the company's social conscience still mourn the day in 2000 when Ben Cohen and Jerry Greenfield sold their business to Unilever and the Ben & Jerry's brand became a sister to Vaseline, Slim-Fast, Ponds, and I Can't Believe It's Not Butter. In a 2008 interview, Jerry Greenfield told Hannah Pool of *The Guardian*, "We did not want to sell the business; it was a very difficult time. But we were a public company, and the board of directors' primary responsibility is the interest of the shareholders. So that is what the decision came down to. It was extremely difficult, heart-wrenching." The buyer didn't matter as long as it paid top dollar. Bottom line: The board and the needs of the shareholders ruled.

Some companies have opted to change their status to become "Benefit Corporations," legal entities that must create a "material positive impact on society and the environment and to meet higher standards of accountability and transparency."[2] One Benefit Corporation, Patagonia, embraces a mission it calls The Change We Seek®, which mandates that the company "Build the best product, cause no unnecessary harm, use business to inspire and implement solutions to the environmental crisis."

Regardless of their legal status, companies must pay equal attention to an expanded universe of people who touch and who are touched by their organization: employees, customers, competitors, suppliers, community leaders and citizens, governments, NGOs, and alliance partners. When they involve all stakeholders, companies can reap the benefits of greater collaboration, innovation, loyalty, and awareness of both challenges and opportunities. Ignoring stakeholders can lead to a tarnished brand image, higher costs, disaffected suppliers, more frequent employee turnover, increasingly dissatisfied customers, and combative governments, communities, and NGOs.

More than ever, companies must reach outside the confines of their own operations to embrace all of their stakeholders. Although they must honor their legal obligations to put the interests of shareholders first, those interests increasingly benefit from positive relationships with all stakeholders. Profits and value now depend on attracting and retaining the most talented workers, enhancing the well-being of communities, creating respectful partnerships with suppliers, thrilling customers with more than a great product and a responsive customer care center, cooperating with regulators, and collaborating with domestic and foreign governments.

It takes but one small spark to ignite a forest fire. In 2011, Molly Katchpole, 22, a nanny living in Washington, D.C., was working two jobs and living from paycheck to paycheck when Bank of America announced that it would start charging her a $5 fee for making even one debit card purchase per month. Irate, Molly broadcast her displeasure on the Internet and started a petition on Change.org. To her surprise, she gathered 306,000 signatures from other folks fed up with big banks squeezing money from working people.

Around the same time, art dealer Kristen Christian vented her outrage with arrogant bankers on Facebook and encouraged her friends to stop doing business with the big banks.[3] Kristen's messages ultimately spawned the November 5, 2011, Bank Transfer Day, when 610,000 people switched from big banks to smaller banks and credit unions. When the targets of consumer wrath, including Citigroup and Bank of America, called in police and security guards to manage the throngs withdrawing their money, they only reinforced their image as care-nothing bullies. Videos of skirmishes with protesters went viral on the Web. Although 610,000 may not seem like an overwhelming number, given the millions of Americans with bank accounts, a Javelin survey reported that 1,456,000 customers cited bank fees as the reason for transferring from big banks in the 90 days following Bank Transfer Day. Bank of America, reeling from pressure from the media, Congress, customers, and Change.org, agreed to drop the fee.

Challenges

Like Molly Katchpole and Kristen Christian, anyone can use smartphones, social media, and the Internet to become a global advocate and citizen journalist. Companies must continuously scan vast sources of information from *The New York Times* to YouTube and Twitter to see who loves and hates them. Potential employees can check out prospective employers on www.glassdoor.com, where people post comments on management and the work environment much as they would a hotel or book review. Advocacy groups target large companies, calling for more ethical business practices and greater responsibility in products, operations, supply chains, and more humane treatment of workers. NGOs harness technology to globally rally people around local environmental and social concerns.

Opportunities

Fully engaged employees bring their best efforts and creative ideas to work. A GreenBiz 2012 article, "Sustainability-Engaged Employees More

Satisfied, Study Shows," shared the story of Jeslin Jacob, a recent business school graduate disturbed by the fiberglass waste that her employer, a roofing company, was sending to landfills. After receiving a lukewarm response to her concerns from senior leaders, she took the initiative to create a market for fiberglass dust that not only diverted waste from landfills but also saved the company thousands of dollars a year. Jacob said, "I feel like I've left an invisible green signature on the products we make. And the more products we sell, the greater the impact of the project. Now that is a great incentive for me to grow business and that makes every day at work satisfying."

Engaging suppliers can also yield far greater results than merely monitoring them. Corporate social responsibility (CSR) and sustainable procurement bring increased emphasis to supply chain management. Companies shifting from a top-down to a collaborative approach to suppliers find ways to operate more efficiently and responsibly throughout the supply chain. Ford Motor Company trains suppliers and works with them on ways they can support the company's sustainable agenda. Companies such as Coca-Cola and Siemens AG recognize and reward suppliers for innovation and performance in helping them achieve and exceed CSR goals. InterfaceFLOR works with suppliers to develop new production processes and reduce costs and to increase profit margins for both their company and their suppliers.

Collaborating with NGOs turns former adversaries into so-called critical friends. At one time, such organizations as Gap, Swiss Re, and the International Timber Trade Organization viewed cooperation with NGOs as sleeping with the enemy. Now they partner with them to improve their products, solve supply chain problems, and operate more responsibly. In 2006, the Levi Strauss Foundation partnered with Business for Social Responsibility to launch HER-Project, a woman's health education program, in factories in Bangladesh, China, Egypt, and Pakistan. Five years later, the program, which focuses on improving women's health and helping factory workers connect to nearby health-care services, had aided more than 90,000 women in 65 facilities. One study found that for every dollar a company invests in factory health clinics, health education, and wellness training, it reaps $3 in increased productivity on the factory floor.

Environmental Degradation

A World Wildlife Fund 2012 report stated that at our current rate we are using 50 percent more resources than the earth can ultimately provide. If developing nations were to match the U.S. rate of consumption, humanity's needs would require 3.6 more planets. The old model that humans can plunder the earth at will and suffer no consequences has become obsolete. Environmental degradation brings drought, floods, unclean water, disease, death, security threats, and pollution. This sad state of affairs should concern corporations every bit as much as it does environmental activists. Negative perceptions of a company's impact on the environment decrease brand value; positive perceptions increase it.

Companies such as Sara Lee that source agricultural products in countries around the world face the problem of food shortages caused by climate change and severe weather conditions in various regions. Australia offers a dramatic case in point. The Deniliquin mill, the largest rice mill in the Southern Hemisphere, once processed enough grain to meet the needs of 20 million people around the world. But six years of drought reduced Australia's rice crop by 98 percent and led to the mill's closing in 2007. In a 2008 *New York Times* article, Ben Fargher, the chief executive of the National Farmers' Federation in Australia, said, "Climate change is potentially the biggest risk to Australian agriculture." The collapse of Australia's rice production contributed to a doubling of rice prices in early 2008, an increase that led to stringent export restrictions, panicked hoarding in the Philippines and Hong Kong, and violent protests in Cameroon, Egypt, Ethiopia, Haiti, Indonesia, Italy, Ivory Coast, Mauritania, the Philippines, Thailand, Uzbekistan, and Yemen.

Companies such as Toyota, Natura Cosmeticos, and Lockheed Martin have already heeded the threats posed by environmental degradation and have chosen to travel the path toward sustainable, profitable growth. The 2011 Carbon Disclosure Project (CDP) by Standard & Poor 500 reported that 91 percent of the S&P 500 publicly discloses greenhouse gas emissions. It makes good business sense because these companies report that a 60 percent emission reduction project will pay for itself in three years or less. As with the other New Corporate Facts of Life, smart companies can convert the threats into opportunities. Not only will the planet and its inhabitants benefit from corporate efforts to protect the environment, but the companies themselves will profit from new sources of energy, less extreme weather events, the approval of investors, enhanced revenues and profits, and more innovative products.

One prominent U.K. retailer, Marks & Spencer (M&S), redefined retail for the twenty-first century. Robert Swannell, the company's chairman, views sustainable business development (environmentally, socially, and economically responsible growth) not as a corporate responsibility program but as a fundamental business factor. With revenues of £9.7 billion ($15.7 billion) in fiscal year 2010–2011, the company attributed £70 million of its profits to sustainability initiatives. M&S calls this approach Plan A. They've created no Plan B because they do not believe in doing business any other way. Adhering to Plan A, M&S works with customers and suppliers to maintain seven pillars: involve our customers, make Plan A how we do business, climate change, waste, natural resources, fair partner, and health and well-being. Between 2006 and 2011, M&S kept growing while reducing total carbon emissions by 13 percent, recycling 94 percent of its waste, and generating 54 percent of its energy from renewable sources. It obtains 90 percent of its wild fish and 76 percent of its wood from environmentally sustainable sources, and its stores now sell energy in addition to clothing and food.

Challenges

Greenpeace's 2011 "Dirty Laundry" report exposed the fact that China's footwear and apparel industry discharges 805 tons of industrial waste every second and that clothes manufactured there often contain toxic, hormone-disrupting chemicals. To prompt change, the advocacy group invited the two largest sports apparel companies, Nike and adidas, to compete in a Detox Challenge to publicly commit to eliminate all hazardous chemicals from their supply chains and products by 2020. Activists and supporters registered their support online and appeared on streets in front of Nike and adidas stores in 29 cities around the world on July 23 at exactly 11:00 a.m. Central European Time, not to picket (that's so 1990s) but to perform a choreographed striptease. Videos (many not appropriate for family viewing) spread across the Internet and attracted coverage by mainstream media and the blogosphere. While Nike and adidas pondered a response, PUMA, third in the industry, made the first commitment. Nike and adidas soon followed. Although the three companies did not know exactly how they could honor their pledge, they knew they needed to come together with others in the apparel industry to find solutions.

Several months later, leading apparel and footwear companies, Nike, adidas, C&A, PUMA, H&M, and Li Ning, announced the creation of a Zero Discharge of Hazardous Chemicals (ZDHC) Programme to eliminate hazardous chemicals over the life cycle of apparel and footwear products by 2020. Through its Joint Roadmap, ZDHC members have set forth a new standard for the apparel and footwear industry, with specific commitments and timelines. Goals include educating suppliers, eliminating certain chemicals from the production process, developing transparent stakeholder engagement programs, and monitoring and publicly disclosing results. Other apparel companies, including Levi Strauss, Jack Wolfskin, Marks & Spencer, and G-Star Raw, signed the Joint Roadmap. As of June 2013, ZDHC participants made measurable progress by setting up seven workstreams, among them training, assessment and auditing, and initiating a chemicals management best practice pilot. Each workstream pursues specific 2015 milestone targets that they hope to achieve by 2020.

Companies must not only protect their brand image; they must stay ahead of increasingly complex regulations both at home and abroad. For example, American automakers began creating lighter, more efficient cars like the Chevy Volt and the Ford Fusion to prepare for 2025 U.S. regulations that will require an average fuel efficiency of 54.5 miles per gallon. When the European Union's 2006 Restriction of Hazardous Substances Directive (RoHS) and the 2005 Waste Electrical and Electronic Equipment (WEEE) directive emerged, smart companies standardized their global operations. Complying with regulatory requirements in each country, state, or city often means a company must manage sourcing, production, and logistics differently in various regions and play catch-up when tougher regulations arise. Companies such as HP and Cisco opt to go beyond the minimum requirements of each country by applying a so-called gold standard to activities throughout the world. Doing so helps them meet or exceed the highest standards while increasing efficiency and staying ahead of competitors.

Each year we experience severe weather conditions like Hurricane Sandy, the 2012 frankenstorm that devastated areas of the Caribbean and the mid-Atlantic and northeastern United States and that adversely affected the southeastern and midwestern states and eastern Canada. Sandy not only killed people and destroyed homes, it slowed energy production, strangled supply chains, and created a ripple effect throughout the entire U.S. economy. A year earlier, the March 2011 Japanese tsunami changed the course of nuclear power expansion worldwide after the nuclear meltdown and release of radioactive materials from the Fukushima I Power Plant. By January 2012, 19 countries had shut down 138 civilian nuclear power reactors, including 28 in the United States, 27 in the United Kingdom, 27 in Germany, 12 in France, and 9 in Japan.

Some companies do not sit around waiting for NGOs, governments, or weather conditions to force changes in their business practices. Instead, they become the force for change. In 2005, Walmart placed sustainability center stage when then CEO Lee Scott presented his vision for twenty-first century leadership. Viewing sustainability as the biggest strategic driver for the next 40–50 years, the company set long-term goals: operating with 100 percent renewable energy, achieving zero waste, and selling products that protect the welfare of people and the environment. Walmart's new requirements for packaging, transportation, plastics, toxins, water use, agriculture, and more sent eco-shock waves throughout their massive global supply chain.

Opportunities

To dispel the myth that going green costs more and hurts the bottom line, business leaders like Coca-Cola Enterprise's CEO John Brock promote the fact that managing resources brings savings, efficiency, and a positive return on investment. Brock points out that most of the company's environmental projects, such as lowering water and energy use and increasing recycling, quickly pay for themselves and enable the company to reinvest in its business and sustainability efforts.

The investment world now respects sustainable investing and impact investing. A 2012 MIT Sloan Management Review report, "Sustainability Nears a Tipping Point," reveals that institutional investors such as pension plans and universities increasingly seek companies that not only make a profit but also adhere to high standards of social and environmental responsibility. Forward-looking investors like companies that compete for a spot on the Dow Jones Sustainability Index (DJSI) because they will most likely outpace less stable, less efficient, and less innovative competitors over the long run. Said Roberta Bowman, SVP and CSO of Duke Energy, "In addition to the more traditional 'socially responsible investors' we are finding that some of our mainstream investors are now looking at *sustainability performance* as an indicator of overall business value."

Globalization

"It's a small world" is a saying that once denoted a coincidence; now it has become a reality. Globalization has created hyperconnected markets where communications technology and rapid transportation link citizens of the world together as never before. Just as information, ideas, talent, products and services, and investments travel the globe, so too do problems stemming from overpopulation, resource depletion, and income disparity. Peace and stability will provide the best solutions not just for individuals and governments, but for the world's business enterprises.

Most global issues defy easy solutions. When a 1993 NBC broadcast exposed child labor abuses in Bangladesh, highlighting a factory that supplied Walmart and other apparel companies, pending U.S. legislation threatened to close the American market to Bangladeshi garments if another case of child labor became public. In response, the Bangladesh Garment Manufacturers and Exporters Association reportedly dismissed thousands of children from garment factories. Unfortunately, this action drove the victims into more dangerous work, such as welding and even prostitution. In contrast, when Levi Strauss faced a similar situation in Bangladesh, it allowed the children of factory workers to leave their jobs and attend school without losing wages and benefits. Jobs would await them when they reached legal age.

Starbucks' strategy to implement sustainable, globally recognizable, locally relevant design sparks innovation and boosts brand loyalty. Works by local artists decorate café walls; school children paint murals for the burlap wall coverings; cement floors remain bare in a SOHO Oregon store; and local green providers supply handcrafted furnishings. In Paris, repurposed wine barrels decorate a Starbucks storefront, with retired champagne bottle racks adorning the interior. Considering itself in "the moment of connection business," Starbucks seeks ways to connect with each local community across 55 countries while promoting its own global commitment to responsible growth. Starbucks serves the world and makes money one community, one store, and one cup at a time.

Challenges

Global supply chains have become increasingly complex and visible. Companies like Starbucks must consider growing conditions, agricultural practices, their effect on trees and wildlife, labor conditions, and worker housing in countries far from its Seattle base. One watchdog, The

Rainforest Alliance, requires a company to meet more than 100 criteria in order to receive sustainable agriculture certification. That certification enhances a company's brand value.

Companies must shield their workers in other countries from violence and navigate a minefield of unfamiliar cultural and ethical mores. When developed nations went into an economic free fall in 2008, many businesses ramped up their strategies to enter emerging markets such as Mexico, Brazil, Indonesia, and China, where local companies routinely pay bribes to get business done. This puts ethically minded multinationals at a distinct disadvantage and in a precarious position. Pressure to make up for declining revenues lured some executives to resort to bribery in order to remove obstacles and speed growth. When Siemens and Walmart did so, they found themselves embroiled in international scandals. A 2012 *Harvard Business Review* article, "Greased Palms, Giant Headaches," reported that bribery and corruption rank a close second to competition and antitrust violations as the most frequent crimes committed by Western companies in emerging markets."[4]

Opportunities

Companies will increasingly tap into emerging markets for growth. As of 2012, Proctor & Gamble reached consumers in 180 countries, Emirates Airline flew to more than 70, and McDonald's sold hamburgers in 119. Globalization often serves as a positive force. Consider how China has liftd 400 million people out of extreme poverty by opening their borders to trade.

Although many people think innovation starts in the richest nations and trickles down to the poorest, some companies tap the power of reverse innovation, where customers in the developing world adopt the newfangled first. A 2012 *Ivey Business Journal* article reported that when U.S.-based Deere & Company decided to produce a new tractor for use in India, it used a zero-based model to design it from scratch and not rely on Deere's current technology. Deere also involved local people on the design team to ensure that the result would match their needs. This approach enabled Deere to enter a new, expanding market with attractive lower-cost models.

Population Shifts

The expanding global population and shifting demographics change the game for all organizations. The UN has declared population growth the biggest problem of the new century, posing serious threats to human health, socioeconomic development, and the environment. The world's population grew from 2 billion in 1927 to 6 billion in 1998 to 7 billion in 2011, with the UN projecting that it will explode to 9.2 billion by 2050. Most of this growth will occur in the poorest countries. Today, 4 billion people, more than half of the world's population, survives on less than $2.50 a day. Pressure from this group, referred to as the Base of the Pyramid, pushes toward the top of society like a volcano about to erupt. A 2012 KPMG report predicted that by 2030 threats to food security due to population growth and related issues of water scarcity and deforestation could escalate global food prices from 70 to 90 percent.

Challenges

The more people on the planet, the more stuff they need, from petroleum products to cucumbers. This puts tremendous pressure on finite resources. The KPMG report also predicted that by 2030, the global demand for freshwater will exceed supply by 40 percent, threatening businesses with water shortages, lower water quality, price volatility, and erosion of their brand image for the wasteful use of water. Water-scarce areas will face the greatest challenges as growers compete for water with consumers and water-intensive industries such as mining and energy. Declining air quality also poses a threat to business. China's average passenger vehicle growth rate of 25 percent from 2000 to 2011 took the country from 10 million to 73 million vehicles. At the end of 2012, approximately 1 billion vehicles careened down the world's roads.

In another game-changing development, more than half of the earth's population now lives in cities. Siemens reports the world's 10 megacities account for 2 percent of the planet's population and a staggering 20 percent of global gross domestic product. City infrastructures cannot keep pace with the explosion. According to Siemens' Sustainable Cities data, in 2010, 82 percent of Americans lived in cities; by 2050 the number will escalate to 90 percent. Cities now account for two-thirds of worldwide energy consumption, 60 percent of water use, and 70 percent of all greenhouse gases. Experts believe China's urban population will reach one billion by 2030. This increase in city dwellers would match the total population of the U.S. Urbanization, driven by economic development, increases consumption and demand for services. While this presents an opportunity for business, it also requires China to shift its emphasis from exports to meeting internal needs, from production to service, and from insensitivity to responsibility with respect to the environment.

A new generation of young people demand change. Mr. Land's students at Sun Valley Elementary School on Happy Lane in San Rafael, California (their real names) have challenged corporate giant Crayola to recycle the 500 million plastic markers the company produces each year. The students' online petition generated 60,000 signatures the first month alone. "I think it really matters," said fifth-grader Olivia McCabe. "We live on Earth and if we hurt it, there's no other place we can go to."[5]

Opportunities

Companies find new consumers by selling to those at the Base of the Pyramid. The more than 900 million mobile phone users in India can buy a SIM card for about 20 cents and pay only 1 cent per minute. This low-cost, high-volume model creates a market for products and services ranging from banking and sandals to health care and government assistance. In 2010, an estimated 2 billion emerging middle-class consumers in a dozen countries spent $6.9 trillion. McKinsey's 2010 research indicates that this amount will rocket to $20 trillion by 2020, which equates to double the 2010 U.S. consumption. Luxury goods have also trickled into emerging nations. Prada opened its first store in China in 1993, joined by other high-priced designers Gucci, Armani, and Louis Vuitton. In 2012, 22 percent of Prada's revenue came from China and other emerging markets.

The challenges of urbanization bring opportunities for sustainable development. Siemens, General Electric, and Cisco view urbanization as an opportunity to upgrade aging infrastructures to more environmentally friendly ones that improve quality of life and reduce costs through energy and resource efficiency. As rural areas shrink and demand for food increases, solutions that emphasize greater agricultural productivity will come from companies such as farm equipment maker Deere and fertilizer makers Agrium and Potash.

Companies today manage employees spanning four or five generations. Having grown up in the digital age, the Millennials and members of Generation Y expect instant connectivity and gratification through their mobile devices. Far from the old world of nine-to-five glued-to-your-desk employment, this new generation merges their work and personal time, requiring employers to rethink performance review and reward systems, technology support, use of social media, working hours, workspace, and telecommuting. Recent college graduates with a strong social conscience seek responsible employers. As G.P. (Bud) Peterson, President of the Georgia Institute of Technology, told me, "Our students are incredibly intelligent; they want to change the world, and they are convinced they are going to do just that."

Applying The New Corporate Facts of Life

Birds do it, bees do it, even business leaders do it. They obey the facts of life. The New Corporate Facts of Life will not go away. These are not flavor-of-the-month fads. They will increasingly determine whether your business strategies succeed or fail. Population growth fattens demand for natural resources while reducing their supply. Environmental degradation threatens the very survival of employees and customers. A rival's innovation renders everything you do obsolete. Access to technology connects folks from Aberdeen to Zambia and enables both brand-enhancing praise and damning criticism. Stakeholders become citizen journalists, creating viral blogs and videos that can make or break a brand. One smartphone can start a revolution. Economic uncertainty makes every investment an agonizing and possibly lethal decision. Globalization connects us all through economic fluctuations, fuel shortages, disease, security, commerce, and human rights.

Every time you make a business decision, whether large or small, local or global, strategic or cultural, you should consider its implications with respect to The New Corporate Facts of Life. Here and at the end of each chapter in this book you can formalize such a review with The New Corporate Facts of Life (NCFOL) Barometer (Figure 1-2). Doing so will help you more deeply understand the issues surrounding the decision, the challenges it poses, and the opportunities it offers. Use it yourself. Invite other organizational leaders and cross-functional groups of people at all levels to try their hands at it. Involving a diverse range of internal and external stakeholders of different ages, experience levels, areas of expertise, and perspectives will raise possibilities that you yourself might miss.

After thinking about all this, do you see areas where you should improve your efforts? Which areas will most dramatically affect your business now and in the future? Who else should you engage in discussions of these trends? What areas should you research more thoroughly? Try to convert your answers into a redefined vision and strategic plan for this year, the next five years, and even the next 10 years.

Figure 1-2. The New Corporate Facts of Life Barometer.

Rating Key:
H–High: We take this very seriously.
M–Medium: We consider this to some degree.
L–Low: We don't think about it much.

NCFOL	Rank How Well You:	H	M	L
Disruptive Innovation	❑ Guard against becoming obsolete. ❑ Foster innovation in many ways. ❑ Seek solutions to societal problems to drive innovation. ❑ Consider new business models for your organization. ❑ Use innovation to learn more about your customers.			
Economic Instability	❑ Manage the fallout from sweeping economic decline. ❑ Capitalize on growth periods. ❑ Invest for the short term and the long term. ❑ Strive for greater efficiency. ❑ Enter emerging and second-tier markets.			
Societal Upheaval	❑ Navigate cultural and political landmines. ❑ Monitor your supply chain. ❑ Protect your brand image. ❑ Bring jobs and prosperity to the communities you serve. ❑ Seek solutions to unmet social needs.			
Stakeholder Power	❑ Foster employee engagement. ❑ Meet stakeholder needs and increase shareholder value. ❑ Follow a business model that considers all stakeholders. ❑ Tap into multiple stakeholders for new ideas. ❑ Partner with NGOs and other external stakeholders.			
Environmental Degradation	❑ Clean and green your supply chain. ❑ Anticipate regulations before they force us to change. ❑ Plan for crises and catastrophes. ❑ Save money by managing resources. ❑ Behave as an environmentally responsible company.			
Globalization	❑ Consider the trade-offs in operating globally. ❑ Operate ethically in all countries at all times. ❑ Protect your people and assets in unstable countries. ❑ Enter emerging markets for growth. ❑ See commerce as a force for good.			
Population Growth	❑ Understand the implications of population growth. ❑ Take advantage of urbanization trends. ❑ Manage multiple generations of employees. ❑ Attract and retain young workers. ❑ Find opportunities in emerging and developing nations.			

CHAPTER 2

Reset Your Mindset

My greatest challenge has been to change the mindset of
people. Mindsets play strange tricks on us. We see things
the way our minds have instructed our eyes to see.

—MUHAMMAD YUNUS, NOBEL PEACE PRIZE WINNER

IN 1976, MUHAMMAD YUNUS, a young college professor at Chittagong University in Bangladesh, decided to do something about the crushing cycle of poverty in a local village. After speaking with the impoverished villagers, he compiled a list of 42 women who needed only a total of $27 to begin the journey out of misery. That's $27 *total*, not $27 each. These women, possessing no money and no education, just like their parents and grandparents before them, could obtain money for their businesses only from loan sharks at exorbitant interest rates. Repayment would keep them trapped in the cycle of poverty. When Yunus approached a local bank on their behalf, seeking merely the $27 the women could use to start their businesses, the bank said no, not without collateral. Nor did bank policies even permit loans to women.

That's when Professor Yunus drew the money from his own savings. With these funds, the women bought the bamboo needed to make furniture and baskets they could sell. Before long, the new entrepreneurs were making enough money not only to support their families but to repay the loans. When Yunus reported this accomplishment to the bank, the bank again turned a cold shoulder. Undeterred, the professor kept making small loans, which the new borrowers also repaid with interest. Still the bank said no.

Although Yunus didn't realize it at the time, he had taken the first steps toward what would become a global microfinance system that reversed conventional banking wisdom by focusing on women borrowers, extending loans only to the poorest borrowers, and setting aside the usual requirement for collateral. In 1983, this resulted in the founding of Grameen Bank (which means Village Bank) with the belief that credit is a fundamental human right. By 2007, Grameen Bank had made $6.38 billion in loans to more than 7.4 million borrowers. By 2010, it was lending more than $100 million each month to poor people, with an almost perfect repayment rate. More than 94 percent of Grameen loans have gone to women, who suffer disproportionately from poverty and who are more likely than men to devote their earnings to their families. Small loans of only a few hundred dollars enabled recipients to start all sorts of businesses and support their families. Over a million families in Bangladesh today have climbed from poverty with their own hard work, a strong set of values, and a little help from a bank started by a man who saw things differently.

In 2006, Yunus and Grameen Bank shared the Nobel Peace Prize for their efforts to "create economic and social development from below." Yunus has received global recognition for his work, including the Bangladesh President's Award in 1978, the Mother Teresa Award in 2006, and the Presidential Medal of Freedom awarded by President Barak Obama in 2009.

While the world's giant financial institutions crumbled and crashed in 2008, Grameen Bank soared. Yunus's 2010 book, *Building Social Business: The New Kind of Capitalism That Serves Humanity's Most Pressing Needs*, details the phenomenon. In one case, a relatively small loan launched Grameen Shakti, a nonprofit enterprise in Bangladesh, where 100 million people aren't connected to the electric grid. This entrepreneurial business, run mostly by women, provides employment and sells affordable solar energy systems to hundreds of thousands of poor people in rural areas.

Grameen has also launched joint ventures with companies around the world, the first in 2005 with the French dairy company Danone (makers of Dannon yogurt) to provide fortified yogurt in Bangladesh at a low price. The name of the yogurt, Shokti+doi, means "yogurt to give strength." Serendipitously, that effort to fight malnutrition led to the discovery of a new preservative. While Grameen Danone's community-based model provides local employment in their factories, Grameen Bank lends money to people to set up nearby microfarms that supply ingredients and to women to set up businesses to sell the product. As of 2012, the venture has created 1,600 jobs within a 30-kilometer radius of the plant, including 900 women in the "ladies network" who sell yogurt door-to-door. The factories rely on renewable energy, rainwater harvesting, and biodegradable packaging. Profits are used to expand the program.

Social businesses supported by Grameen must be self-sustaining. The owners must not take any money out of the business beyond their initial investment. Additional profits must be spent on improving society. Grameen Danone measures success not by counting profit but by counting the number of children it nourishes. However, as its discovery of the new preservative underscores, the company gains more than feel-good satisfaction. It also reaps the rewards of greater innovation, creativity, engagement, and learning. These returns on the investment help the company's businesses in more affluent regions. Other large corporations, including Intel, BASF, adidas, and Veolia Water, have started joint venture social businesses with Grameen, the profits from which make the world a better place to live.

Yunus, believing that "poverty is not created by the person, it is created by the system—concepts, policies, institutions," envisioned a new system that succeeded. His vision defied conventional wisdom. As Yunus said of the conventional banks, "The whole struggle was the mindset." If we don't first shift our thinking and reshape our old perspectives, we can't change behaviors, foster innovation, or create new solutions.

Perennially successful companies prosper by replacing conventional business assumptions with new ones that can create shared value for the company and society. Patagonia prospers by promoting the counterintuitive notion that customers should buy less. On Black Friday, November 25, 2011, typically one of the busiest U.S. shopping days of the year, the company ran a full-page ad in *The New York Times* urging readers, "Don't buy this jacket." The company has adopted a model whereby it aims to make fewer products of higher quality in order to encourage customers to buy only what they need and to sell or recycle garments they no longer need. The *Times* ad appeared after the company had experienced its most successful two years ever. Conventional wisdom would have dictated the opposite approach—"Buy more!"—but Patagonia targets the most discerning consumers who more likely buy higher quality at a higher price point. Patagonia even promises to repair its fleece jackets at no cost to the buyer and invites customers to sign a pledge to repair the garment if necessary and to resell or recycle it through one of the stores.

The company's commitment to responsible and sustainable business practices extends to using material from old clothes to remanufacture apparel, thus reducing the consumption of raw materials. In the 1990s, Patagonia started turning plastic bottles into fleece garments, a practice now used by many other companies. The company manages the investments in new processes by applying two budget cycles, the usual annual one and a ten-year one that measures long-term payback. Patagonia has reset its mindset.

It takes some effort to reset a mindset. We cling to our existing beliefs because they make us feel safe and comfortable. When we question and replace them, we take a big risk: the bigger the change, the bigger the risk, and the bigger the risk, the greater the fear of failure. While it takes courage to rethink approaches that have made us successful in the past, the forces of change keep gaining speed. If we don't respect them and reset our mindsets, we risk losing it all.

The average Fortune 500 company survives for only about 30 to 40 years for one major reason: failure to change. Blockbuster refused to change its video store model, downplaying the potential threat of an online video model. Kodak invented digital photography and X-ray technology but kept its focus on film while the world rapidly went digital. On the other hand, IBM, which stands for International Business *Machines*, no longer builds machines. It has transformed itself from a hardware seller to a supplier of business solutions. Another global giant, United Parcel Service, began life in 1907 as a bicycle messenger service. Since then, UPS has continuously changed its business model to grow itself into a global commerce and logistics leader. To alter the way we look at our business, as IBM, UPS, and Patagonia have done, we must understand why and how we developed our mindsets in the first place.

Understanding Mindsets

Mindsets, mental models, paradigms, perspectives, whatever you call them, they consist of all the basic assumptions, beliefs, images, and stories that shape the way we define ourselves, other people, organizations, and every facet of the world. They determine how we interpret and respond to situations. They are the lenses through which we view the world. Of course, these lenses often distort what actually exists to match our own individual way of looking at the world. We don't see Reality with a capital *R*. We see our own unique brand of reality. As any detective will agree, two people who witness a felon grabbing a woman's purse and bolting into a crowd will offer markedly different descriptions of the event. Jane recalls a short, bearded man in a red hooded sweatshirt; Joe insists he saw a tall woman wearing an orange vest and ski mask. The same applies to the arrival of a new competitor on the scene or a sudden decline in demand for our company's products. Most importantly our mental models affect how we behave in challenging situations and how we make crucial business decisions. When a major change alters the business terrain, Jane may focus on the problems it creates and avoid addressing it with a major investment, whereas Joe might see it as a golden opportunity on which he should bet the farm.

Since many of our subjective beliefs lie below our level of awareness, we seldom examine them closely. Do they really make sense, or might they lead us down a dangerous path? Whether you realize it or not, you start shaping your mental models as an infant, when you need to make sense of the world and all the events that affect you. As Dr. Nicole Lipkin, psychologist and author of *What Keeps Leaders Up at Night*, told me, "We're so over-stimulated in our lives. Our brain protects us by organizing our thinking and filtering the information we receive."

Psychologists call this natural human tendency *confirmation bias*. We prefer and accept information that supports our mental models, and we discount and reject information that does not. Two people read the same news report about the rising national debt. One sees it as support for tax cuts for the wealthy; another views it as proof that the government should spend more money stimulating the economy. Same event, two radically different reactions.

Here's a little game that illustrates the point. Count the number of times the letter F appears in this headline:

FINISHED FILES ARE THE RESULT OF YEARS OF SCIENTIFIC STUDY COMBINED WITH THE EXPERIENCE OF MANY YEARS.

How many did you count? Three? Four out of five people would agree with that number. Take another look. Did you notice that *of* appears three times? Aha! The letter *F* appears six times. So why do most people miss half of them? Because we tend to ignore things to which we attach little value. *Of* is a little word, which, incidentally, we pronounce "ov." Because we tend to focus on key words when we scan a sentence, our eyes easily skip over little old *of*.

The Problem with Mindsets

We see what we expect to see, hear what we expect to hear, and think what we expect to think. Unfortunately, this can cause some pretty big problems. Recently a strong-willed executive I'll call Sarah confided that she felt "blindsided" when her company fired her. In her own mind, she was performing well and simply could not understand what had so displeased her superior. After we chatted for a while, Sarah began to see her predicament from a fresh perspective, finally admitting, "I guess I overlooked a lot of signals over the past few months that should have warned me to examine my actions more closely." Sarah admitted that she held much more conservative opinions than her employer's leaders. Firmly believing that her perspective on issues the organization faced was always the right one, she repeatedly made decisions that alienated key customers, colleagues, and the organization's CEO. When one of her decisions made national headlines and put the company in an embarrassing position, costing it tens of millions of dollars in revenue, her boss finally fired her. Looking back on it all, Sarah could see that she had ignored data that would have counteracted her belief that she was doing a good job. She had let her subjective beliefs evolve into the truth about her situation.

Dr. Diane Kramer, a psychologist and executive coach, encourages clients to decide whether their perception of reality belongs in the "truth bucket" or the "belief bucket." If you file it under beliefs, you can choose to change it. Even if you label it a truth, you must bear in mind that today's truth can quickly become tomorrow's falsehood. When it comes to the future, you need to keep your eyes and ears open and your data collector humming at full speed.

From each event we experience, we observe data in the world around us, select which data we will use, add meanings to the data, and draw conclusions based on those meanings. These conclusions become beliefs that spur us to take action. To make matters worse, our beliefs continue to influence the data we select and accept. The Circle of Perspective (Figure 2-1) illustrates how we continue to reinforce our beliefs and justify our actions based on how we view the world around us.[1]

Figure 2-1. The Circle of Perspective.

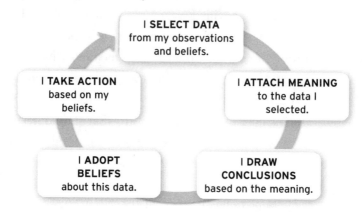

Not long ago, I was working with several colleagues on a client project. During a team meeting, we shared our views about what had worked well so far, what we could have done differently, and where we should go from here. After I expressed my thoughts, one of my colleagues, Amanda, shot me a puzzled look. When I asked whether I had said something that bothered her, she said she took my comments about what we might have done differently as a personal affront. I couldn't believe my ears. "Hey, I was talking about myself, not you!" I explained. It immediately dawned on me that Amanda had read between the lines and inferred that the specific points I'd made applied to what she had or had not done.

The incident taught me something about confirmation bias. No matter how clearly you speak or write, others will insert their own subjective interpretations between the lines. In this case, a conflict between two different views led to laughter and a stronger bond going forward.

Overriding Our Mental Models

The world of mental models is not some abstract playground for academics and intellectuals. It's a concrete laboratory for change. Operatives at the Central Intelligence Agency know this. That's why they use extensive analysis of situations and information to uncover and test their own opinions and thought processes. Sometimes a raw recruit will detect a small change in a mountain of data before an experienced specialist sees it. The veteran sees what she expects to see, whereas the newcomer notices it immediately because he brings fewer expectations to the situation. In other words, the freshman may need to learn a lot, but the senior may need to *unlearn* a lot.

Often, even the most prominent leaders in their fields resist new ideas that eventually replace the old facts of life. When Hungarian obstetrician Ignaz Semmelweis recommended that doctors sanitize their hands before delivering babies, colleagues ignored him, despite published reports that hand washing reduced mortality to less than 1 percent. His colleagues' obstinacy in the face of hard facts eventually drove Semmelweis into a mental asylum, where he died at the hands of his guards. Not until the nineteenth century did doctors change their minds after Louis Pasteur confirmed the germ theory. In another remarkable case, biologists initially derided Charles Darwin for his bizarre theory of evolution, which took 50 years to become widely accepted in the scientific community. In 1977, Ken Olsen, founder and CEO of the mini-computer maker Digital Equipment Corporation, insisted that "There is no reason for any individual to have a computer in his home." You can find the gravestone in the dinosaur cemetery: RIP DEC.

Anyone want to argue about climate change? Despite the fact that 97 percent of qualified scientists agree that humans have been contributing to changes in the earth's climate that will cause tremendous environmental and societal problems, many people in the general public choose to ignore the science and treat climate change as an unproven opinion. Nevertheless, many countries, cities, universities, and businesses do accept climate change as a new fact of life and have begun taking steps to address it. For many companies, the response has already reaped significant rewards in terms of enhanced innovation, efficiency, and profits. A 2012 Deloitte study, "Towards Zero-Impact Growth: Strategies of Leading Companies in 10 Industries," praised PUMA, Nike, Nestlé, Natura Cosmeticos, Unilever, and Ricoh for their strategies to grow and prosper with zero environmental impact. According to another 2012 report, "The Sustainability Movement Nears a Tipping Point," conducted by *MIT Sloan Management Review*, 70 percent of respondents say that their companies have put environmental sustainability squarely on their management agendas, whereas two-thirds believe that they must do so to remain competitive.

Replacing Old Rules with New Facts

Forward-thinking businesspeople are replacing the old shareholder-centric mindset with a much more inclusive shared-value one. They know that sustaining long-term growth in the twenty-first century will depend on both businesses and governments recognizing the fact that they cannot survive if the 7 billion people inhabiting our planet cannot attain healthy standards of living without depleting the earth's resources or running up colossal public debt. The survival of all depends on developing a new view of growth that balances economic prosperity with societal and environmental well-being. It's not a matter of *either* making a profit or protecting the planet; it's a matter of doing both or, as author Jim Collins suggests, applying "the genius of the 'and' instead of the tyranny of the 'or.'"

Unilever stands out as a forward-thinking company. Its leaders see themselves as part of society, not separate from it, and therefore believe that their company must respect the needs of the general public and communities as much as they do the needs of their shareholders. Unilever's CEO, Paul Polman, has said that "in the future this will become the only acceptable model of business. If people feel that the system is unjust and does not work for them, they will rebel against it. And if we continue to consume key inputs like water, food, land, and energy without thought as to their long-term sustainability, then none of us will prosper."

Every day, 2 billion people use Unilever's food, home care, and personal care products, which include such popular brands as Dove soap, Ben & Jerry's ice cream, Lipton Tea, Q-tips, and Suave shampoo.

Unilever delivers those products while maintaining an unwavering commitment to its mission:

➤ *We work to create a better future every day.*

➤ *We help people feel good, look good and get more out of life with brands and services that are good for them and good for others.*

➤ *We will inspire people to take small, everyday actions that can add up to a big difference for the world.*

➤ *We will develop new ways of doing business with the aim of doubling the size of our company while reducing our environmental impact.*

Think about that last tenet. Unilever aims to double its size *and* reduce its negative impact on the environment. To achieve this mission, the company implemented its 2010 Sustainable Living Plan that sets three key targets the company expects to achieve by 2020:

➤ *To help more than one billion people improve their health and wellbeing.*

➤ *To cut our environmental footprint for making and using our products in half.*

➤ *To have 100 percent of our agricultural raw materials come from sustainable sources.*

CEO Paul Polman repeatedly stresses that Unilever's Sustainable Living Plan isn't just a piece of its business plan, it *is* the business plan.

During the worldwide economic decline that began in 2008, Unilever continued to grow profitably and received global recognition for its accomplishments. LinkedIn's 2012 Global In-Demand Employers index ranked Unilever as the world's fifth most desirable employer, acknowledging the company's Sustainable Living Plan as a major attraction for employees. In 2010, 2011, and 2012, Polman himself received the Best Investor Relations for a CEO award, and in 2012 he won the prestigious

C. K. Prahalad Award for leadership in sustainability from the Corporate Economic Forum. That award honored him for bold visions and actions that combined a commitment to long-term capitalism with sustainable business practices. When Corporate Economic Forum founder M. R. Rangaswami presented the award, he said, "Unilever under Paul Polman's leadership is a true pioneer of emerging 'next practices' in the private sector." To put it another way, Polman and his company have successfully replaced the old rules with The New Corporate Facts of Life. Their new perception of reality has guided them to exceed the best practices of today by creating the even better practices of tomorrow.

As Unilever exemplifies, a forward-looking leader thinks beyond the old notions of philanthropy, compliance, and tree hugging. By looking through a fresh lens and adopting a shared-value model, a new breed of companies are finding ways to save money, make money, enter new markets, and create new products and services that delight customers, improve their quality standards and processes, and attract talented and engaged employees. Such organizations develop greater resiliency, responsibility, accountability, transparency, and innovation. They come up with creative answers to the complex questions that businesspeople must ask themselves today:

- ▶ Do we inadvertently finance terrorism in the Congo when we buy tin, tantalum, and titanium to make our products?
- ▶ How will we get China to remove hormone-disrupting chemicals from the clothing they make for us?
- ▶ How can we use sustainable wood sources and stop cutting down ancient Canadian boreal forests?
- ▶ Why do workers at our Chinese supplier commit suicide due to poor working conditions?
- ▶ How can we use renewable energy and save money?
- ▶ Can we produce our products using 90 percent less water?
- ▶ What chemicals should we remove from our products?

► Does using certain ingredients in our products contribute to deforestation and wildlife extinction?

► How should we react when population growth puts pressure on food and water supplies?

► What innovations can we bring to market that will solve human problems and earn a profit in the long run?

► How do we attract a new generation of workers who want meaningful work, flexible hours, and balanced lifestyles?

► How do we grow our business in new countries without succumbing to locally accepted practices of bribery and corruption?

► How can we engage lots of people from diverse stakeholder groups, including competitors, to find sustainable, profitable business solutions?

► Can we learn to look at our business in truly, even radically, new ways to profit through responsible practices?

Probing questions like these help you see the problems posed by the New Corporate Facts of Life as opportunities for growth and increased profitability. They ignite the sort of brainstorming that can overturn conventional wisdom and viewpoints and replace them with insights that can ensure a brighter future for your organization. Figure 2-2 can help set you on the right path.

Shifting Mindsets

Changes in our day-to-day experiences gradually shift our most deep-seated beliefs. However, leading in this NCFOL world requires fast-tracking certain changes in our current perspectives, which have grown out of our past experiences. Resetting our mindsets with the profoundly different perspectives we need to prosper in the future starts with opening our minds and our hearts.

Figure 2-2. Compare Old Rules to New Facts.

NCFOL	Old Rules	New Facts
Disruptive Innovation	Remain competitive by developing the next logical step in your products and processes.	Leapfrog ahead of competitors by tackling societal problems with radical new thinking and game-changing innovations.
Economic Instability	Respond to short-term economic fluctuations by investing aggressively during good times and cutting back ruthlessly during bad times.	View current economic conditions within the larger and more long-term context.
Societal Upheaval	Promote corporate social responsibility through philanthropy and community relations.	Take a leadership position to improve the well-being of all citizens in countries where you do business.
Stakeholder Power	Manage the business for shareholder returns and stock market value.	Engage and communicate transparently with all stakeholders who come into contact with your business.
Environmental Degradation	Comply with environmental and safety regulations, but do not worry about depleting resources until scarcity forces you to look elsewhere for them.	Set your own high standards and use environmental responsibility to drive efficiency, profitability, and innovation.
Globalization	Move manufacturing to developing nations, modify your products for other countries, and observe the standards and practices of each individual country.	Lead the industry to responsibly and positively impact all aspects of your global value chain.
Population Shifts	Monitor and adapt to shifting demographic patterns, such as an aging population and increasingly diverse populations.	Anticipate and create sustainable strategies to capitalize on population growth, urbanization, and multigenerational workforces.

Since we generally tend to heed those experiences that match our customary way of thinking and filter out contradictory information, opening our minds takes real effort. Jessica Owens, general manager of a five-star resort in Mexico, knows all about it. She kept hearing about the profitability of sustainable practices, but never having experienced this phenomenon, she needed to replace an old mindset that says, "Going green *costs* you money" with a new one that argues, "Going green can *make* you money." I encouraged Jessica to "see with the eyes of a child," opening her mind to new possibilities. As she learned about other hotels and many major corporations that were saving money by reducing energy and waste with sustainable business practices, Jessica began to see the light but still could not translate her knowledge into action. Before she could do that, she needed to open her heart as well as her mind.

Opening our hearts helps us connect emotionally to a future we had not previously imagined. As I continued working with Jessica and her leadership team, I urged them to consider different scenarios. "How must we rethink our strategy to succeed five and ten years from now? How will our strategy affect the environment and all the people we touch?" These questions stimulated a range of emotions as the team considered the difference between their current practices and the more sustainable ones they might adopt for the future. Some felt guilty for not acting more responsibly. Others became defensive. Several grew excited about new possibilities. However, as the group pondered ways more sustainable practices could help communities where their own employees live, everyone started to believe that running a world-class resort and behaving like a good citizen could go hand-in-hand down the path to profitability.

It took time for Jessica's people to discard old perspectives and begin thinking and feeling differently. Psychologists tell us that confirmation bias causes people to cling to deep-seated status-quo thinking. A new idea pops up on our radar screen. We weigh it against our long-held beliefs. If it suggests that our old beliefs are wrong, we prefer to ignore it as a freak event or an anomaly. We'd rather stay in our comfort zone than admit the fallacy of an old idea. Getting out of that comfort zone would place us in a vulnerable position. Fear of the unknown, fear of change, fear of ridicule, and fear of failure immobilizes us.

The human brain responds to change the same way it responds to any physical threat, as our fear urges us to flee or fight the danger. It can't tell the difference between a deathtrap and an opportunity offered by a New Corporate Fact of Life. No wonder we find it so challenging to shift a single mindset, not to mention the mindset of an entire organization.

In Jessica's case, she and her team began to overcome their fears as I helped them formulate plans for the short, medium, and long term. With small, celebrated early wins, they gained confidence in the new approach. Some simple changes reduced energy and water use. Guests loved the gourmet meals the chef prepared with organically grown, local food and sustainable seafood. Pride and engagement spread throughout the staff as people offered their own ideas. A whole organizational mindset had changed one small step at a time.

Transformational change toward a better future in this NCFOL world always requires us to conquer our biases and fears. Jessica and the other leaders you'll meet in this book have done just that.

Questioning Organizational Mindsets

Before you can adopt a new mental model, you must comprehend the existing one. Most of us seldom look closely at our mindsets; we feel so comfortable with them that we no longer question their value. It all starts with developing an inquiring mind and engaging in deep reflection and introspection. Ask the hard questions. Capture a belief in one sentence, and then ask yourself, "Why do I believe this? What facts support this belief? Will this belief withstand the test of time?" Then frame a new belief, and ask the same questions.

You can perform the same exercise with groups. Ask a group of people with divided opinions on a topic such as nuclear energy expansion to reverse sides and make a case for the opposite perspective. In group situations, people tend to argue for and defend their position on an issue and need a lot of coaxing before they willingly explore other possibilities. Their confirmation and status quo biases rule their thinking. Each person becomes more firmly entrenched in his or her point of view. When forced to choose among competing beliefs, the group may settle for a compromise or reluctantly accept what the most senior person believes. Compromising and accepting authority seldom changes hearts and minds. Real change must run deeper. Teams can also fall prey to group think, a trap in which everyone goes along to get along, that is, agrees with the prevailing thinking so as not to make waves.

Resetting the prevailing mindset of an organization begins and ends with hard questions, open minds, keen ears, respect for the opinions of others, and a willingness to weigh all options. That sort of environment not only generates the best ideas and solutions, it paves the way for people to take new directions. Researchers Marcial Losada and Emily Heaphy evaluated the conversations of high- and low-performing business teams with respect to three key issues (Figure 2-3): (1) Were people generally positive or negative? (2) Did they inquire about or advocate positions? (3) Did they talk more about themselves or others?

Figure 2-3. High-Performing Versus Low-Performing Teams.

Team Conversations	High-Performing Teams	Low-Performing Teams
Positivity Versus Negativity	5:1	1:20
Inquiry Versus Advocacy	1:1	1:3
Other Versus Self Comments	1:1	1:30

Highly effective teams focus on the positive aspects of a situation, concentrating on strengths and assets. That approach induces optimism about the future and keeps team members open to far-ranging possibilities. People ask more questions and think about the welfare of the group, not just their own self-interests. The next time you attend a meeting, sit back and analyze the conversations. How would you rate your own group in these three areas (on a scale of 1–10, with 10 representing the highest)? Once you know the scores, you can look at ways to raise them.

Although we can't go through life without making certain assumptions and attaching meaning to events, we can learn techniques to understand and question our own assumptions and those of others. The inquiring mind:

➤ **Reflects:** Examine the thoughts and assumptions that lead you to your beliefs.

➤ **Informs:** Share your thoughts and assumptions with others.

➤ **Inquires:** Ask questions to learn about the thoughts and assumptions of other people, especially if they differ from your own.

You must look beyond the facts surrounding a specific belief because a person's unique experiences and emotions always add a good deal of subjectivity to their thinking. That's why you cannot easily change a mindset by simply stating the logical business case for it. Suppose a team at an imaginary health-care provider, Prime Healthcare, decides that it must make crucial changes in light of new health-care laws. Bob White, the firm's Chief Financial Officer, lays out a logical adjustment in dealing with insurance reimbursements. Randall Black, the Chief of Nursing, and Barbara Green, the Chief Medical Officer, attack Bob's plan, concerned that it could reduce the quality of patient care. "We can't just go by the numbers," they argue. "Well, your concern won't do patients a lot of good if we go out of business," Bob angrily counters. It doesn't take long for emotions to derail the discussion.

No matter how hard you try to change a mindset, you may reach an impasse where you're just not making any progress. When that happens, the group needs to pause, step back, and reflect on why they have gotten stuck in their thinking. To get unstuck, you might try the following technique to view a situation through different perspectives. Imagine that everyone in the group is studying an issue through his or her own lens and that they are then asked to examine it from many different perspectives:

1. **Facts Lens:** "What do we know for sure?"
2. **Benefits Lens:** "How will we gain from this change?"
3. **Dangers Lens:** "What could go wrong?"

4. **Emotions Lens:** "What emotions will this change ignite?"

5. **Innovations Lens:** "Can we imagine innovative alternatives?"

6. **Process Lens:** "What approach should we use to achieve our goals?"

Suppose the team at Prime Healthcare applies this approach to its business problem by focusing on the basic question, "Can we find ways to improve the quality of patient care that also make us more efficient and cost-effective?" The team first starts by asking questions from the Facts perspective in order to uncover what they know for sure. Then they rotate through each of the other perspectives:

1. **Facts:** "What do we know for sure about high-quality patient care and clinical errors?"

2. **Benefits:** "What changes can we make to improve quality and reduce costs?"

3. **Dangers:** "What could go wrong if we make these changes, or if we do not make major changes?"

4. **Emotions:** "How do we feel about each of these options?"

5. **Innovations:** "What creative ideas can we come up with?"

6. **Thought Processes:** "What are we missing in considering this issue?"

Whatever approach you use to look at possibilities from many different perspectives, you want to probe new solutions with as many penetrating questions as possible. Probing helps ensure that you do not replace one outdated mental model with another, equally flawed one. At Prime Healthcare, the exercise resulted in a new model for patient care that linked efficiency to effectiveness without reducing quality. A careful study of patient–provider contact revealed that providers spent much more time completing the required paperwork than they did working directly with patients. In just one year, a new mobile-based documentation program ended up saving money on paperwork, reducing clinical errors, and increasing the amount of time providers spent with patients.

Preparing People to Adapt to Change

Engaging people in the process of looking at issues from many different perspectives not only surfaces opportunities and reduces risks, it also fosters closer working relationships. Research has shown that change occurs faster and is more likely to stick over time when the people involved enjoy strong interpersonal relationships—when they care deeply for one another and about the results they achieve together. If they believe change will help them get better results, they'll work harder to implement it. On the other hand, people don't much care for what they didn't create.

Over the years, Royal Dutch Shell has popularized adaptive scenario planning as a way to consider how various forces may impact a company and its industry in the future. Basically, this form of scenario planning prepares people to adapt to change by encouraging them to imagine a variety of possible futures. They don't try to predict the future. They just use their imaginations to paint concrete pictures of how change in the business landscape might affect the company and how various responses might propel it to a brighter future. By doing so, they gain both a heightened awareness of the forces driving change and a keener sense of the fact that "we're all in this together." Not only can this exercise expose previously unquestioned assumptions and beliefs, it paves the way for a successful collaborative response to change. During the process, people feel free to express their ideas in an open, nonjudgmental environment where no one dismisses an idea just because it may initially seem crazy or outrageous. People step up, speak up, and listen up. Once a group captures several future possibilities, they develop strategies for implementing them.

Shell has used adaptive scenario planning for over 40 years. It helped the company anticipate and manage the great global gas shortage of 1973. While the crisis caught other oil giants off guard, Shell emerged as an industry leader. Scenario planning also helped Shell prepare for the 1979 global energy crisis, the 1986 collapse of energy markets, the fall of the Soviet Union, the rise of terrorism in the Middle East, and mounting pressure for corporate environmental and social responsibility.

Adam Kahane, author of the book *Transformative Scenario Planning*, believes we need to go beyond merely preparing for the future: We need to shape it. Kahane, who once worked for Shell's scenario planning department, has used his version of scenario planning in situations where it initially seemed impossible to shift perspectives. In his book, he describes working with South African leaders to overcome deep-seated racial prejudice in a postapartheid country. Thinking about the consequences of a number of different scenarios, the leaders began to see the need to take action by making specific decisions that would smooth the path to a peaceful transition.

One of these scenarios was nicknamed Icarus after the mythological boy whose excitement over his ability to fly with wings held together by wax caused him to fly too close to the sun. When the heat melted the wax, the boy plunged into the sea. In this scenario, participants imagined a newly elected South African government spending heavily to address the apartheid inequities of the past. Although they saw a lot of short-term benefits, they concluded that such an expenditure would ultimately bring budgetary constraints, inflation, and currency depreciation, all of which could bring down the fledgling government and return the country to authoritarian rule.

When the African National Congress government took over in 1994, it took steps to establish prudent economic policies that would bring a degree of fiscal stability to a new South Africa. This fiscal discipline propelled the country's economy from 1 percent growth in the preceding decade to 3 percent between 1994 and 2004, a number that helped the country survive a global recession.[2]

Engaging multiple stakeholders early on contributed to a successful transition from a prejudiced mindset to one imbued with mutual trust and respect. The country's peaceful transformation came about because people changed their thoughts, actions, and relationships with each other.

As the South Africa example illustrates, you can find ways to reset mindsets in even the most contentious and complex situations. My research has led me to a number of companies who deserve special recognition for their success in shifting perspectives in ways that will secure their competitiveness and profitability. Space constraints prevent me from telling their full stories here, but Figure 2-4 briefly notes each of these organizations. I urge you to do your own research into some of these companies, who may provide a model for your own efforts to shift perspectives.

Figure 2-4. New Mindset Hall of Fame.

Disruptive Innovation

- Google aims to organize the world's information and make it universally accessible and useful.
- AkzoNobel seeks sustainable solutions by doing great science, undertaken by great people and in partnerships with others.
- BMW puts what-if? at the core of innovation to develop leading mobility solutions and a state-of-the-art driving experience.

Economic Instability

- RBS Group strives to serve as a model for how banks can contribute to society and make shareholders money along the way.
- Coca-Cola commits to the economic empowerment of 5 million women around the world by 2020.
- UPS invests resources to ensure that it will continue to thrive over the long term while managing short-term fluctuation.

Societal Upheaval

- Unilever vows to help more than 1 billion people improve their health and well-being.
- Coca-Cola fights obesity by promoting active, healthy living to employees, their families, and the communities they serve.
- Valid Nutrition partners with corporations to create a profitable business model to treat and prevent childhood malnutrition in developing countries.

Stakeholder Power

- PUMA, adidas, Nike, H&M, Levi Strauss, and other apparel brands and retailers joined hands in 2011 to lead the industry to zero discharge of hazardous chemicals (ZDHC) in their supply chains by 2020.
- Campbell's Soup turned its business around by making employee engagement a priority.
- SC Johnson taps into multiple stakeholders to achieve business goals and stay abreast of emerging societal needs.

Environmental Degradation

- Walmart sets its sights on producing zero waste and relying 100 percent on renewable energy.
- Unilever seeks to double its business while cutting their environmental footprint in half.
- Novelis seeks to double its profits and obtain 80 percent of its aluminum content from recycled materials.

Globalization

- Levi Strauss strives to protect worker rights and ensure safe, healthy, and humane labor conditions throughout its global supply chain.
- Novo Nordisk values uncompromising quality and business ethics.
- Google believes the need for information crosses all borders.

Population Shifts

- Siemens leads the way in sustainable urban development with green, efficient products, solutions, and financing models.
- Google seeks energetic, passionate, diverse people with creative approaches to work, play, and life.
- Dow expects to meet the intensifying demands from population growth through cutting-edge science, technology, and human ingenuity from across the company and the world.

Companies like these share one important trait: They leap ahead of their competitors because they hire and cultivate people with inquiring minds who constantly challenge old models. Because they often fail to follow the conventional rules of business, leaders need to make sure that they channel inquiring minds toward business results. Bill Seidman, a consultant and author, bases his leadership advice on research into what social scientists call positive deviants:

Positive deviants are purpose-driven people with a good social core. Unconstrained by the tactics of today, they are always "checking the edge" looking toward the practices of tomorrow and asking "Is there

a better way to achieve my purpose?" If a company wants to change their existing business, positive deviants are likely already thinking about and may already be acting in new ways. Organizations should go to them and ask "How should we think about this?" They can tell you and they will bring a richness to the process.

Most importantly, they will look for ways for their organizations to profit from The New Corporate Facts of Life.

Applying The New Corporate Facts of Life

Using the NCFOL Barometer, rate how well your organization seeks to shape the future of your business and industry in each area.

After completing this exercise, consider the current mindsets you may need to reset for your organization to go beyond reacting to change to actively imagining and influencing the future.

Figure 2-5. The New Corporate Facts of Life Barometer.

Rating Key:
H–High: We actively seek to shape the future for our industry.
M–Medium: We consider this to some degree.
L–Low: We don't think about it much.

NCFOL	Rank How Well You:	H	M	L
Disruptive Innovation	❑ Redefine the industry's future with disruptive innovation. ❑ Develop innovations that profitably benefit society. ❑ Question assumptions and redefine the business model.			
Economic Instability	❑ Anticipate and react to economic fluctuations with speed and resilience. ❑ Balance short-term profits with investments that ensure long-term growth. ❑ Lead the industry in sustainability indices and rankings.			
Societal Upheaval	❑ Ensure safe and fair working conditions throughout your supply chain. ❑ Create healthier products and promote well-being. ❑ Use commerce to lift people out of poverty.			
Stakeholder Power	❑ Respect the views of all stakeholders. ❑ Engage external stakeholders for ideas and buy-in. ❑ Develop a highly engaged workforce.			
Environmental Degradation	❑ Find ways to decouple growth from natural resource consumption. ❑ Green the entire value chain. ❑ Achieve aggressive environmental goals.			
Globalization	❑ Operate ethically everywhere, all the time. ❑ Insist on supply chain transparency and traceability. ❑ Audit and address global business issues continuously			
Population Shifts	❑ Lead sustainable growth in emerging nations. ❑ Embrace and benefit through sustainable urbanization. ❑ Redefine work to attract and retain the new generation.			

Create a Compelling Vision

The future ain't what it used to be.
—YOGI BERRA

RAY ANDERSON GRADUATED with honors from Georgia Institute of Technology (Georgia Tech) with a degree in industrial and systems engineering in 1956. He spent 14 years working for various carpet manufacturers before he decided to launch his own company. While visiting Europe, he had noticed carpet tiles in commercial office buildings and saw a vision of that product sweeping the United States. Many in the industry thought the idea ridiculous. Why would anyone take perfectly good carpet, cut it into squares and expect to sell it for twice the price, especially in the midst of a recession? Yet Anderson combined his life savings with funds from supportive investors and founded Interface in 1973. He built a plant, installed equipment, acquired raw materials, and hired employees, all before booking a single order. Anderson stayed the course over the next 21 years, watching Interface exceed his initial vision, growing from a hopeful start-up to a global enterprise with nearly a billion dollars in annual sales. Vision accomplished.

But now the story gets really interesting. Vision goes far beyond chasing the latest business trend or making incremental changes. Enduring companies reach for the stars, aiming to accomplish the seemingly impossible. Their leaders do not rest with turning just one imagined future into reality. They keep aiming higher and higher, constantly applying their imaginations in ways that others cannot and even in schemes that many find foolish.

In 1994, Jim Hartzfeld, then a research associate at Interface, gave Ray Anderson a handwritten note from a salesperson who wanted advice on how to respond to a major customer's questions about the company's environmental policies. The request got Anderson thinking about what Interface might do beyond merely complying with government regulations. Given the fact that carpet manufacturing involves a lot of petroleum-derived chemicals, Anderson wondered whether his company could be causing unseen environmental problems, such as harmful toxins seeping into the ground. Anderson asked Hartzfeld to form an environmental task force to examine the issue. Hartzfeld, less than enthusiastic about an assignment that struck him as a relatively minor recycling initiative, reluctantly agreed.

When Hartzfeld invited Anderson to launch the task force by sharing his "environmental vision" with the team, Anderson drew a blank. The company had developed no strong position on environmental issues.

Serendipitously, that same week someone had given Anderson a copy of *The Ecology of Commerce*, written by Paul Hawken (HarperCollins, 1993), cofounder of the Smith and Hawken garden supply firm and a champion of the environment. As Anderson turned the pages, a new vision began to form. Could his company become more environmentally responsible and still turn a handsome profit? It was a moment Anderson later described as a "spear in the chest epiphany." He thought, "My God, someday what I do here will be illegal. Someday they'll send people like me to jail."

Anderson had celebrated his 60th birthday the year he read Hawken's book. At that age, he had naturally begun thinking about the next phase of life for both himself and his 21-year-old company. What legacy would Anderson leave after he retired? What would drive the next generation of leaders at Interface? These thoughts had created a context for Anderson's reshaping the company in a way that would enable it to thrive, at the same time transforming itself into a leading practitioner of sustainable environmental practices. What had begun as a simple question from a customer had grown into a whole new way of looking at how the company operated in the world.

Soon after his epiphany, on a hot and humid day in late August 1994, Anderson stepped into a cold, air-conditioned hotel conference room where he could almost see his breath. He told the task force he had come at Jim Hartzfeld's request to share his ideas about environmental responsibility with the group.

Anderson spoke from his heart, insisting that only the most powerful institution on earth could take the necessary steps to avert a global catastrophe. Business, not government, must take the lead:

> **Every business has three big issues to face: what we take from the earth; what we make with all that energy and material; and what we waste along the way. We're going to push the envelope until we no longer take anything the earth can't easily renew. We're going to keep pushing until all our products are made from recycled or renewable materials. And we're not going to stop pushing until all our waste is biodegradable or recyclable, until nothing we make ends up as pollution. No gases up a smokestack, no dirty water out a pipe, no piles of carpet scraps to the dump. Nothing.[1]**

Anderson went on to say that this commitment would, paradoxically, enable it to grow and prosper more than ever. Anderson then challenged the team to figure out what to do and how to do it. He wanted them to tell him how Interface could become a restorative enterprise that puts more back into the earth than it takes out and leaves the world a better place with every yard of carpet it sells.

Before anyone could offer any objections to what he had said, Anderson turned and left the room. People sat in stunned silence.

Gradually, however, the team moved past their initial shock and began questioning their leader's sanity. "We're carpet makers, not environmental engineers." Although he was also stunned, Hartzfeld pressed the group to move past their shock to discuss the challenge.

At a key point in the meeting, Graham (Scotty) Scott, employee number six at Interface, stood up and began talking about compromise. "If we can make these changes, if we can transform a company that uses so much energy, so much oil, that wastes so much—if we can do all that profitably, then any business can do it. No one will have an excuse."[2] Scotty paused briefly before continuing. "I can dedicate the rest of my career to making up for all the compromises I have had to make. I can dedicate myself and that's just what I'm going to do." These stirring words sparked a major shift in the team's mindset.

Interface refers to its sustainability plan as Mission Zero. It boldly commits to eliminating the company's negative impact on the environment by the year 2020. To accomplish this goal, Interface redesigned processes and products, pioneered new technologies, and reduced or eliminated waste and harmful emissions, at the same time increasing the use of renewable materials and sources of energy. Innovations included reverse logistics and postconsumer recycling technologies, where they collect old carpets and turn them into new carpets. As a result, between 1996 and 2011, the company lowered greenhouse gas emissions by 32 percent, fossil fuel use by 90 percent, and water consumption by 84 percent. It cut its energy use by 47 percent per unit and increased renewable energy use to 31 percent. Forty-four percent of the materials used in 2011 came from recycled or bio-based materials. The carpet factories slashed the total waste they shipped to landfills by 76 percent, equivalent to more than 253 million pounds of waste. By the end of 2010, the company had saved $438 million in costs through waste reduction efforts, most of which came from employee suggestions.[3] At the same time, sales increased by two-thirds, profits doubled, and they gained market share during a rough recession.

This story speaks to the power of vision, initially one man's vision that became a company's vision and ultimately spread across the globe. One midsized company started a movement that continues to transform industries and helped set the foundation for the U.S. Green Building Council (USGBC). *Fortune* magazine twice included Interface in its annual list of the 100 Best Companies to Work For, and The GlobeScan (2007) Survey of Sustainability Experts ranked Interface atop the list of global companies with the greatest commitment to sustainability, followed by Toyota and GE.

Before he died in 2011, Anderson wrote several books about his journey. In 1998 he published *Mid-Course Correction*, followed in 2010 by *Confessions of a Radical Industrialist*. Both books described how a new outlook on doing business in the world helped his company replace the old environmentally damaging industrial model with a more responsible one dedicated to profitable sustainability.

Understanding Vision

The term *vision* can mean many things to many people. Many equate it with mission, strategy, or goals. In this book, we define it as a compelling, vivid image of an aspirational future that aligns to your values and purpose and that requires substantial effort to achieve. Consider this definition's component parts:

- ► A "compelling, vivid image" paints a picture people can see in their mind's eye and that inspires them to action.

- ► A vision must "align to your values and purpose." As you move boldly into an increasingly uncertain future, you must hold fast to your core values.

- ► An "aspirational future that . . . requires substantial effort to achieve" means aiming high at results that may seem almost impossible to accomplish. Ambitious and far-reaching, the desired results require a lot of hard work to make them happen. Visions seduce us to dream the impossible dream and then motivate us to make it possible.

Interface's vision did not emphasize selling more carpet tiles than any other company. It aimed "To be the first company that, by its deeds, shows the entire industrial world what sustainability is in all its dimensions: People, process, product, place, and profits—by 2020—and in doing so we will become restorative through the power of influence." Ray Anderson often said, "It's not a vision unless it takes your breath away."

I'm not talking about paying lip service to change. Nor am I proposing warm and fuzzy idealistic dreams. As the renowned philosopher and poet Santayana observed, "Words without action are the assassins of idealism." Great organizations use their visions to guide them toward an ideal world built with 10 percent aspiration (vision) and 90 percent perspiration (execution). They develop strategies and a series of specific accomplishments that will take them successfully into that future in both the short term (one to five years) and the long term (10 to 30 years).

As happened at Interface, people often don't know how they are going to achieve the impossible. That takes a lot of hard thinking, painstaking research, and the development of a radically new mindset. Remember, when President John F. Kennedy vowed to a joint session of Congress in 1961 that the United States would put a man on the moon in ten years, no one knew how that could possibly happen.

Interface's vision goes beyond the walls of their own operations and even their industry. Internally, it guides every aspect of their work and permeates their culture. The people there believe they are protecting the world, not merely making carpets. Every Interface leader I interviewed for this book told me they never thought they would spend most of their career working for a carpet company. However, the new direction turned a mere career stepping-stone into a lifelong commitment to making a difference, through their work, in ways they had never dreamed possible. In this way, Interface attracts, retains, and gets the best work from employees at all levels.

Externally, the company publicly reports the status of its sustainability efforts on four fronts: environmental footprint reduction, product innovation, culture change, and the challenges ahead. Some large companies such as Walmart approach Interface to find out how they can achieve similar results. People at Interface continue to mentor global leaders in the transportation, retail, home building, and food and beverage industries on environmental action, quality, innovation, enthusiasm, hope, and profits. Without profits, no company can sustain itself for long.

Today farsighted companies look past traditional business boundaries when they shape their visions because they know that, despite the importance of profits, value extends beyond the bottom line. Interface's success proves the point. Visionary leaders like Anderson know they must peer far into the future. A 2010 United Nations and Accenture study reported that over 93 percent of chief executives from 800 global companies across 25 industries in 100 nations acknowledged that sustainability was "important or very important" to the future success of their businesses.[4]

Creating That Compelling Vision

The best vision provides a guiding beacon. In creating your own North Star, you should adhere to four important principles to discover more than just a lot of fancy words to insert into your annual report.

1. **Keep true to your organization's purpose and core values.** What should remain intact despite whirlwind forces reshaping the business landscape?

2. **Engage key stakeholders to co-create your vision.** Which influential stakeholders can provide new and diverse perspectives?

3. **Think big, bold, and beyond today's obvious possibilities.** Can you imagine a seemingly impossible future for your organization?

4. **View the future through the NCFOL lens.** Which sweeping changes will most dramatically affect your business?

Let's imagine you run Childco, a toy company that specializes in plush toys and stuffed animals. Having read stories about forward-thinking companies such as Interface and Patagonia, you begin to imagine a better way to do business by combining your need for profit with your desire to become a better corporate citizen in the world. How can Childco redefine the future? As you create a new vision for your company, you look beyond the toy industry for trends, inspiration, and creativity. You think beyond your specific products as you proceed through the four steps to creating a compelling vision.

Keeping True to Your Organization's Purpose and Core Values

While looking for examples of values-driven companies, you come across a magazine article about Anita Roddick, founder of The Body Shop, who decided to do more than just manufacture high-quality cosmetics. The company Web site lists her as a human rights activist first, and as founder of the company second. With over 2,500 stores in more than 60 markets globally, Roddick's company has led the industry in addressing environmental issues and attacking poverty around the world.

The Body Shop makes all of its products with nonpolluting ingredients, and it opens stores in poor neighborhoods where it can provide employment and return profit to the community. It follows a strict Against Animal Testing policy, has developed fair trade standards with over 30 suppliers in more than 20 countries, and has provided income to over 25,000 people across the globe. Five core values guide everything the company does:

1. Support community fair trade.
2. Defend human rights.
3. Stand against animal testing.

4. Activate self-esteem.

5. Protect our planet.

In 2006, L'Oreal acquired The Body Shop as part of the global cosmetics giant's quest to become a leader in sustainable practices and prove that "beauty is more than skin deep."

Roddick's original vision for The Body Shop was, "I just want The Body Shop to be the best, most breathlessly exciting company—and one that changes the way business is carried out. That is my vision."

You think about Roddick's vision and how it applies to your business: Why does Childco exist at all? No matter what else changes, what should remain intact? Childco's mission statement proclaims the company's purpose: "Childco's mission is to delight and nurture children by being the best and most respected toy company in the world."

Then you consider Childco's core values:

- ▶ **Fun:** Create fun by having fun.
- ▶ **Responsibility:** Act with integrity at all times.
- ▶ **Respect:** Treat all people with respect.
- ▶ **Quality:** Make the highest-quality and safest products.
- ▶ **Learning:** Encourage learning in both our products and our workplace.

You keep Childco's mission and core values front and center as you reach out to others for insights and support.

Engaging Key Stakeholders to Cocreate Your Vision

While the responsibility for creating vision ultimately rests with you as the CEO, involving others will help you avoid falling in love with your own bright ideas. Keeping that rule in mind, you speak with your senior leadership team about their concepts of the company's future. Unfortunately, each Childco executive expresses the view that his or her function should receive the most emphasis. That doesn't surprise you. People tend to see the world through their own personal perspectives.

Perhaps you need to cast a wider net and include a broader range of stakeholders to shape Childco's vision. Whom should you include? What questions should you ask? How should you approach them? You worry a bit about the Emperor's New Clothes syndrome, where people tell the CEO only what they think he wants to hear. You're a business leader, not an expert on stakeholder engagement and vision creation. Ultimately, you decide to hire a consultant to help you identify the right people to help formulate Childco's new vision.

She asks you, "Whom does Childco influence? Who influences Childco?" Employees, shareholders, children, and parents naturally come to mind. She presses you to consider other possible internal and external stakeholders. As you ponder this question, you come up with a few surprises: Childco's suppliers; the board of directors; teachers; a software developer; an expert psychologist who has written a book on the effects of media exposure on young children; a well-known animal trainer with a deep knowledge of canine and feline behavior; NGOs such as the International Council of Toy Industries, Greenpeace, and Save the Children; a representative from the federal government's product testing lab; and three other toy manufacturers who develop video games and educational software. This unusual assembly could brainstorm ideas that your own people would never come up with on their own.

You want to create a stakeholder council comprised of some selected people you believe will probe and question all ideas, no matter their source. The council will, you hope, bring some out-of-the-box thinking to the undertaking, smoke out the unintended consequences of well-intentioned decisions, and boil it all down to a truly actionable vision. This approach also ensures that all those affected by Childco's vision will understand and support it. Without their buy-in, you might as well fold your tent and do something else with your time.

Think Big, Bold, and Beyond

You try to imagine a seemingly impossible future for Childco. Your research introduces you to Toyota's global vision, which transcends the automotive industry:

> Toyota will lead the way to the future of mobility, enriching lives around the world with the safest and most responsible ways of moving people. Through our commitment to quality, constant innovation, and respect for the planet, we aim to exceed expectations and be rewarded with a smile. We will meet our challenging goals by engaging the talent and passion of people, who believe there is always a better way.

Although Toyota struggled through massive vehicle recalls beginning in 2008 and weathered severe supply chain disruptions caused by Japan's 2011 earthquake, the company continually renewed its commitment to innovation, a commitment that had resulted in such breakthroughs as a more flexible manufacturing process to enable quick adjustments in the production line, the incorporation of new materials, the installation of the latest technology in its vehicles, and the production of a wider range of alternative-fuel models. While other automakers shied away from alternative-fuel vehicles, Toyota persevered and in 1997 introduced the Prius, the world's first mass-produced hybrid. In 2012, the Prius became the world's third best-selling car, propelling it out of the planet-saving niche into the mainstream market.

Exploring yet another industry, you study the Virgin Group, founded in 1970 by Sir Richard Branson. The company has become one of the world's most recognized and valued brands. Virgin's business interests span travel, music, mobile communications, financial services, leisure, holidays, and health and wellness. Its units employ approximately 50,000 people in 34 countries. In 2011, Virgin's global branded revenues reached £13 billion ($21 billion). Branson did not envision creating one of the largest enterprises on the planet but aimed instead at earning the utmost respect of everyone with whom his businesses came into contact:

> **Virgin believes in making a difference. We stand for value for money, quality, innovation, fun, and a sense of competitive challenge. We strive to achieve this by empowering our employees to continually deliver an unbeatable customer experience.**

In his book, *Screw Business as Usual*, Branson wrote about "turning business as we know it upside down and really making it a force for good in the world." That core value drives all of his companies. That's what a great vision does. It reflects core values and motivates people to honor them in all the work they do.

You bring together stakeholder groups in what you call visioning summits, meetings designed to get people peering 10 to 20 years into the future. Visioning does not involve incremental changes but rather the sort of monumental changes we can scarcely imagine. If Interface can do it with carpets, Childco can do it with plush toys. At the summit, people discuss the company's greatest strengths and project them into the future. What would its ideal future look like in 10 or even 20 years? What good does the company bring to the world? How do people feel about working at Childco in this ideal future?

You engage many people to ask these so-called dream questions and listen for the key elements of connection and possibilities. You ask for big, bold ideas that go beyond current thinking. As people get excited about blue-skying the future, you hear a lot of astonishing, even outrageous ideas, and it pleases you no end to hear such excitement about bringing joy, comfort, learning, and caring to children and communities around the world. The same enthusiasm accompanies discussions of the sort of unique, vibrant corporate culture it will take to do that.

Viewing the Future Using
The New Corporate Facts of Life

In your effort to shape a better future, you continue researching how the major forces of change are affecting your own and other industries. Your efforts include visits to organizations in different industries to obtain new ideas. Your hosts actually enjoy answering such questions as, "What vision drives your strategy? How far ahead do you look? What do you see there?" Scanning the media for news of emerging trends, you try hard to keep abreast of future possibilities. You also collect reports from organizations such as Forum for the Future and the World Resources Institute. All of this looking through the NCFOL lens helps you imagine a vastly different future for your organization and industry. For each NCFOL, you consider what Childco might do.

Disruptive Innovation

What sort of toy animals will delight children ten years from now? Twenty years from now? How about robotic teddy bears? Why not marry the iconic toy with robotics and interactive computer games to create a simulated pet that provides the companionship of a beagle and the interactive instruction of a gifted teacher? You spend time learning about the latest developments in robotics and interactive gaming. A few news reports capture your imagination. One details robots with video conferencing capability that can gather in one room while their operators sit at their desks at remote sites around the world. Another proposes a new category of video games that do not use sex and violence to entertain players. One tells of a 3-D printer technology that allows people to make their own toys.

How might such breakthrough innovations shape a better business model and bring new and different products to market? Can Childco discover innovative ways to promote learning? You make a note to include innovation in the company's vision in a way that aligns it with your core values.

Economic Instability

While the toy industry remained fairly stable during the worst of the recent recession, you weigh some other economic factors. The declining economy combined with technological advances has spurred an increase in microentrepreneurs, so-called slasher-workers (e.g., a lawyer/artist), and patchwork careerists. The U.S. Bureau of Labor Statistics in 2005 reported that one-third of U.S. workers, more than 42 million people, belonged to a growing freelance segment of the labor force, earning a living as independent contractors, working as temporary or part-time employees, moonlighting, or doing other contract gigs or projects. As *Daily Beast* editor Tina Brown wrote in 2009, "No one I know has a job anymore. They've got gigs." Many workers transition from their full-time jobs by first becoming career slashers—the lawyer/artist, the accountant/chef, the professor/speaker, or the psychologist/writer.

How will this trend affect Childco in the future? How can you take advantage of the growing gig economy? You begin to imagine a virtual organizational structure using entrepreneurs to bring greater design innovation that will expand the market for your products. You make a note to consider flexible labor, manufacturing, and supply chain cost models that tap into emerging economic trends. Childco must remain profitable in good times and in bad.

Societal Upheaval

You have been hearing about unsafe and demeaning working conditions in factories around the world and wonder if you really know what happens in Childco's extensive supply chain. Are our suppliers' factories safe? Do they pay a fair, livable wage? Do children work in these factories? How do we find out if any suppliers use forced labor? You do think a company must take steps to improve people's lives by lifting up a society with meaningful jobs, ethical commerce, equal treatment of women, and respect for natural resources. Societal upheaval occurs because oppressed people yearn for education, jobs, homes, equality, safety, health, and a bright future for their children. Fulfillment of these desires creates stability, prosperity, and peace. Businesses, you conclude, should abandon the old model of chasing cheap labor and ripping apart the environment for profit and go beyond merely complying with local laws and bestowing handouts. Everyone profits when you help people build a sustainable future where trade replaces aid and where hope and pride conquers the despair that ignites violence.

While reading Fast Company's "100 Most Creative People in Business 2012," you learn about Tal Dehtiar, who founded the shoe and leather goods company, Oliberté, in 2009. Although Canadian-based, the company manufactures and sources its materials in Africa, with the expressed goal of creating and maintaining sustainable jobs.

Oliberté refers to its vision as "The Change We Seek®":

We believe that no one should feel they have to rely on aid to get by in a place with a potentially booming economy. Oliberté's goal is to create sustainable jobs in Africa by staying local—sourcing materials there as well as hiring and manufacturing locally—so that people can start, or continue to, define their own lives. Beyond creating sustainable jobs, Oliberté aspires to demonstrate that Africa creates quality, handcrafted goods that can shine in any market and is a continent of pride, power, and liberty.

Dehtiar talks in the article about creating a business beyond charity through trade, not aid. "I'm not a fan of giving things away. If we want to help Africa, we have to create manufacturing jobs—and I don't mean cheap labor. Through the local production of Oliberté shoes, we can create 1 million jobs in Africa by 2025." Sales soared when the company moved away from Western-styled shoes to reflect African culture in its design and craftsmanship. Oliberté now sells its products in countries such as Canada, the United States, Hong Kong, Singapore, the United Kingdom, Denmark, Oman, and South Africa, to name a few.

Oliberté commits to environmental responsibility with respect to livestock, water use and treatment, and recycling. The company makes the soles of its shoes from natural crepe rubber that is harvested from rubber trees and untreated with toxic chemicals. Insisting on fair and ethical business practices, Oliberté staffs its factories with diversity in mind, placing women in 50 percent of the production and senior administrative jobs. Factories surpass local labor regulations, and workers receive such benefits as subsidized or free lunches, tea breaks, and maternity leave.

Back at Childco, you decide to develop a higher level of social conscience by going beyond conventional notions of corporate social responsibility and philanthropy. You vow to find ways to improve working conditions within your own supply chain. Perhaps your company might economically empower women in impoverished areas by enabling them to handcraft some of Childco's products. The money they earn would feed their children and help them rise out of poverty. Mothers and grandmothers would appreciate the handmade quality and take a lot of pride in the fact that they are helping other women and families by purchasing their handiwork.

Stakeholder Influence

A colleague tells you about Next Generation, a U.K.-based financial industry association of young professionals from asset management companies, banks, insurers, business schools, and consulting, accounting, and legal firms.

Founded in November 2010, this collection of young talent from across the financial services industry convened to develop a shared understanding of where the industry stands today, with the hope of forming a collective vision of where forward-looking leadership could take it over the next 10 to 15 years. The industry employs a million people, contributes more to the United Kingdom's income tax revenues than any other sector, and includes global leaders offering products ranging from cross-border banking to carbon trading.

To formulate their vision, Next Generation tapped into every imaginable stakeholder: the general public, customers, employees, shareholders, business partners, management, government, and regulators. In the end, they proposed this vision:

We judge the strength of our industry not just by how it benefits the strong, but by how it encourages the ambitious, empowers the family, nourishes the community, inspires the public, and benefits the nation. Our vision aspires not to determine the battleground of short-term tactical advantage, but occupies the high ground from which our industry's future and our nation's well-being will be shaped.

This organization inspires you. You, too, have learned a lot by engaging a diverse group of internal and external stakeholders. Some input did not surprise you. Children want toys that are fun, cute, and comforting. Parents add safety, high quality, and affordability to the mix. Along with teachers, they value toys that promote positive learning experiences and help develop social skills. Retailers want to satisfy those desires. Shareholders and the board of directors expect strong profits and growth. Regulators insist you comply with a myriad of laws concerning trade, materials, safety, and labor.

You also learned much you didn't know. Input from animal behaviorists, robotics engineers, developmental psychologists, and parents convinced you that your idea of robot pets might not make sense because they would interfere with the natural bonds children form with other human beings and animals.

Retailers now insist you sign an agreement committing you to ethical practices in your supply chain. One NGO, Organic Baby University, claims to have found a chlorinated tris in the flame retardant used in some of Childco's stuffed animals. Scientists eventually connected this chemical, once widely used in children's sleepwear, to cancer. Another NGO criticizes an unsafe factory in Childco's supply chain that employs children and gives its employees only one day off per month. Although Childco doesn't own this factory, you feel obligated to make sure that all of your suppliers comply with your ethical business practices.

Childco employees bring good and bad news. Although they take great pride in their work and express high levels of dedication, enthusiasm, and creativity, they feel that management does not listen to their ideas, especially criticisms of how Childco operates.

You commit to maintaining engagement with multiple stakeholders inside and outside the company and to insisting that all managers encourage new ideas, listen carefully to complaints, and never exact punishment for honest opinions that differ from their own.

Environmental Degradation

When you study the "State of Green Business 2013" report by GreenBiz and the research firm Trucost, you learn that, for more than a decade, Trucost has been placing a monetary value on the resources businesses use and the pollution they generate. The report shows that, between 2007 and 2012, the number of S&P 500 firms reporting profits from better environmental practices has grown by 61 percent. In that same period, despite the economic slump, investment in environmental research and development more than doubled. In addition, a 2012 Ernst & Young–GreenBiz report found that 76 percent of survey respondents expected that natural resource shortages would affect their company's core business objectives in the next three to five years. Many have already been encountering problems with limited supplies, geopolitical confrontations, and escalating prices, all of which add urgency to the quest for sustainable solutions.[5]

Caterpillar, for instance, weighs environmental issues as it strives to fulfill its vision, which doesn't even mention the company's iconic large yellow construction machines: "Our vision is a world in which all people's basic requirements—such as shelter, clean water, sanitation, and reliable power—are fulfilled in a way that sustains our environment."

You assume that someday Childco might be required to measure and report on the materials and energy it uses and on its impact on the planet. Will Childco find itself paying taxes on these natural capital costs? What if the resources you need grow scarce? How might you cut energy and resource costs while increasing profits? How can environmental innovation lead to product innovation? What if we could totally recycle our products into new products? Although your questions outnumber your answers at this point, you know you must ensure the safety of every toy and know what materials each contains and the circumstances under which they are manufactured. Once again, you resolve to go beyond compliance and adopt a vision of Childco as a responsible steward of the environment.

Globalization

Technologies such as wind turbine generators, electric vehicle motors, batteries, fuel cells, and energy-efficient lighting rely on rare earth minerals, a collection of 17 scarce and therefore costly elements such as neodymium, dysprosium, and cerium. Ninety-seven percent of these materials come from China. Obtaining, refining, and using them creates a host of problems, ranging from limited supply and rising global demand to environmental damage. China began restricting exports of these materials in 2010. Conscious of China's history of restricting exports, Japan has been finding ways to reduce its dependence on rare earth elements over the past few years. Honda extracts rare earths from used car batteries. Panasonic found a way to recycle neodymium from old electronic appliances. TDK, which creates magnets for motors, conserves its use of dysprosium by spraying the element on motors rather than mixing it in. Because of efforts like these, Japan's demand for rare earth metals dropped by more than 25 percent from 31,000 tons in 2010 to 23,000 tons in 2011.

Considering the global reach of your supply chain, you commit Childco to use raw materials that will not force it to raise the price of the next generation of plush toys to levels that most families cannot afford and that will not cause irreversible harm to the areas from which the materials are obtained. You think about minimizing reliance on any one country and find alternative materials and technologies. Perhaps you can situate manufacturing operations closer to points of sale. You'd love for Childco to adopt a global perspective for every aspect of business: design, supply chain, marketing, and distribution, all the way through to the end of each product's life. Childco impacts the world; the world impacts Childco.

Population Shifts

A 2010 Organization for Economic Co-operation and Development study estimates that between now and 2030, the global middle class will grow from 1.8 billion to 4.9 billion people.[6] A 2011 Ernst & Young study reported that between 2009 and 2030, expenditures by the global middle class could increase from $21 trillion to $56 trillion.[7] As markets grow, the strain on natural resources can lead to critical shortages and significant business risks.

As with the other NCFOL, you anticipate both opportunities and threats. Parents in developed nations are spending more per child. With the right approaches to design, distribution, and pricing, Childco could tap into the rising middle class in other countries.

Childco must continue to keep a sharp eye on population shifts and demographic changes around the world. Of course, you also know that the company must look beyond numbers and income to evaluate the social and environmental implications of entering new markets and remaining in current ones.

Articulating the Vision

Back at Childco, after progressing though the various stages of vision creation, you pull your core team of forward-thinking stakeholders together to consider all that you have learned. You share a quote by author and management guru Charles Handy: "The companies that survive the longest are the ones that work out what they uniquely can give to the world—not just growth or money, but their excellence, their respect for others, or their ability to make people happy. Some call those things a soul." The consultant you've hired shares a summary of key findings, highlighting ways in which the NCFOL can shape Childo's future:

► Innovate to promote learning.

► Operate more efficiently and profitably.

► Profit with a purpose.

► Thrive in both good and bad economic times.

► Remain a positive force in the lives of all the people and societies you touch.

► Engage, value, and learn from all stakeholders.

► Accept responsibility to serve as stewards of the environment.

► View Childco from a global perspective.

► Address changing demographics to grow responsibly.

Although no one could stress all these elements in one vision statement, you want to include them in a way that makes the vision tangible and ties it to specific goals. The vision team contemplates some key questions: "What business are we in? What do we want our brand to mean? What kind of company do we want to become?"

A passionate discussion takes place. How can Childco grow and remain a steward of the environment? Childo makes stuff, and that stuff ends up in landfills. Does the world really need another teddy bear? How do we grow responsibly? What, exactly, does it mean to act—as Interface, Patagonia, and Virgin do—as forces for good?

The team comes up with a working draft of a new vision for Childco:

We create products that delight and educate children in ways that respect the world's resources and communities. Our innovative peo-

ple and partners do this by merging profit and purpose to protect the future for the generations to follow. We have fun. We make people smile.

You'll refine this draft vision statement before launching it throughout Childco.

Translating Words into Actions

Ray Anderson's compelling vision inspired people to dream—and do— the impossible. He engaged the minds and hearts of all of his people because he knew that achieving Mission Zero required engaging the entire company and everyone else with a stake in Interface's future. He remained constantly open to new ideas. A great vision must never remain static but should evolve as the future unfolds. In his last book, *Confessions of a Radical Industrialist*, Anderson wrote, "If you have better ideas, I hope you will share them with me; for as long as I live, I will be looking for a better way."

As Pablo Picasso said, "What one does is what counts and not what one had the intention of doing." Dreams are only as strong as the actions they inspire. A powerful and compelling vision guides people on a journey where they deal creatively with challenges and obstacles, where they feel highly motivated to contribute to the cause, where they continually learn and grow, and where they feel that they are doing something relevant with their lives. Research has repeatedly shown that people are motivated by doing meaningful work, where they can make more of a difference than merely putting bread on the table. They also want to know that their leaders will invite, listen to, respect, and embrace their best ideas. Whatever your company's vision, you want to embed it into every fiber of your organization's being so that it serves as a guiding beacon. That means doing a lot more than printing it in your annual report and posting it on the cafeteria wall.

MIT's Peter Senge, a highly respected author and thought leader on organizational learning, has said that vision statements often lose their power as soon as they are laminated. Cocreate a vision that embodies the desires and dreams of all your stakeholders, one that engages their hearts and minds and that then encourages actions consistent with that vision. Connect it to the bottom line by making it the heartbeat of your organization's leadership, strategy, culture, and business model. Compelling visions do more than inspire. They create a vivid image of the future where great purpose and great profits intersect for enduring prosperity.

Applying The New Corporate Facts of Life

Using the NCFOL Barometer in Figure 3-1, rate how well your organization seeks to shape the future of your business and industry in each area. Then consider how each NCFOL might influence or impact your organization's vision. Try to look at this from the perspective of the future, not with the mindsets of the past.

Figure 3-1. The New Corporate Facts of Life Vision Barometer.

Rating Key:

H–High: We take a leadership role in influencing change.
M–Medium: We consider this factor when envisioning our organization's future.
L–Low: We don't generally pay much attention to this factor.

NCFOL	Rank How Well You Consider These in Creating Your Vision	H	M	L
Disruptive Innovation	❑ Create a radically different future with disruptive innovation. ❑ Develop innovations that address society's problems. ❑ Go beyond today's best practices to create tomorrow's next practices.			
Economic Instability	❑ Develop ways to prosper in periods of economic instability. ❑ Redefine the measures of success for long-term results. ❑ Become economically efficient and effective.			
Societal Upheaval	❑ Use business to solve difficult societal issues. ❑ Introduce products that improve quality of life. ❑ Bring prosperity to communities and to the organization.			
Stakeholder Power	❑ Consider the future impact on all stakeholders. ❑ Obtain input from many stakeholders when shaping vision. ❑ Engage stakeholders often as you move forward.			
Environmental Degradation	❑ Transform the industry through ecology leadership. ❑ Create sustainable value chains. ❑ Rethink all operations to be environmentally sound.			
Globalization	❑ Adhere to the highest standards for global ethics and values. ❑ Use commerce as a force for global peace and prosperity. ❑ Recognize how nations and regions will evolve over time.			
Population Shifts	❑ Plan for the impact of rapid population growth. ❑ Harness the demographic changes affecting your business. ❑ Position the next generation to lead.			

CHAPTER 4

Map the Strategic Journey

Words without action are the assassins of idealism.

—George Santayana

IN 2011, the La Jolla–based regenerative medicine company Advanced BioHealing was growing at a rate of 30–40 percent a year. After the company bought the rights to a bioengineered skin substitute called DERMAGRAFT®, a leading treatment for foot ulcers in people with diabetes, its revenues exploded from $9 million in 2007 to $147 million in 2010.

DERMAGRAFT® requires prompt delivery within extremely tight time constraints and insists that its product remain at –75 degrees Celsius. People who handle it in highly sanitized environments must cover themselves head-to-toe with white suits, gloves, shoe covers, and masks. Packages ready for shipment display large signs on their sides: "Urgent: Human Tissue Enclosed" and "time/temperature sensitive product." If a shipment to a surgical unit does not adhere to its strict delivery schedule, the product can quickly deteriorate and become unusable. Signs posted around the facility remind employees, "It's a patient, not a package."

As Advanced BioHealing expanded, it partnered with UPS to manage its growing logistical needs: warehousing, packaging, distributing, tracking, and reporting. UPS seemed the ideal partner, given its history and commitment to service in the health-care industry and its ability to handle the company's requirements with respect to time, temperature, packaging, and handling. As part of their operating agreements, the two companies collaborated to create contingency and disaster recovery plans that included an additional distribution center near UPS's hub in Louisville, Kentucky.

These plans were put to the test when at 3:38 p.m. on September 8, 2011, a massive power failure struck nearby San Diego. The entire metro area shut down, including the airport. Advanced BioHealing's outgoing shipments were stranded in the warehouse. If the shipments could not move, the company's business and the health of thousands of patients were at risk. That's when the UPS contingency and disaster recovery plans went into high gear.

Mike Whitmore, Associate Director of Global Logistics at Advanced BioHealing, recalled that day: "There was no hesitation. There was no 'We'll see what we can do.' It was 'Absolutely!' They (UPS people) did exactly what they were trained to do,"[1] including calling in additional employees to process all of the day's orders from the Louisville location. UPS frequently proclaims, "We love logistics." Customers such as Advanced BioHealing often say, "We love UPS."

Ross McCullough, UPS's Vice President of Corporate Strategy, explained that the company has invested significantly in solutions for the health-care industry: "We want to be in complex parts of supply chains [such as health care] because ... we bring unique information, knowledge, solutions, and execution."

When Advanced BioHealing, today a part of Shire Regenerative Medicine Inc., decided to outsource its logistics, it made a strategic decision. Its vision to transform the regenerative medicine marketplace could not become a reality without the right strategy. Although vision paints the picture of where you want to go and how you want to grow your business, strategy sketches a roadmap to your destination. A great strategy does not follow an arrow-straight path but allows for surprising twists and turns along the way. It provides a way of thinking about your future in concrete and tangible terms.

UPS serves as a good example of strategy in action. The company, started in 1907 as a messenger operation called the American Messenger Company, initially delivered messages, packages, and food, in addition to running errands on foot or by bicycle. When a major disruptive innovation, the telephone, rendered message delivery obsolete, the company focused on delivering small packages from department stores to customers' homes. It eventually added motorcycles and then its first Ford Model T in 1913. That same year, it merged with a competitor to form Merchants Parcel Delivery. In 1919, with its first expansion from Seattle to Oakland, it changed its name to United Parcel Service. In 1929, it ventured into air service delivery but abandoned that effort within months due to the Great Depression. It reintroduced air service in 1953 and became the first in the industry to offer two-day delivery. Arch rival Federal Express delivered another market disruption when it launched overnight air service in 1973, to which UPS responded by initiating UPS Next Day Air in 1982.

UPS now operates one of the largest private ground delivery fleets and one of the largest airlines in the world. Clearly, its strategic planning and execution have passed the test of time. Imagine your company dominating its market 100 years from now.

UPS leaders constantly ask fundamental questions, such as, "What does this company really do? Why does what we do matter to the world? What will we be doing 15 years from now?" And they respond to all the inevitable roadblocks and detours the organization encounters. McCullough believes that UPS never gets comfortable with its market position, remaining "constructively dissatisfied." The company's strategic planning team constantly brings employees with cross-functional backgrounds together with external experts to scan the business environment, test the company's own assumptions, and inspire innovations.

Like any smart company, UPS continually tries to balance efficiency with innovation. Although it has taken pride for many years in running "the tightest ship in the shipping business," it must frequently step out-side its comfort zone to keep reinventing itself with more than mere incremental changes. How, its leaders ask, can we *transform* our compa-ny and our industry to better serve our customers?

Delivering Today's Commitments and Tomorrow's Promise

NCFOL strategies go beyond lip service and incremental changes. Merely tweaking an organization's current operation will not propel it to greater results. Smart organizations look for truly transformational ways they can maximize their core business while re-creating themselves for a dramatically different future. This process usually occurs in three over-lapping phases, as illustrated in Figure 4-1. In Phase 1, the company grows and protects its core business, enabling it to finance the future while preserving the present. At the same time, in Phase 2, it develops business opportunities that it can begin to grow today. In Phase 3, it invests in initiatives that allow it to experiment with opportunities that might fuel future growth and profitably propel it well past its competitors.

Figure 4-1. Deliver Today's Commitments and Create Tomorrow's Promise.

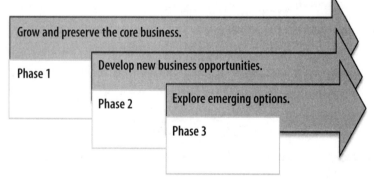

UPS has always strived to integrate short- and long-term business plans, emphasizing growth that preserves its core business (Phase 1,

package delivery), while investing in new ventures (Phase 2, global logistics management) and exploring future opportunities (Phase 3, harnessing big data, alternative-fuel vehicles, and next-generation technologies).

The company uses scenario planning to assess a range of likely and unlikely possibilities for the future. This mental exercise gets people asking the what-if questions that help them prepare for every imaginable contingency, from political instability to soaring fuel prices and labor unrest.

In the pages ahead, we will look closely at how UPS has remained true to the company's core values while continually changing its business model, technology, services, and global reach. At times, it changed the game in its industry; at other times, it reacted adroitly to a competitor's game-changing move.

Mapping Your Strategy Using The New Corporate Facts of Life

The New Corporate Facts of Life present game-changing opportunities. Interestingly, UPS has contemplated them all as it continuously monitors global and industry trends and seeks ways to build greater capabilities. It does so with its basic purpose and vision in mind: to "enable global commerce" and "synchronize the world of commerce by developing business solutions that create value and competitive advantages for our customers."

As we follow the story of UPS's unfolding strategy, consider how you might integrate each of the NCFOL into your own company's strategy. What, specifically, must you do to put it at the forefront of your industry? How will you preserve and grow your Phase 1 core business while ensuring future growth and profitability by investing in Phases 2 and 3?

Disruptive Innovation

When you think of disruptive innovation, Netflix, Apple, Skype, and Google may spring to mind. It might surprise you to learn that UPS deserves a place in that pantheon due to its willingness to adopt new technology and refine its business model.

Not so many years ago, if a frantic bride called the UPS customer service line to locate her wedding dress just days before her big day, the service rep would dig through reams of carbon copies of delivery slips to track down the missing package and then try to decipher a scribbled recipient signature. Fast-forward to 2013. This morning, I clicked on a link in an e-mail from UPS to track delivery of my new iPad Mini. UPS Quantum View software showed my order traveling on Friday, February 15, through Incheon, South Korea; Chek Lap Kok, Hong Kong; Shenzhen, China; and Anchorage, Alaska, before arriving in Louisville, Kentucky, on Saturday the 16th and in Atlanta, Georgia, on Sunday the 17th. It will arrive by 10:30 a.m. at my office just north of Atlanta on Monday the 18th. If I were a nervous bride, I would have taken great comfort from that information. Strategy leader McCullough describes UPS as a "deceptively complex company" that has grown rapidly beyond small package delivery. Customers do not see it, but an amazing technology and logistics network drives even the smallest delivery.

UPS has become such a data-rich company that a Wall Street analyst once commented that it is really an information technology company that delivers packages, rather than the other way around. Big data accumulates as UPS harnesses technology to achieve greater efficiency, speed, customer service, and safety. One multiyear initiative, the company's Package Flow Technology (PFT), required a massive overhaul of routing, loading, and sorting processes. PFT shortens delivery routes, minimizes engine-idling times, and instructs on the proper package-loading sequence. The technology minimizes left-hand turns, which saves fuel, labor costs, carbon emissions, and delivery time. Between 2003 and 2012, PFT shaved 100 million miles from UPS's delivery routes, reduced fuel use by 10 million gallons, and cut carbon emissions by more than 100,000 metric tons.

Innovation applies to business models just as much as it does to technology. UPS has constantly evolved its model to fit the times. By the late

1990s, e-commerce, expanding supply chains, and outsourcing of various business operations forced changes in how it served the global market. Size alone could no longer prevail. UPS's specialty, small-package delivery, accounted for only 6 percent of global shipping. How, it wondered, can we protect our core small-package delivery business (Phase 1) while growing to become a global commerce leader (Phase 2)? Looking back on that period, the company's CFO, Kurt Kuehn, says, "Enabling global commerce was a 'man on the moon' mission for our company." However, he goes on to say:

> Change is the coin; opportunity and risk are the two sides. And what we saw was a threat. We had a profitable business in our U.S. domestic small-package operation. It generated 90 percent of our profits and it had been the source of consistent earnings growth year-over-year. We had perfected that. We knew how to deliver packages smoothly and efficiently, but we also knew...that just focusing on domestic transportation would not keep the company vital in the years to come.

Becoming a global commerce leader also demanded innovations in the company's approach to supply chain management. To make that happen quickly, UPS embarked on a buying spree, purchasing some 40 companies that would add capabilities in logistics and distribution, transportation and freight, trade management, brokerage services, and freight forwarding. Its strategy aimed at making its name synonymous with *logistics* just as *Xerox* once stood for all photocopiers and *Kleenex* for all tissues. By becoming the one-source solution for all shipping needs, UPS frees customers such as Advanced BioHealing to focus on their own core business.

How does disruptive innovation present challenges and opportunities for your organization?

➤ **Phase 1:** What aspects of your core business must you protect and defend against disruptive innovation?

➤ **Phase 2:** What new technologies or business models should you start growing to disrupt the market yourself?

> ▶ **Phase 3:** What innovation investments should you make to create a radically different future?

Economic Instability

The great recession that began in 2007 dramatically hit industries such as newspaper publishing, retail, building and construction, automotive, and banking. The September 2008 bankruptcy filing by Lehman Brothers, the largest in U.S. history, plunged financial markets and an unsuspecting world into chaos. In the midst of the decline, however, certain industries grew, among them renewable energy, Internet companies, online publishing, and e-learning.

UPS has survived and thrived through multiple recessions, the Great Depression, and two world wars. It went public in 1999 to obtain the funds needed to invest in acquisitions and global growth. As a private company, UPS had always shied away from risk and had seemed to some critics as overly conservative in its effort to protect its employees' ownership value. But to expand globally, it needed to take on more debt to finance acquisitions into new markets.

As challenges of global recession, major company bankruptcies, and worldwide credit crises have taken center stage, UPS's Kuehn sees the role of a CFO changing from "being fancy accountants to co-drivers of corporate strategy. We no longer worry only about quarterly results. We also focus on strategies for long-term growth."

At UPS, Kuehn became one of the first CFOs of a major corporation to broaden his focus to include sustainability. Kuehn realized that embracing sustainability could further reduce the company's energy costs, drive innovation, and open up new competitive and revenue opportunities. "A CFO's job really is about using resources wisely and ensuring that an enterprise is strong enough to thrive for decades to come," Kuehn explains. "Sustainable, if you want to call it that." A strategy emphasizing sustainable business practices also helps UPS manage risk. Wall Street hates surprises. Investors want to feel confident that the companies whose stock they own pursue a responsible business strategy that will enhance stock value over the long term.

UPS buffers itself against economic instability by continuously assessing and reducing its long-term risks. Of course, fuel represents a huge risk factor for a company that operates so many trucks and planes. One of the company's scenarios, dubbed Oil 200, considers what would happen if oil prices jumped to $200 a barrel. That could easily occur in a perfect storm of political unrest in oil-producing nations, carbon taxation, drilling limitations due to environmental concerns, and a lack of affordable alternatives. Other UPS scenarios evaluate such potential risks as economic declines, protectionism, and freezes on trade agreements, which countries might use in an effort to retain jobs within their own borders.

Managing economic uncertainty means figuring out how to grow profitably in good times and bad. With a strong cash position and a culture of carefully evaluating opportunities, UPS continues to grow through well thought-out strategies, the efficient use of capital, and a culture of dedication, execution, and accountability. Kuehn believes that businesses shouldn't pull back in tough times. "Great, long-term companies continue to execute. You've got to be responsive. You must have a flexible cost structure, but taking one of the wheels off to save some money ultimately will slow the vehicle down."

Wall Street analysts have generally viewed UPS as a company that should weather the recent economic recession because it has proven its management prowess and leadership stability for more than 100 years. In 2008, its stock sank as low as $49 per share; in early 2013, it had risen to $84 per share, more than a 70 percent increase. In 2012, UPS achieved record earnings per share and generated free cash flow of approximately $5.4 billion.

How does economic instability present challenges and opportunities for your organization?

> ► **Phase 1:** What aspects of your core business must you protect and defend against economic peaks and valleys?

► **Phase 2:** What new business opportunities for profitable
growth should you start seizing right now?

► **Phase 3:** What investments should you make to create an economically resilient future?

Societal Upheaval

Societal problems pose serious difficulties, of course, but they also offer
strategic opportunities for greater innovation, economic development,
and achievements that can even promote peace among nations that rely
on each other for commerce. The best strategy extends beyond financial
health to the well-being of employees, suppliers, customers, and all communities affected by the organization. People matter.

To manage risk and keep their people safe and their business operating, UPS, like other multinational companies, must anticipate all manner
of disasters, from terrorism to tsunamis. UPS hires local people to work
in their communities. Patrice André, its Vice President of Human Resources, International Operations, believes in the importance of local
intelligence. "Two weeks ago, when several bombs exploded in India, we
knew about it within an hour and that our people were safe."

André describes UPS as part of a network of logistics professionals
supporting crisis management and disaster relief. They also willingly act
as first responders in a catastrophe. For example, in its disaster relief program, UPS trains logistics staff to participate in the World Food
Programmes' Disaster Relief Team, which deploys helpers to Honduras,
Indonesia, Darfur, Haiti, Thailand, and other countries in need.

UPS Vice President, Global Human Resource Services, Mike Johnson
views corporate social responsibility as an engagement tool. After the big
2008 earthquake in Haiti, several UPS employees volunteered with the
Salvation Army there. While still in the country, one of the volunteers told
his colleagues in Sacramento about the difficulty of monitoring members
of the 2,000 families living on a soccer field in tents fashioned from bed
sheets. Eager to solve this problem, several employees spent a weekend
reconfiguring an existing UPS package-tracking technology to keep track

of those families. In addition, the company donated handheld UPS Trackpads that Salvation Army workers could use to scan special badges on each person and that other officials could use to record vital data such as family size, the head of the household, location, and supplies received or needed. It did not take long for other relief agencies to express interest in using the system, which remains in operation today.

UPS employees volunteer 1.8 million hours of their time each year. HR VP André has seen volunteer activities shift with the times. "Ten years ago it was mostly to address poverty and literacy. For the last five years, especially in Asia, it's been about protection, relief, and rescue of the environment, planting trees, and cleaning the landscape." One program emerged from employees wanting to reduce teenage deaths due to distracted driving. In 2009, they launched UPS Road Code, whose volunteers use youth-oriented video game technology to teach teens about driving hazards. The program has now spread around the world. When making philanthropic grants through its foundation, the company considers the extent to which employees support a particular cause.

What societal issues present challenges and opportunities for your organization?

➤ **Phase 1:** What aspects of your core business must you protect and defend in the event of societal upheaval?

➤ **Phase 2:** What new business opportunities should you grow to meet a societal need profitably?

➤ **Phase 3:** What investments should you make for a dramatically changed world in the future?

Stakeholder Influence

Technology, global reach, and an increasingly transparent world require every company to consider stakeholder needs more carefully than ever before. UPS pays attention to a wide variety of interest groups: employees, labor unions, customers, Wall Street, investors, the board of directors, regulators, NGOs, communities, and suppliers. Engaging a broad range of stakeholders increases the chance of surfacing important insights. It also fosters greater creativity, alignment, collaboration, and greater ownership of the evolving strategy.

Tools such as its Materiality Matrix, a sample of which appears in Figure 4-2, help company leaders consider the impact of its business strategy not just on its own success but on the welfare of all its stakeholders. The most important issues for both stakeholders and the business appear in the top right quadrant of the matrix. For UPS, these strategic factors included megacities/infrastructure, labor relations, emerging markets, health and safety, global unrest, trade barriers, ethics, transparency, accountability and reporting, responsible marketing, and greenhouse gas policy and advocacy.

Figure 4-2. Sample Materiality Matrix.*

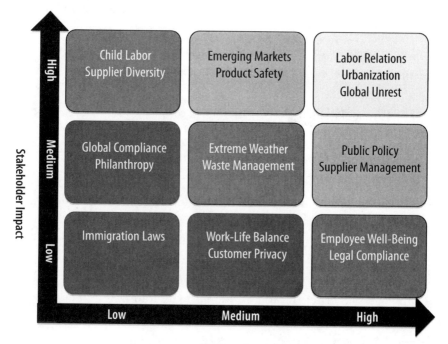

Business Impact

* To view the UPS Materiality Matrix, read the 2012 Sustainability Report on ups.com.

To create a materiality matrix with your leadership team, list both your important stakeholders and all issues important to your business success. Ask each leader to plot each business issue on the matrix in terms of its importance to stakeholders and to the business. Discuss areas of disagreement to discover different perspectives and to move toward a strategic consensus. For example, since highly unionized UPS employs more Teamsters than any other company, it views labor relations as an extremely critical business and stakeholder issue.

UPS views its managers as partners in the company. This stems in part from the fact that for more than 70 years before the company went public, its managers owned all the stock. UPS has been recognized quite often for its employment practices and reputation as a desirable place to work. *Fortune* has placed UPS on its list of the World's Most Admired Companies for more than 20 years. In addition, *Diversity-Plus* magazine named it one of its 30 Champions of Diversity in 2012, and the Minority Corporate Counsel Association gave UPS one of its coveted 2011 Employer of Choice Awards.

Eighty percent of its employees work not in office buildings but in the skies, on the roadways, or in one of the company's hundreds of warehouses or air hubs around the world. More than 70 percent of the company's managers started in nonmanagement positions, gaining valuable boots-on-the-ground experience with customers and frontline operations. Valuing people provides a tremendous payback to UPS in terms of employee engagement.

Employees remain loyal to the company, to the union, and to their customers. UPS must constantly negotiate with labor unions on issues that affect the welfare of its huge workforce, especially those related to job changes and safety. It also diligently promotes and tracks safety, thereby improving the workplace, protecting employees, and reducing business risk and costs. The UPS Telematics system uses sensors to track all sorts of data about a vehicle and driver performance, recording instances of seatbelt use, harsh braking, and backing up in residential areas. The company does all this to ensure the ultimate in safety, fuel efficiency, and customer delight. And while these types of systems provide useful data, the grassroots efforts of employees have done even more to improve safety. Every business unit has a health and safety committee aligned to the company's Comprehensive Health and Safety Program (CHSP). As one employee in the Chicago area quipped about the importance of safety, "My most important stop of the day is going home." CHSP committees took this idea and ran with it. Efforts such as the My Most Important Stop program have dramatically reduced injuries and costs and greatly improved employee health and safety.

Safe, engaged, well-trained employees result in happy customers, another critical stakeholder group. At UPS, everyone learns to think like the customer, constantly asking how each action or decision contributes to or detracts from the customer experience. Doing so has led to many innovative service offerings that benefit both company and customers. The most profound change has come with the rise of e-commerce. Strategy leader McCullough said that although UPS predicted "the empowered consumer" created by e-commerce, the phenomenon has become "bigger than we ever imagined" and remains a key driver of the company's strategy. UPS lets customers control their shipments by easily looking up delivery schedule dates and times and changing the time or delivery address to make sure someone can accept and sign for the package. While customers get their packages at the time of their choosing, UPS also saves time and fuel by avoiding multiple delivery attempts.

When UPS went public in 1999, it had to deal with a whole new set of stakeholders. It now needed to consider the effect of its strategy on investors, Wall Street, and government regulators. At the time of the initial public offering, Kuehn served as head of investor relations for the company. Looking back, he says that these external stakeholders served as a catalyst for change. Its steady expansion onto the global stage required UPS to look beyond its own walls, augmenting its internal focus with a broad international perspective. When you operate as a public company, you must also practice transparency and build currency in trust, not just in dollars.

Competitors figure prominently in UPS's strategy. The company looks for ways to collaborate with them in some areas, while still competing with them in others. The United States Postal Service (USPS), one of its most direct competitors, has become a major customer and strategic alliance partner in a prime example of business co-opetition, where competitors collaborate on solutions, then compete based on their own strengths such as brand image, customer loyalty, ability to execute, and operational excellence. One USPS/UPS partnership, Blue and Brown Make Green, combines more than the color of the partner's uniforms, it facilitates smoother package delivery. Because snail-mail delivers to every address and post office box in the country, the USPS can often transport a delivery that last crucial mile or two, especially in rural areas. The reverse occurs when the USPS uses the UPS ground and air fleet to help deliver mail across the country and internationally. The partnership reduces fuel consumption, labor costs, and carbon emissions while speeding delivery to customers. Everyone wins with a sustainable solution that Postmaster General Patrick R. Donahoe proudly calls "leaner, greener, smarter, and faster."

What strategic issues most concern your key internal and external stakeholders? How can you tap your stakeholders to enhance your strategic thinking?

> ► **Phase 1:** How can you ensure continued stakeholder support for your core business?

> ► **Phase 2:** What new business opportunities should you pursue to meet stakeholder needs profitably?

> ► **Phase 3:** What investments should you make to benefit stakeholders and the bottom line in the long term?

Environmental Degradation

A number of companies around the world deserve recognition for their efforts to address environmental degradation, among them SAP, IBM,

Nike, IKEA, Marks & Spencer, and Natura Cosméticos. Companies such as Nike, IKEA, Marks & Spencer, and Walmart estimate that between 80 and 90 percent of their carbon footprint occurs in the supply chain, starting with raw materials and flowing through the logistics chain of packaging, storage, and transportation. Recognizing this as both a challenge and an opportunity, UPS has made supply chain sustainability a strategic focus. To fulfill its goal of "running the tightest ship in the shipping business," UPS turns lean to green by reducing waste and energy use, using more efficient materials, investing in new technology, and making decisions that lower risks and save money.

UPS Chief Sustainability Officer (CSO) Scott Wicker says, "One of the largest problems in society is climate change. That's our focus." The United States, Canada, and the United Kingdom have joined the ranks of countries now requiring companies to report the methods they use to assess and address risks posed by climate change. When a major storm hits anywhere in the world, it invariably disrupts UPS operations. Imagine the challenges presented by the 2010 tsunami in Japan, the 2011 floods in Thailand, and the so-called 2012 Superstorm Sandy in the Northeast United States.

The company chooses to operate more sustainably because it's the right thing to do for both the company and the environment. Wicker emphasizes the importance of collecting good, solid data. "We have to map every source we burn fuel in our network worldwide, and we get better at it every year." When customers asked UPS for environmental supply chain data in 2009, it built a carbon calculator. "Data allowed us to provide this service," Wicker says. Business customers can purchase data from the carbon calculator to determine the environmental impact of the transportation and distribution of the packages and freight they send and receive. The company expects that more and more business customers will eventually need this service both to meet new regulations and to calculate their own carbon footprint for life cycle analysis and sustainability reporting.

UPS views sustainable practices as a way to maintain a competitive edge. For instance, as part of its carbon-neutral shipping option, it purchases high-quality, verified standard carbon offsets on behalf of each customer using this service. The UPS team that developed the carbon-neutral shipping option beat competitors to market with this option. The strategy worked well, and the company found its first major customer for this service before the team had even completed it. When Bill Strang, President of Operations of plumbing fixture maker TOTO America, heard about it, he jumped at the chance to use the service. "Sign us up. TOTO will be your first customer. We will pull any shipping that we are doing with FedEx and use UPS for all of it." TOTO willingly pays a little more per package for this service because it fits their values to run a highly sustainable, responsible company. UPS salespeople include this story in their sales pitches. Strang says. "It's like having UPS promoting the TOTO brand every time they show that page." The company wins, the customer wins, and the environment wins.

At UPS, fuel represents about 5–6 percent of overall costs. Reducing the number of driving and flying miles cuts expenses, reduces fossil fuel use, and lowers carbon emissions. Wicker estimates that in 2012, UPS delivered more packages by air than it had in 2011 but did it in less air flight time, saving more than 9.5 million gallons of fuel. Through the company's rolling laboratory, it partners with vehicle manufacturers and the EPA to develop and test alternative-fuel technologies. In 2011, UPS expanded its green fleet by 35 percent and now operates one of the largest and most diverse private green fleets in the world with more than 2,600 alternative-fuel/advanced-technology vehicles in service. UPS aggressively pursues the technology to help create a hedge against future disruptions of fuel supply. UPS, FedEx, AT&T, Verizon, PepsiCo's Frito-Lay, and Coca-Cola have also partnered with the U.S. Department of Energy and their competitors, forming the National Clean Fleets Partnership to replace vehicles using diesel fuel and gasoline with cleaner, greener fleets.

Whenever possible, the company uses more carbon-friendly transport modes for delivery, investing in newer, more efficient aircraft, and offering sustainable packaging alternatives. Wicker believes intermodal shipping, using trucks instead of planes and trains instead of trucks, greatly reduces the company's carbon footprint. The UPS Smart Pickup service lets customers opt out of regularly scheduled UPS visits, then call for a pickup when they need one. The company estimates that this service alone saves 8 million miles driving each year in the United States, 793,000 gallons of fuel, and 7,800 metric tons of CO_2 emissions. CFO Kuehn says, "It's lean, it's green, and it's a no-brainer."

Producing internal reports on environmental impacts since 1994, UPS once again led its industry by publishing its first annual public "Sustainability Report" in 2003. It uses the data collected for its reports to achieve sustainability goals such as reducing energy use and costs, while adopting practices that benefit people and society.

The company regularly receives accolades for its sustainability efforts. In 2012, it received the EPA Climate Leadership Award, was recognized as a Best Global Green Brand, and scored 99 out of 100 in Carbon Disclosure Project's Leadership Index of S&P companies, the best score in the United States in 2011 and 2012. UPS has also appeared on the Dow Jones Sustainability Index (DJSI) since 2004. It helped the EPA develop its SmartWay Program and later got involved in creating similar programs in other parts of the world, such as the Green Freight Asia and Green Freight Europe networks.

UPS's sustainability reputation and award-winning recognition by the U.S. Environmental Protection Agency (EPA) for environmental leadership has helped increase the company's government business. When an executive order by President Barack Obama required federal agencies to report and reduce their carbon impact, UPS won status as a preferred vendor for U.S. government delivery services and for other companies who do business with the government.

What environmental issues present challenges and opportunities for your organization?

▶ **Phase 1:** What aspects of your core business must you protect and defend from resource constraints, changing regulations, or damage to brand image?

▶ **Phase 2:** How can environmental responsibility create new business opportunities?

▶ **Phase 3:** What investments should you make for an emerging future of scarce resources, new regulations, and energy-efficient innovations?

Globalization

Scott Davis, Chairman and CEO of UPS, has said, "[T]he world is changing dramatically as we become a global economy, and it takes big ideas and bold moves to keep up." Strategy leader McCullough notes that a growing middle class has begun to drive retail consumption outside the United States: "We've got to ensure that we are well-prepared, not only in developed parts of Europe, Asia, and Canada, but in the developing nations. I think that is huge and will cause fundamental shifts in the way trade patterns move, and trade patterns are a critical component of our business."

Globalization stretches the investment capabilities of most companies. UPS didn't turn a profit from going global for more than ten years, but the company stayed the course because it made such good sense from a long-term perspective. Currently operating in more than 220 countries and territories, the company's strategy has proven a smart bet.

UPS began its international growth when it first entered Canada in 1975 and then Germany in 1976, moves that put it in direct competition with each country's postal service. It continued global expansion with several acquisitions in Europe and Asia, financing this strategic move by opening up stock ownership beyond the management team to all employees.

The company greatly expanded its global presence by adding broader capabilities to its offerings. According to CFO Kuehn, to become a logistics leader, UPS needed "to be able to go in credibly and talk to companies of all sizes about their global strategy and how we can help facilitate it." Kuehn sees the continued acceleration of e-commerce and the increase of the middle class in emerging markets as two key drivers of the company's global growth strategy.

UPS Director of Organizational Development Paul Nieminen sees globalization as a major strategic factor to consider when developing the company's people practices. Leaders must expand their perspective by strengthening their grasp of global issues. Understanding culture and managing change become high priorities when you cross borders for acquisitions. Nieminen insists that you must pay attention to both "the national culture and the organizational culture."

Global expansion poses other cultural challenges as well. Respecting that fact, UPS flipped the old saying "go global, act local" to "think local, act global." This means honoring local customs, yet operating with the same rock-solid values and operational excellence everywhere in the world. Although it adapted the vast bulk of its practices to match the needs of individual countries, it remained true to its core values. For example, German workers, with a propensity for living in the same area where they grew up, did not feel comfortable with the idea of moving somewhere else to accept a promotion. This cultural trait ran counter to the UPS tradition of promoting from within. It took time and patience, but UPS gradually convinced its German employees that its corporate values respected the workers' own interests, not just those of the company. UPS also found cultural similarities in many countries, especially in Asian nations with a strong work ethic, group dedication, and a sense of partnership. In any event, respecting cultural similarities and differences requires an open mind and sets the tone for a smoother entry into new markets.

With some forecasts estimating that 70–80 percent of total global gross domestic product will cross borders by the year 2025, UPS wishes to position itself as a leader that smoothly moves products across the entire supply chain while providing a consistently excellent customer experience.

How does globalization present challenges and opportunities for your organization?

▶ **Phase 1:** How do you protect and defend your core business in this globally connected world?

▶ **Phase 2:** What new business opportunities should you begin growing right now to tap into the global marketplace for customers and suppliers?

▶ **Phase 3:** What investments should you make for the long-term global future?

Population Shifts

Urbanization, new generations entering the workforce, hordes of Baby Boomers retiring, and population growth all influence strategy at UPS. In the United States, Generation Y (those born between 1980 and 1999) makes up more than 25 percent of the workforce and will grow to nearly 75 percent of the global workforce by 2025. Meanwhile, more than 40 percent of the current workforce will enter retirement within the next decade.

UPS knows that it must harness, develop, and retain the next generation of leaders, at the same time keeping its more experienced workers fully engaged. Those entering the workforce now differ markedly from their seniors. Impatient and often feeling entitled, they nevertheless want meaningful work that satisfies them with more than a mere paycheck. Many aspects of the NCFOL speak to that desire. UPS's Mike Johnson says this generation asks different questions. Until recently, young recruits would say, "Where do you want me to go, and when do you want me to go there?" Now they say, "What does this do for me? What about my spouse?" HR International Operations VP André says of this generation, "I think we have to...recognize that there are very significant variations across the world." Using China and Singapore as examples, André points out that young people want "fast learning and fast career development." Furthermore, "[t]o a young Chinese employee, a year seems like forever." This generation is "fast-connected and fast-disconnected. The ability to provide new learning is critical." In Europe, which has suffered high unemployment rates for many years, André believes that "long-term employment seems quite attractive again." The UPS philosophy of promoting from within propels people up social and economic ladders. Today, a blue-collar UPS worker in China can aspire to rise through the ranks and become president of Asian operations.

André notes that in his 20-plus years with the company, he has seen community involvement receive more and more support and recognition around the world. Johnson attributes that progress to the fact that "[t]his generation is very much interested in working for organizations that care and are doing the right thing."

As people of all generations flock to cities, Walmart plans city store models, Zipcar replaces automobile ownership with borrowing, and businesses look for ideas in places such as Singapore, the original urban country. UPS considers scenarios wherein most of the world's population could live in megacities by the year 2050. This shift drives the need for innovation and green growth at companies such as UPS, DHL, and others that play a critical role in managing city logistics, utilities, and transportation. CSO Wicker points out that the strategic implications for UPS go far beyond restrictions on delivery vehicles during peak traffic hours. UPS has already planned on adding more electric vehicles to its fleet in London, where such restrictions have already taken place.

Beyond swelling cities, population growth in emerging nations presents companies with both opportunities and challenges. With 95 percent of the world's people living outside the United States, future growth will depend on attracting new consumers in emerging markets. To do so, UPS intends to create a profitable business model that depends on serving the Base of the Pyramid with appropriate pricing, equipment, and quality. To accomplish this, it must sometimes modify its practices. For instance, when drivers cannot rely on costly tablet technology to collect data in remote regions, they get the job done with cell phones instead.

How do shifts such as population growth, urbanization, and multiple generations present challenges and opportunities for your business?

▶ **Phase 1:** How do you protect and defend your core business in the face of these population shifts?

▶ **Phase 2:** What new business opportunities or risks do these population trends present for the near term?

▶ **Phase 3:** What investments should you make to address even more dramatic population shifts in the future?

Evolving Your Strategy

For more than a century, UPS has defined, refined, and transformed its strategy, extended its business model, and expanded its core capabilities. To succeed in the next century and beyond, it must continue to lead, not follow, and it must constantly serve as a catalyst for industry change in order to keep fulfilling its desire "to enable global commerce." The culture, leadership, structure, and engagement of many UPS employees and partners around the world help the company bring their strategy to life. The remaining chapters in this book will show you how to do the same for your organization.

Applying The New Corporate Facts of Life

Using the NCFOL Barometer (Figure 4-3), rate how well your organization considers each factor when it engages in strategic thinking. After reviewing your responses, do you see factors that should be better integrated into your organization's strategy? Which of these might have the greatest impact on strategic, sustainable growth for the short, intermediate, or long term? What potential risks and opportunities would each of these NCFOL have on your strategy? How are you aligning your efforts across your organization?

Figure 4-3. The New Corporate Facts of Life Strategy Barometer.

Rating Key:

H–High: We emphasize this factor as part of our strategic thinking.
M–Medium: We consider this factor in our strategic thinking.
L–Low: We don't consider this factor when thinking about our strategy.

NCFOL	Rank How Well You Incorporate These into Your Strategy	H	M	L
Disruptive Innovation	☐ Consider disruptive business models and practices. ☐ Create innovations good for society and our business. ☐ Understand factors that could transform our industry.			
Economic Instability	☐ Anticipate and plan for economic instability. ☐ Enhance resilience and risk management. ☐ Develop greater efficiency and effectiveness.			
Societal Upheaval	☐ Anticipate and plan for potential societal upheaval. ☐ Develop products and services that solve societal problems. ☐ Strengthen the communities and people we touch.			
Stakeholder Power	☐ Consider the strategic impact on all stakeholders. ☐ Obtain stakeholder input in creating strategy. ☐ Engage stakeholders on how to implement strategy.			
Environmental Degradation	☐ Develop environmentally responsible products and services. ☐ Redefine supply chains for positive environmental impact. ☐ Integrate environmental responsibility into all operations.			
Globalization	☐ Consider cultural differences and global impact. ☐ Promote global peace and prosperity through commerce. ☐ Adapt approaches and priorities by location.			
Population Shifts	☐ Manage risks and opportunities of rapid population growth. ☐ Plan for the impact of urbanization. ☐ Develop new leaders and replace capabilities of retirees.			

CHAPTER 5

Build a Unique and Vibrant Culture

If you do not manage culture, it manages you.

—EDGAR SCHEIN, PROFESSOR,
MIT SLOAN SCHOOL OF MANAGEMENT

NOVO NORDISK, the Danish-based global leader in diabetes treatment, has built a deeply caring corporate culture. On a recent visit to the company's Clayton, North Carolina, plant, I strolled down a long hallway that connects two buildings. People have dubbed one wall, which is painted the same vivid blue color as the company's logo, The Blue Mile. As I walked, I scanned the stories printed below the many large photo portraits that adorned the wall. Each story reveals how much the company's products have made each person's life healthier and happier.

One of the photos shows Charlie Kimball, a highly successful professional race car driver. Charlie knew from the time he began racing go-carts at age nine that he was born to drive fast. He even passed up the opportunity to attend Stanford University to pursue his dream of championship racing. In 2005, he became the first American in 11 years to win a British Formula 3 race and later went on to set two track records and rack up several more Formula 3 victories in Europe. His racing career nearly came to a crashing halt in 2007, when at the age of 22, doctors diagnosed Charlie with type 1 diabetes, forcing him to stop racing mid-season. When he discovered that some states would not issue a commercial driver's license to people who take insulin, Charlie feared that he might never race again. Working with his doctor, people at Novo Nordisk, and his crew, he took control of his diabetes and got back behind the wheel in 2008, winning a spot on the winner's podium in the first race he entered. Charlie now collaborates with Novo Nordisk, using his celebrity to promote the fact that diabetes need not slow anyone down or take their dreams off track.

My escort, Diane Cox, the organizational development leader for the plant, proudly pointed out that these photos depict employees and people related to employees at that very facility. As employees walk The Blue Mile to and from the cafeteria, they see this powerful reminder that the work they do makes a big difference in people's lives. They have aligned with a higher purpose. They don't make drugs; they save and improve the lives of people around the world. Their culture runs through their veins.

The story behind The Blue Mile offers an example of the company's unique and vibrant culture. Such a culture stands out from moribund ones, and everyone who comes into contact with it finds it engaging, dynamic, energetic, and vital.

One category in this location's employee engagement survey, "The mission of my company makes me feel my job is important," consistently receives a nearly perfect score year after year. Diane recalled how this score gave her an idea. "We believe in building on our strengths, so let's build on this sense of mission and purpose." Knowing that "people have the greatest attachment to those they know and love," she imagined installing a collage of photos. The committee she put together to explore the idea took it further. Bruce McCarthy, one of the site's human resource business partners, offered to take the photos and interview people who volunteered to appear on the wall. According to Diane, "This gave Bruce a chance to do what he does best" by uniting his passion for photography with his pride in the company.

Culture contains deeply felt assumptions, values, and beliefs. We see it reflected in behaviors and decisions that produce results. Often described as "the way we do things around here" or the "glue that binds people together," culture consists of both visible elements—such as behaviors, decisions, conversations, workspace design, written materials, mission statements, websites, policies, reward systems, and performance expectations—and invisible elements—such as core values, basic assumptions, beliefs, and mindsets that drive the visible elements.

Picture culture as an iceberg, with only the tip visible to the eye. Ninety percent lies below the surface, where you can't see it. That's the part that sunk the *Titanic*, and that's the part that could sink your company's strategy.

Novo Nordisk's Blue Mile exemplifies just one of many visible aspects of the company's culture. When visitors to their sparkling clean plant must put on a protective gown, shoe covers, a cap, and gloves, they see the company's dedication to safety and quality in action. The white boards outside each department show the day's progress toward goals. The displays, continuously updated by managers and employees, make the department's work visible to all. Office employees, including executives, work in open, bright spaces with low walls to promote collaboration. You can see your colleagues at work.

Even the intangibles, such as company pride, take concrete form. Numerous awards adorn the lobby's walls, including the 2012 Global Knights plaque commemorating Novo Nordisk's selection as the most sustainable company in the world. The company's Web site proclaims its dedication to corporate social responsibility and highlights stories of patients, employees, and the work they do to advance health in communities from Kansas to Kenya.[1] When you talk with the people at Novo Nordisk, you hear such comments as, "Accountability is really important—lives are in our hands…We care about the community and the environment as much as the bottom line…My opinions count."[2] Located near the prestigious Research Triangle area of North Carolina, employees can pick and choose among many great employment opportunities. Diane says they stay with Novo Nordisk because they "value having a purpose and making a difference in people's lives, contributing to the community and making the world a better place for their children."

These and many other concrete examples of the company's culture spring from a core set of values, including responsibility, accountability, quality, patient focus, respect, continuous learning, and more. All organizations can reap the rewards of building their own unique and vibrant culture.

A well-managed culture can catapult a company to achieve record-setting results. A poorly managed one can send it crashing to the ground. Research consistently proves a strong correlation between culture and all aspects of business performance: profitability, productivity, revenue growth, shareholder value, customer loyalty, employee satisfaction, and return on investment.[3]

Culture and the Bottom Line

Strategy alone won't bring success. Nor will culture alone. A great company harnesses both. A vibrant, high-performance culture brings a smart strategy to life. Dysfunctional cultures crush strategy, frustrate people, and hamper business success. Just scan the daily business press to see the sad news of cultures that have run amok:

- ► The robo-signing practices that led to foreclosure-gate, a disaster for tens of thousands of home buyers when scores of mortgage servicers and employees at several large banks signed affidavits that led to wrongful home foreclosures.

- ► The fining of GlaxoSmithKline to the tune of $3 billion by the Food and Drug Administration after it came to light that GSK employees were bribing doctors and illegally promoting Wellbutrin, Paxil, Advair, and Avandia for unapproved off-label uses.[4] Three years earlier, Pfizer had paid $2.3 billion in fines for off-label marketing of several drugs.[5]

- ► Accounting improprieties involving Enron, Worldcom,

Andersen, and many others that resulted in damaged companies, tens of thousands of lost jobs, and the loss of retirement savings for countless people.

On the positive side, the exposure of these misdeeds led to major reforms in the financial and pharmaceutical industries. For such changes to make any material, lasting difference, a culture must maintain an abiding commitment to the underlying values reflected by the reforms. On the negative side, thousands of employees and their leaders broke laws and ethical rules, behaving in ways that brought shame and financial ruin to their companies and hurt millions of innocent people in the process. How could that happen? Because culture can both build and destroy. Vibrant cultures create desired results; toxic cultures inevitably wreak havoc on both people and performance. When people get swept up in a cultural riptide, they think and behave in ways they never could have imagined.

How do you build a vibrant culture like the one I observed firsthand at Novo Nordisk? How do you develop a positive, vibrant, ethical, innovative culture that motivates high-performance behaviors and achieves enduring results? You make it consistent with The New Corporate Facts of Life.

Culture and The New Corporate Facts of Life

Great cultures capture people's hearts and minds to drive greater creativity, collaboration, engagement, and excellence. To capitalize on opportunities in a world of constant and accelerated change, companies need to replace outdated, dysfunctional cultures with ones imbued with commitment, courage, customer focus, and innovation.

In 2004, DIRTT—a Calgary, Canada–based company that employs nearly 1,000 employees throughout North America and whose acronym stands for "Doing It Right This Time"—burst onto the so-called "agile interior" scene with a different perspective on how to build office interiors that goes beyond simply constructing workspaces. The company's movable walls and other architectural elements create plug-and-play infrastructures that clients can repurpose and redesign with little or no waste.

DIRTT's culture aligns to the company's mission and vision: to radically and profitably modernize the multibillion-dollar construction industry. Their previously unimagined mass-custom modular solutions offer top speed, state-of-the-art design, high performance, and environmentally responsible products. The company's shared-value business model and culture enhance both their clients' and their own success in ways that also respect the environment. Between 2008 and 2012, DIRTT expanded while the building industry as a whole dropped by 60 percent and decades-old competitors went broke. The company attributes its success to two factors: groundbreaking interior design software created by Barrie Loberg, one of the company's founders, and the DIRTT culture.

Referring to themselves as DIRTTbags ("Ya gotta problem wit dat?"), the firm's passionate people strive to help clients attain the best solutions, experiences, and environments possible. They also help each other. They volunteer. They get goofy. And, like Novo Nordisk employees, they thrive on the idea that their efforts make the world a better place. Working at DIRTT means more than installing workspaces and earning paychecks.

While every organization develops its own unique set of desired traits and no organization does everything right all the time, the best ones keep considering The New Corporate Facts of Life. Figure 5-1 compares the cultural actions of companies embracing The New Corporate Facts of Life with those who do not. Jot a checkmark along the continuum at the point where you think your company stands with respect to each action.

Whenever I begin work with a new client or research a company, I look for traits such as those on the right side of the chart in the organization's culture. Companies embracing this new business model define and align their cultures to achieve their visions of a different way of doing business, constantly questioning, refining, and even replacing the business models of the past.

Figure 5-1. Assess Your Organization's Cultural Traits.

Old School Cultures	New Facts of Life Cultures
Focus primarily on shareholders	Strive for the success of all stakeholders
Inhabit our own island	Operate as part of an ecosystem
Protect functional silos	Collaborate across boundaries
Encourage maintaining the status quo	Emphasize continuous learning
Make decisions with limited input	Engage all stakeholders
Lead from the top	Install leadership at all levels
Focus on the bottom line only	Adhere to a shared-value model
Motivate with a carrot-and-stick approach	Instill company pride
Allow the end to justify the means	Require ethical and responsible behavior
Set attainable goals	Reach for the stars
Accept mere incremental improvement	Strive for disruptive innovation
Let the past dictate the future	Create a bold future
Share on a "need to know" basis	Remain highly transparent

Creating Your Unique and Vibrant Culture

Organizational culture starts the very day a company comes into existence with its founder's vision. Like a growing organism, it steadily evolves, either on its own or at the hands of the company's leaders. Manage it, or it will manage you. Even though you can't see your culture on paper as you can your financial statements, or hold it in your hand as you can your company's products, you can still manage it carefully. You can't duck responsibility for your company's culture any more than you can ignore a child's upbringing. And, like a parent's job, the work of nurturing culture never stops.

In an ideal world, an organization's founders decide what kind of culture they need to fulfill their vision, mission, and strategy. The leaders of companies like DIRTT, Novo Nordisk, Southwest Airlines, and Starbucks have done just that. If you have paid scant attention to your own firm's culture or find it suddenly challenged by an acquisition or new leadership, you must think about transforming it by building on what works well and eliminating what doesn't.

As shown in Figure 5-2, culture creation or transformation progresses through four key phases:

1. **Define** your ideal future-state culture.
2. **Assess** your current culture.
3. **Create or transform** your culture with a three-step process: lead, engage, and align.
4. **Monitor and measure** the results and keep managing it as carefully as you do every other crucial aspect of your business.

Figure 5-2. Four Steps to Culture Transformation.

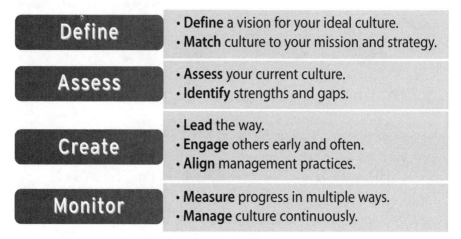

Define
- **Define** a vision for your ideal culture.
- **Match** culture to your mission and strategy.

Assess
- **Assess** your current culture.
- **Identify** strengths and gaps.

Create
- **Lead** the way.
- **Engage** others early and often.
- **Align** management practices.

Monitor
- **Measure** progress in multiple ways.
- **Manage** culture continuously.

As we take a closer look at each of these steps, we'll discuss many of the tools and resources you can use to create or transform your own unique culture. You want to identify the resources you can tap into within your company, such as your organization development professionals. Also, consider adding external resources, such as consultants, who can bring extensive expertise on culture change and an outside perspective to the undertaking. A combination of internal and external players often works best. The internal people know the company well. External professionals see aspects of the company differently and can offer more candid feedback to those involved in the change effort.

Define

Step 1: Define Your Desired Future-State Culture

Whether you are creating a brand-new culture or altering a current one, you must form a clear vision of what future culture you need to implement your strategy and accomplish your mission. Try listing the attitudes and behaviors that you want your people to adopt. You might begin with the traits of the game-changing cultures discussed earlier. Whatever list you use, you want it to paint a clear picture of the cultural traits and values needed to achieve your company's strategy and fulfill its mission. Let's examine how Novo Nordisk and DIRTT, two very different yet highly successful companies, defined their cultures.

After Mogens Smed sold his company, Smed International, to Haworth for $300 million, he decided to launch a new venture. Troubled by the waste and harm to the environment caused by traditional building methods, he vowed to "do it right this time." From the beginning, Smed envisioned DIRTT as a company that values people, planet, and profit, in that order. He puts people's needs first because he believes that they determine the fate of the business. The efficient use of resources makes reusable workspaces and recycled materials more profitable. Smed, who refers to himself as the "head DIRTTbag," runs a flat organization without formal titles. "We want to drive from the bottom up, not build a hierarchy." He believes in empowering and constantly challenging people in ways that motivate them to work hard and have fun at the same time. Operating with a high level of transparency, DIRTT seeks to meet the needs of customers, with environmentally responsible, functional, high-quality, and attractive designs. Smed says, "This business is sustainable. If I left tomorrow, it could continue to grow to several billion dollars, as long as they keep the culture growing." Nothing empowers effective succession planning more surely than a vibrant and dynamic culture.

A decade after introducing their values, Novo Nordisk's leaders decided to update the Novo Nordisk Way of Management. As a key part of the process, CEO Lars Rebien Sørensen and other company leaders spent five months traveling to seven corporate sites around the world, eventually meeting with 350 employees and 100 patients, health-care providers, and other stakeholders. More ideas and suggestions came through social media. This input helped the company's leaders reinforce core values and principles and condense the message. Engaging others in the process also fostered greater ownership of these values across the company.

Today, the ten Novo Nordisk Way Essentials capture the beliefs, aspirations, and expectations that drive the company's culture:

1. **We create value by having a patient centered business approach.**

2. **We set ambitious goals and strive for excellence.**

3. **We are accountable for our financial, environmental, and social performance.**

4. **We provide innovation to the benefit of our stakeholders.**

5. **We build and maintain good relations with our key stakeholders.**

6. **We treat everyone with respect.**

7. **We focus on personal performance and development.**

8. **We have a healthy and engaging working environment.**

9. **We optimize the way we work and strive for simplicity.**

10. **We never compromise on quality and business ethics.**[6]

Diane Cox described the importance of these essentials to employees: "People are pretty passionate about living the Novo Nordisk Way and for holding others accountable to do the same."

Defining Your Desired Unique Culture. Although DIRTT operates with far less structure than Novo Nordisk, both clearly define the company's cultural attributes. Your organization needs to decide how to define the unique culture it desires.

➤ **Start with your strengths.** Every company, no matter how troubled its culture, does some things well. Identifying your company's strengths and assets provides a foundation of pride and optimism on which people can build new cultural traits. Focusing just on what's wrong leads to a dangerous it's-broke-so-we-must-fix-it mindset. Retain and strengthen the positive core—those traits you must keep no matter what changes you plan to make. Use these strengths to help eliminate damaging and inappropriate traits.

➤ **Engage all stakeholders.** Stay in constant touch with all the people affected by the way your company operates. Involving your employees promotes greater ownership and strengthens their commitment to creating the new culture. Suppliers and alliance partners can provide insights on how you meet, exceed, or fail to meet their expectations.

➤ **Research the state of the art.** Scan the business media, including news articles and books; visit with leaders at other organizations; review the research on how culture differentiates top-performing companies from the also-rans; and remain on the lookout for cultural traits that honor The New Corporate Facts of Life. Also consider your competitors, who may have cultivated traits you should emulate or avoid.

➤ **Review your company's strategy and vision.** (See Chapters 3 and 4 for more on these subjects.) Consider whether your strategy and vision have changed and whether they need to change. Identify the cultural qualities needed to fulfill the vision and execute the strategy.

➤ **Communicate the desired cultural traits to all stakeholders.** Broadcast the cultural traits you desire for your organization widely and frequently. Test whether stakeholders understand and embrace them. Ensure that the behavior, comments, and decisions made by leaders reflect the desired culture.

DIRTT executives regularly ask their employees to answer five critical questions:

1. Does working at DIRTT improve me?

2. What do you need from the company that you are not currently getting?

3. Are there genuine opportunities for advancement?

4. Is there a culture here that creates an enjoyable working environment?

5. Is it rewarding to have a career as a DIRTTbag?[7]

DIRTT and Novo Nordisk share a number of traits, such as their responsible business practices, environmental and social consciousness, and customer (or patient) focus. Yet each has crafted a unique culture. What works for one company may not work for another.

Cultural norms may vary somewhat in different departments or functions within the organization. Take UPS, for example. Certain traits, such as customer service, corporate responsibility, and quality, sit at the core of the organization, but UPS business units apply them differently:

Think outside the box: The UPS research and development people must think creatively, seeking the best cutting-edge technology and experimenting with prototypes.

Deliver the box: The driver must adhere to numerous rules to ensure safe delivery of a shipment to the customer, on time, intact, using the least amount of fuel. Yet the driver must also think outside the box to delight customers, overcome traffic delays, and even deal with emergency situations.

Assess

Step 2: Assess Your Current Culture

Offering a prescription without making an accurate diagnosis amounts to nothing but management malpractice. Once you have defined your desired future-state culture, you need to assess your current culture. Only a thorough assessment will reveal sometimes surprising strengths, undetected weaknesses, and other insights leaders need before they tinker with anything.

A proper assessment involves much more than employee satisfaction, workplace quality, and engagement surveys. Such surveys may tell you how much people enjoy working for the company and what they like or dislike about their jobs, but they do not reveal the whole picture.

While certain core cultural traits may cascade across an entire organization, the overall culture actually consists of a patchwork quilt of idiocultures, meaning cultures at the group level. Understanding the ways idiocultures form helps achieve the consistent display of desired traits throughout the organization. Specific leaders, locations, practices, and history influence each and every business unit. Organizations created through acquisition may retain remnants of their previous cultures, and even longstanding units may evolve in different directions. A good assessment will reveal these cultural variations.

Because Novo Nordisk considers culture a crucial and game-changing business variable, the company's leaders hold themselves accountable for managing culture as much as they do sales, profitability, quality, and production. Because they know that culture affects all other success factors, they make sure that every one to three years a team of facilitators audits culture in the firm's facilities around the world.[8]

During my work with Novo Nordisk, I spoke with leaders and other employees to uncover their perspectives on whether they align with the company's culture and its higher purpose, as well as on ways the senior leadership team might operate most effectively. The comments I heard echoed the values proclaimed in the Novo Nordisk Way:

- ▶ "We make life-changing and life-saving drugs."

- ▶ "It's not just about cost and efficiency; we are expanding access to diabetics around the world."

- ▶ "I can express my views here."

- ▶ "Lives are in our hands. This impacts our way of thinking and acting."

▶ "We want things to be done right and will pay the price for high-quality solutions."

▶ "We care about community and the environment as much as the bottom line."

▶ "I learn every day."

You can use a lot of different tools to assess your culture, including:

▶   Contextual observation.

▶   Group and individual interviews.

▶   Organizational practices review.

▶   Crowd sourcing.

▶   Culture surveys.

As in the defining phase, look for what's working well and not so well. When you find pockets of innovation or people who feel exceptionally empowered and connected to their work, study the reasons for their motivation and engagement. What differentiates the highest-performing locations from the lowest-performing sites? What do their leaders do differently? What principles and values guide their practices? What sets them apart from other teams or groups? How can you get more people doing what they're doing?

Assessing Your Culture through Contextual Observation. I love observing cultures in action. Watching people do their work provides valuable insights into culture that go far beyond the opinions and statistics derived from formal surveys. Walk around the office areas or plant floor. Immerse yourself in the work. Ask a worker to train you. Act like a customer, not just a buyer of what your company sells; imagine yourself a worker upstream or downstream who sends work to or receives work from other departments or teams. Visit far-flung sites to study variations from location to location. Compare the highest-performing and lowest-performing sites. What do the top performers do that others don't? Watch how people solve problems. Eavesdrop on meetings without exerting your influence. Hang out in the break or lunchrooms. Consider body language and facial expressions. What makes them nod, smile, scowl, or swear? Do they eagerly offer ideas, or do they prefer operating under the radar? Does their workspace display fun, personal items, or does it look sterile and bleak? Who wields the real power? Providing senior leaders with a list of the cultural traits and specific behaviors you've observed helps open their eyes to the true nature of the culture. When faced with specific examples, leaders will more likely look beyond what happens and try to figure out why it happens. The why sheds light on how shared values play out in terms of people's beliefs and behaviors.

When visiting the DIRTT Savannah plant, I saw people wearing shirts designed by an employee with a saying on the back: "It's not the destination, it's not the journey, it's the DIRTT you pick up along the way." The night before, the plant hosted a pie throwing contest to raise funds for breast cancer in honor of the wife of a coworker in the Calgary location. When they ran out of whipped cream, they filled the pie tins with barbeque sauce or ketchup. DIRTT closes its plants early one day a month for beer meetings, where employees can engage in freewheeling discussions with their leaders.

Assessing Your Culture Through Group and Individual Interviews.

Seek and ye shall find. Ask and they will tell. It often amazes me how much people will share about what's going on in an organization when you approach them the right way. Too often, a leader falls prey to the Emperor's New Clothes Syndrome, where people say what they think the leader wants to hear rather than what they truly think. To avoid that trap, try these approaches to getting the most out of individual and group interviews. In doing so, leaders should openly encourage feedback and promise no retribution for total honesty that may make leaders feel uncomfortable.

▶ **Tap into external resources.** Some employees may feel more comfortable speaking to someone from outside the company;

others may prefer keeping it in the family. The external person doesn't bring biases to the interview and can more easily tell the truth about the Emperor's New Clothes. Yet an internal person knows the culture more intimately and can more easily get to the truth of the matter. Quite often a combination of the two approaches works best.

▶ **Promise anonymity, not confidentiality.** Regardless of the method for obtaining information, you want it to paint an accurate picture. Let people know you will share quotes or examples or modify feedback to avoid revealing the specific sources of the information.

▶ **Seek stories.** Ask for examples of the culture in action, which create a far more compelling image than a list or ranking of traits. Stories resonate with people and evoke emotions. Novo Nordisk's Blue Mile provides a great example of constantly sharing stories to promote pride and commitment.

▶ **Find out what's working.** Rather than embarking on a witch hunt to find out what's wrong, focus on what's right. The positives provide a foundation on which to build the future. More importantly, discussing what's right with the culture reinforces pride in the company and gets people excited about the future. Ask questions to elicit stories and examples of an organization's strengths and assets, as well as ideas for creating a desired future. Focusing on strengths and channeling efforts toward the future motivates and engages people. You can freely use the sample interview guide on our Web site: www.strategic-imperatives.com.

▶ **Don't ignore what's not working.** People naturally complain about the problems they encounter at work. To avoid a lot of negative and unproductive finger-pointing and blaming, you can get people talking about problems in a more positive way by asking, "If you were in charge, what would you do to make working here a more gratifying experience?" Consider the difference between these two answers: "People don't collaborate around here; everyone's trying so hard to get ahead of their peers." Or, "I'd set up more rewards for team success that emphasize greater collaboration over self-promotion." Positive-based questions move people from whining to defining. Also, determine whether examples represent the rare exception or the norm by asking how often they occur.

Assessing Your Culture Through Organizational Practices Review. Reviewing a company's organizational practices provides great insight into what people do or do not value. Take a look at governance, hiring practices, communications channels, training and development programs, compensation plans, recognition and reward systems, organization design, and performance management practices.

Review the list of management practices in Figure 5-3. Note where your organization falls on the left-to-right continuum.

Assessing Your Culture through Crowd Sourcing. As with obtaining input on an ideal culture, you can employ social media to gather a wide spectrum of feedback about your current culture. In the case of Novo Nordisk, employees and customers can provide input at any time through the company's website.

Assessing Your Culture through Culture Surveys. Surveys specifically designed to assess culture can help identify cultural variations, particularly across large or diverse organizations. Although you will find culture surveys helpful, you should view them as supplements to your other assessment efforts. To gain a full understanding of your current culture, you also need to talk to people, observe behaviors, and examine organizational practices. This gives you the full context in which to analyze all the input you have gathered.

Once you have completed your assessment, compare your current culture with your desired future-state culture. Identify and prioritize the gaps between the two, and then turn your attention to creating the one you want.

Figure 5-3. Assess Your Management Practices.

Old School Practices		New Corporate Facts of Life Practices
Hire the breathing	Recruitment and Hiring	Hire the best
Prefer baptism by fire	New Staff Orientation	Provide thorough orientation to the way people do things here
Let people figure it out for themselves	Training and Development	Develop the right skills
Let the ends justify the means	Compensation	Reward the right results/behaviors
Focus on problems	Recognition	Celebrate success
Do the minimum required	Employee Benefits	Display true concern for employees' well-being
Keep people in defined compartments	Goal Setting	Make sure people know how their goals fit within the larger context
Let people learn through the grapevine	Communication	Emphasize two-way, timely, respectful dialogue
Punish risk-taking	Risk-Taking	Reward prudent risk-taking
Allow whatever gets the job done	Business Ethics	Insist that people do the right thing
Follow policies that aren't customer-friendly	Customer Service	Strive to delight customers
Stress competition within and among teams	Teams	Build collaborative groups
Tolerate poor managers	Management	Develop and hire the best managers

Create

Step 3: Create Your Culture by Leading, Engaging, and Aligning

Whether transforming or creating a culture, you need to simultaneously exercise leadership, engage your key stakeholders, and align your organizational practices with the new culture.

Leading. Any fisherman will tell you, "A fish rots from the head down." Dysfunctional cultures come from the top. So do vibrant cultures. As with other aspects of business success, the right culture starts with the right leadership.

Leaders at mosquito control company Clarke recognized the need for cultural changes. CEO John Lyell Clarke III knew from age 13 that he would one day take the helm of the firm his grandfather had founded in his garage in 1946. The Clarke company kills mosquitoes. At one time their logo showed a giant C on top of an upside-down dead mosquito. However, the nature of the business began to trouble the third-generation CEO. Trained as a scientist, Lyell understood the importance of protecting the environment. Approaching 50, Lyell wanted to engineer a makeover for his company. Oh, he still liked the idea of killing disease-carrying mosquitoes, but he didn't like the harshness of many of the products used to get the job done. To solve that dilemma, he set Clarke's scientists to work creating organic compounds that would knock off mosquitoes just as effectively as decades-old poisons, yet embody the principles of green chemistry. With those safer products in hand, Lyell set about completely redefining and rebranding Clarke, from an insecticide maker to a public health company. This meant significantly changing and realigning the company's products, practices, buildings, equipment, and, most of all, culture.[9]

Through their words and deeds, leaders must embody and promote the desired culture. Disconnects between the walking and the talking erode trust, foster cynicism, lower satisfaction, and raise employee turnover. We'll talk more about effective leadership in Chapter 6. At this point, however, you can determine the extent to which all your leaders accept accountability for culture and champion it by rating how much they demonstrate the following behaviors by placing an H (high), M (moderate), or L (low) in Figure 5-4. Then rate how well you champion culture by asking yourself the same questions.

Leaders who do not fare well in these areas of culture building may need coaching and development on how to promote the organization's

Figure 5-4. Leaders As Culture Champions.

How well do your leaders:	H	M	L
Clearly define what needs to be done and how it will be done?			
Define and embrace the organization's code of conduct and values?			
Promote two-way communication and provide multiple avenues for feedback?			
Align management practices to the company's values and strategy?			
Role-model desired behaviors?			
Reward progress, preferred behaviors, and results?			
Hold others accountable for embracing and promoting cultural traits?			
Continuously monitor and adjust the culture to meet changing needs?			

culture. Those who simply cannot fulfill the role of culture champion may find more satisfaction working somewhere else. Of course, you want to ensure leadership buy-in by hiring and promoting the right leaders, rewarding them for desired behaviors and results, insisting on high ethical standards and transparency, and monitoring ongoing efforts by everyone to keep the culture humming.

When DIRTT set about hiring plant managers as it expanded plant operations into Savannah and Phoenix, it found that many potential recruits preferred the command-and-control style that wouldn't suit the company's empowered work culture. COO Tracy Baker ultimately decided to promote a current plant leader, Mike Greer, to run Savannah. She knew Mike held the respect of the DIRTTbags at the plant and would lead in ways that matched the culture. After seeing Mike's leadership in action and valuing the high performance of the Savannah plant, she later asked him to oversee Phoenix as well.

Engaging. Smart leaders recognize the importance of employee engagement because it results in a highly motivated, self-developing, continuously improving, creative, innovative, and productive workforce. You know you've got it when you see people going above and beyond their job descriptions by investing extra time, brainpower, and energy into their work.

At Clarke, Lyell introduced his vision of a new business model at an all-employee meeting in 2008, a time when the economy was caught in the downdraft of the recession. Some thought him crazy, but most embraced the idea and wanted to be part of the new order. Employees contributed hundreds of ideas on how to make the new Clarke a reality. The next few years brought great change. An initial ad hoc group evolved into a formal sustainability board and five sustainability committees. At the time of this writing, these committees prioritize actions and lead the way to engage people throughout the organization to make changes large and small. Ideas come from inside and outside the company. Twenty percent of the people at Clarke's 2013 summit, Clarke Plus: Accelerating Sustainability, represented external stakeholders such as customers, bankers, government representatives, and fellow business leaders.

In your own organization, you want to engage employees early and often during every phase of a culture-building or culture-transformation process, inviting their help with defining the desired future-state culture, assessing the current culture, supporting necessary adjustments, and measuring results. Chapter 7 provides additional information, tools, and resources for fostering greater stakeholder engagement, but at this point you should consider specific steps you can take to fulfill your organization's unique needs by fostering greater employee engagement in your corporate culture:

1. Understanding what drives employee engagement: meaningful work, the big picture, leadership, personal growth, and pride

2. Discovering the levels and variations of employee engagement within your organization

3. Designing a system that fosters employee engagement by:

    ► Providing meaningful work clearly linked to key goals

    ► Clarifying the context of the work

    ► Strengthening leadership

    ► Practicing full transparency with open, honest, retribution-free two-way communication

➤ Emphasizing collaboration, trust, and initiative

➤ Involving people early and often

➤ Building pride in the organization

4. Linking engagement efforts to your strategy and critical initiatives (When people see the whole field of play as well as the goalposts, they will more likely do what it takes to score points and apply their imaginations to the effort.)

5. Measuring and monitoring engagement as diligently as you do the bottom line

If you want to chat with Preben Haaning, Corporate Vice President and General Manager of the Novo Nordisk Clayton facility, don't look in his office. You'll more likely find him on the plant floor, where he spends most of his time talking to employees, asking questions, and inviting ideas. Diane Cox describes him as "very inclusive, a great communicator, and a great coach to his senior leadership team." Preben keeps his finger on the pulse of his organization and its culture.

Once you've engaged your people, you want to make sure that your management system keeps everyone rolling in the right direction.

Aligning. Every organization operates with a management system. That system—consisting of all of an organization's management practices, from hiring, training, compensation, and communication, to the physical workspace, organizational design, governance and decision making—should harmonize to support the culture. That's just another way of saying that culture depends on alignment.

Clarke's leaders and employees collaborated to redefine operations, facilities, processes, and management practices. Bicycles replaced trucks, and company Priuses bear the phrase, "Love the Earth, Not Mosquitoes." Handheld devices increase efficiency and reduce fuel use. Green building initiatives lower energy use, and all new facilities are built to LEED (Leadership in Energy and Environmental Design) certification standards. A waste management operation dubbed Starve Oscar (after the garbage-devouring monster on *Sesame Street*) reduces waste and costs. It evolved from an employee grassroots effort to attain an aggressive zero-waste-to-landfill goal. An Extraordinary Health and Happiness committee finds ways to improve employee health and wellness, while an integrated product design team focuses intently on creating more Next Generation products.

To determine the degree to which your management practices support your desired future-state culture:

- ▶ Review the results of your earlier assessment of formal and informal management practices.
- ▶ List practices that require adjustment.
- ▶ Take steps to modify ineffective or damaging practices and/or create new ones.

The assessment of formal and informal practices should have provided you with areas that cry out for improvement. This list could include desired practices that you need to tweak, undesired ones you should eradicate, and new ones you want to install. Formal practices include such items as recruitment, hiring, training, compensation, performance management, and recognition programs. Informal practices matter just as much. Consider how communication occurs, how people collaborate as teams, and whether they willingly take risks that might help them learn and the business advance. Look at the workplace to see what changes need to occur.

Although you can learn from the practices of other companies, make sure you implement those that best suit your unique organization and bring you closer to the vibrant culture you desire. DIRTT and Novo Nordisk operate with wide-open environments supporting their belief in open, transparent interactions. Novo Nordisk's performance appraisals include triple-bottom-line goals with respect to people, profit, and planet. While DIRTT embraces similar values, they don't use performance appraisals.

Once you've identified traits you hope to change, take steps to modify ineffective or damaging practices and/or create new ones. It often makes sense to take small first steps because those initial successes, though not monumental, help you gather momentum toward more sweeping, long-term improvements. Sometimes, however, you need to make big changes to address major cultural problems, such as the unethical behavior at GSK and Pfizer. Whether you want to implement large or small changes, find ways to engage people along the way, sharing your aspirations for the future and inviting suggestions and support. Doing so helps create the buy-in you need to imbed new traits in the culture. I recommend a simple list like the one shown in Figure 5-5. Notice how this list goes beyond a narrow approach to include a variety of options such as engagement, communication, measures, people practices, and innovation.

If you want to change the game, you need to change the culture. Lyell Clarke did just that at Clarke. And he did it in measurable ways.

Figure 5-5. Align Practices to Achieve Goals.

Changes	Options to Implement Change
Promote corporate-wide social and environmental responsibility	Engage stakeholders in creating the vision and strategy.
	Educate employees on the importance of responsible practices.
	Regularly encourage them to contribute ideas.
	Recognize and reward contributions and progress.
	Add systems for energy efficiency and waste reduction.
	Promote and fund innovation.
	Continuously communicate success stories.
	Identify programs for community involvement and volunteerism.

Measure

Step 4: Measure the Results

As with any meaningful initiative, you want to monitor and measure the results of your culture creation or transformation. Have the new compensation, recognition, and reward programs fostered the right behaviors and results? Do performance reviews confirm the desired changes? Are all training and orientation programs raising awareness and improving performance on the job? Has turnover decreased and employee engagement increased? Do customers express greater levels of satisfaction? Have people offered innovative ideas? How have your efforts improved the bottom line? Are you achieving your strategy? While you can easily quantify results, you can't reduce cultural traits to mere numbers. Thoughts and relationships reveal themselves only through behaviors. Clearly define how core values translate into job-specific behaviors.

Decide at the outset exactly how you will determine whether new beliefs drive new actions that, in turn, drive business results. Go beyond the customary financials to include factors as employee happiness, customer satisfaction, brand image, community appreciation, and environmental impact. Maintain total transparency by frequently communicating your measurements, both positive and negative, to all stakeholders.

For each priority area, indicate how you will measure progress, as shown in Figure 5-6.

Figure 5-6. Define Key Measures.

Priorities to address	Steps to take	Measure progress by
Promote corporate responsibility	Engage employees to obtain their ideas and input	Number and diversity of employees engaged
		Quality of ideas aligning to the vision
		Number of ideas implemented
		Results of these changes
	Implement energy reduction initiatives	Energy reductions
		Related savings
		Behavior changes
	Insist on ethical business practices around the globe	Percentage of employees trained
		Incidents reported
		Frequency and severity of calls to the compliance hotline

For the Clarke company, redefining itself as a "global environmental products and services company" meant adopting new business indicators. When company officials started measuring environmental factors such as energy and waste reduction, they discovered, to the delight of all concerned, that Clarke was saving a half million dollars a year by operating more sustainably. Each sustainability committee determines measureable goals, then carefully tracks and reports on progress. Volunteer hours, the number of bed nets distributed to Nigeria, and lives touched by the company's work appear alongside the usual financial indicators. As for financial growth, every single customer does more business with Clarke than they did a few years ago because they feel drawn to the company's sustainability strategy and products.

Bringing It All Together

A vibrant and unique culture captures people's hearts and minds to drive greater innovation, more productive collaboration, deeper engagement, and higher degrees of excellence.

Organizations that choose to embrace The New Corporate Facts of Life define and align their cultures to achieve their visions of a strikingly different tomorrow, where their workforce moves from compliance to commitment to creation. At Clarke, Lyell discovered a pent-up desire for greater purpose, both in his own heart and in the hearts of his people. By engaging his employees with his new vision, he unleashed a pent-up whirlwind. It turned out that the people there didn't really want to work for an insecticide company, but they did want to work for one that benefits public health and the environment. Whereas Clarke once struggled to fill jobs in their peak summer season, the firm now enjoys a waiting list of people who yearn to join the cause. Amazingly, it not only remained profitable throughout its cultural transformation, it ended up growing its revenues during the recession. To date, Clarke's dynamic new culture has touched 300 million lives through mosquito control and aquatic protection services, with a goal to reach 660 million, nearly 10 percent of the world's population. In 2010, the EPA awarded Clarke the Presidential Green Chemistry Challenge Award for their next-generation Natular, a product listed with the Organic Materials Review Institute (OMRI). What does the future hold for this forward-looking enterprise? When the time comes, Lyell hopes one of his five children will lead this dynamic, ever evolving company into its fourth generation of family ownership.

When I interviewed Lyell about the transformation, he quoted Paul Hawken, the environmentalist and founder of Smith & Hawken, whom he greatly admires: "Once you see, you can't un-see." Once Lyell saw a changing world and his company's place in it, he couldn't un-see it. He had to figure out a better way. I personally rank him at the forefront of executives who know how to *lead* cultural change, how to *engage* others in the endeavor, and how to *align* business practices with a game-changing culture.

Applying The New Corporate Facts of Life

What steps have you taken to integrate The New Corporate Facts of Life into your business? Using The New Corporate Facts of Life Barometer, see where you stand and possibly where you need to go.

After applying The New Corporate Facts of Life Culture Barometer to your organization, list areas where you would like to make some changes. *Define* your desired future-state culture. Assess your current culture. Then consider how you would *lead*, *engage*, and *align* to acquire or strengthen each cultural trait. Finally, indicate how will you *monitor* results.

Figure 5-7. The New Corporate Facts of Life Culture Barometer.

Rating Key:

H–High: We totally get this. Our organization widely embraces and reflects this trait.
M–Medium: We sort of get it. This cultural trait exists to some extent, but we could do more.
L–Low: We're not doing this. Our organization does not really exhibit this trait.

NCFOL	Embedding the NCFOL into Culture	H	M	L
Disruptive Innovation	❑ We actively encourage risk-taking and experimentation. ❑ We recognize and reward innovations small and large. ❑ We continuously ask: What's possible? What if?			
Economic Instability	❑ We educate people on economic variables that affect us. ❑ We insist on fiscal responsibility. ❑ We manage for the long term, not just quarter-to-quarter.			
Societal Upheaval	❑ We help people in communities locally and globally. ❑ We promote diversity, wellness, fair pay, and respect. ❑ We choose ethical suppliers with safe workplaces and fair labor practices.			
Stakeholder Power	❑ We engage our people at all levels early and often. ❑ We understand our customers and regularly seek their input. ❑ We involve external stakeholders and experts to solve problems, to come up with new ideas, and to learn.			
Environmental Degradation	❑ We feel passionate about reducing our environmental impact. ❑ We strive to achieve ambitious environmental goals. ❑ We encourage our people to come up with ideas on how to reduce our environmental footprint.			
Globalization	❑ We respect and value the cultures and norms of countries around the world. ❑ We keep abreast of global changes that may affect us. ❑ We build relationships with global suppliers and customers.			
Population Shifts	❑ We monitor population growth and demographic changes. ❑ We have installed workplace practices suitable to multiple generations of employees. ❑ We design and align our business to stay ahead of shifting demographics.			

CHAPTER 6

Lead on the Edge of Change

A leader takes people where they want to go.
A great leader takes people where they don't
necessarily want to go, but ought to be.

—ROSLYN CARTER

IN 1991, Steve Nygren and his wife Marie were living in Atlanta with their three young daughters. Steve's company, Peasant Restaurants Inc., had grown to 34 restaurants in eight states. He also served on several boards of directors. Looking back, he says they were living on the "treadmill of life." Then one weekend, during a family visit to the countryside just outside Atlanta, the Nygrens surprised themselves by buying a 60-acre farm. It would, they thought, make an ideal weekend retreat. Three years later, Steve sold the restaurant business, resigned from all the boards, and retired, stepping off the treadmill.

By 2000, the Nygrens had opened a bed and breakfast inn and expanded their landholdings to 300 acres. One day, while out jogging along their property with his daughter, Garnie, Steve saw bulldozers clearing some adjacent land. When he asked one of the workers about the project, the worker replied, "We're clearing the trees. I guess they're going to build houses here; that's what usually happens." Steve didn't realize it at the time, but that chance conversation would propel him out of retirement. Concerned about the potential harm to the area's rural character, he called other landowners and began buying up land. Within five weeks, the Nygrens owned another 600 nearby acres. Although this protected their little slice of rural heaven, some 40,000 surrounding acres in Chattahoochee Hill Country, roughly the size of Napa Valley, remained vulnerable to development.

That's when he called his good friend Ray Anderson, founder of the carpet manufacturer Interface and the former co-chair of Bill Clinton's President's Council on Sustainable Development. When Steve sketched out his vision for creating a sustainable community with an abundance of protected green space where people could live a healthier, more environmentally responsible life, Anderson expressed interest and happily connected Steve with experts on the subject.

Steve and Marie forged ahead with their vision. After a little research revealed that 36 people owned half of the targeted 40,000 acres, the couple invited a few owners at a time to small dinner parties where the conversation turned to the topic of responsible development. Having laid this groundwork, the Nygrens invited all of the 36 landowners to their home for coffee and Marie's fabulous desserts. "It was an absolute disaster," Steve recalls. Some folks wanted to preserve the land; others wanted to sell their parcels and cash out. The meeting deteriorated into a verbal brawl, with the "stupid tree-huggers" battling the "greedy developers."

The setback did not deter Steve. After conducting more research, he persuaded the group to reconvene. Again, Steve shared his vision, this time with the help of experts on sustainable community practices. In the end, the group came to a consensus. They would preserve 70 percent of the land and still allow for the construction of nearly 30,000 homes. By comparison, a traditional suburban development would use 80 percent of the land for 5,000 fewer homes.

The group then set about convincing the more than 500 people who owned the other 20,000 acres to work with them on a design that would both protect the land and allow for growth. Hundreds of people ultimately agreed on a plan. Eventually the group convinced Fulton County to replace existing zoning regulations with new ones for this particular area.

The Nygrens themselves offered their land, now 1,000 acres, for the first groundbreaking. Steve's solid reputation as a businessman in Atlanta eventually convinced one bank to help finance the project, provided the Nygrens put up their valuable midtown Atlanta properties as collateral. They eagerly took the risk. With funds secured, the project went forward and soon resulted in the first street in the first hamlet in a community Marie called Serenbe.

Serenbe consisted of 40 initial properties on which buyers could build homes and businesses. Rawson Haverty, an executive with Haverty's Furniture Companies, added his nearby 80 acres to the initial hamlet and agreed that he and his wife would construct a home. Steve's sister-in-law wanted to buy a cottage lot. Marie and Steve agreed to build a townhouse as their own residence, proving that a family could live fabulously on only an eighth of an acre in the middle of the countryside. They also decided to open a small café and bakeshop, now known as The Blue-Eyed Daisy. Steve contacted acquaintances about the opportunity to be part of this unique community. Momentum gathered, and in a few short months buyers had snapped up all the remaining lots.

Today, about 370 residents live in this beautiful community nestled among undeveloped fields and woods. Their homes adhere to EarthCraft House green building specifications, with heating and cooling supplied by solar energy and the community's geothermal system. Beautiful gardens landscaped with plants suited to this southern climate replace the chemically treated lawns popular in most suburbs. Three distinct hamlets include homes and businesses surrounded by wildflower meadows, preserved forests, a lake, and an organic farm. The Blue-Eyed Daisy bakery, the smallest Silver LEED-certified business in the United States, has become a popular gathering spot in a totally walkable community.

Serenbe has evolved into much more than a serene, healthy place to live. The community has drawn international attention as it evolved into a center for research, learning, and teaching. It hosts artist and scholarin-residence programs, attracting brilliant and creative people from around the world. In 2012, Steve and others formed the Serenbe Biophilic Institute, a center for sustainability education and research, and for sharing best practices with other community leaders.

Serenbe also attracted the first Bosch Experience Center, showcasing the Bosch Home Net Zero suite of products and appliances. Opened in 2013, the center offers consumers, trade professionals, and governments the opportunity to learn about Bosch solutions and serves as a world-class gathering spot for conversations on sustainability research and education. In addition, the University of Georgia and the Department of Agriculture have converted the office and conference room at the Serenbe stables into an agricultural center where interns from the university work with the town's farms and the farm cooperative. What's more, the Urban Land Institute named Serenbe as one of the ten best environmental communities in the United States, and people from the Gates Foundation have come to Serenbe to study the effects of the built environment on people's health.

This saga began with one man's vision for change and his willingness to set aside his retirement to provide the necessary leadership for that vision to become a reality. Change under the influence of the NCFOL always requires such bold leadership.

Creating Great Futures Through Bold Leadership

We have met the future, and the future is us. As Woodrow Wilson, the 28th President of the United States and Nobel Peace Prize winner, put it, "You are not here to merely make a living. You are here to enable the world to live more amply, with greater vision and a finer spirit of hope and achievement. You are here to enrich the world and you impoverish yourself if you forget that errand." Steve Nygren does more than earn a good living. He didn't set out to change the world; he simply wanted to protect his community's rural way of life. He met each problem, challenge, and obstacle with passion, vision, and a sense of responsibility. He drew on all his skills, resources, and relationships to create a community that has become a model to inspire and educate others around the globe. He stepped up and led the way.

As our incredibly complex world continues to change, so too must our leaders. Huge but not insurmountable challenges loom on the horizon. Tackling these challenges and turning them into breakthrough opportunities requires a new breed of leader. Responsibility for a better world does not fall only on the shoulders of the Steve Nygrens of the world. We must all take responsibility to lead. As Emmett Murphy wrote in his book *Leadership IQ*, "Every worker leads; every leader works."

Defining the BOLDEST Leadership Needs

Over the past two decades, as I have developed leaders and created effective leadership programs, I've learned a lot about what makes great leaders tick. While working on a graduate project at Case Western Reserve University, I developed the basis for a new model of leadership competence for an emerging breed of leaders who will help create more profitable organizations and a better world. Ultimately, with The New Corporate Facts of Life in mind, I captured all those lessons in my BOLDEST Leadership Competency model. You can find the full model at my company's website (www.strategic-imperatives.com). For the purposes of our discussion, I've created a more concise version (Figure 6-1).

At first glance, many of these leadership traits may seem familiar. Haven't we always wanted visionary leaders who can build relationships and develop their people? The difference lies in the scope and complexity of each of these capabilities. In a world where our organizations must transform themselves in light of the NCFOL, leadership must also evolve. For instance, Old School leaders shaped vision on the foundation of past successes, merely extending the status quo with a few new wrinkles, such as new technology and new marketing channels. An NCFOL

Figure 6-1. BOLDEST Leadership.

B	**Boundaries** ☐ Build coalitions across borders. ☐ Influence key stakeholders. ☐ Break down functional silos.
O	**Opportunities** ☐ See around the bend. ☐ Create compelling visions. ☐ Promote optimism.
L	**Learning** ☐ Quickly absorb complex information. ☐ Emphasize innovation. ☐ Foster a continuous learning culture.
D	**Deliverables** ☐ Deliver today and create tomorrow. ☐ Hold people accountable. ☐ Produce both profit and purpose.
E	**Emotions** ☐ Lead with integrity and self-confidence. ☐ Display empathy and social skills. ☐ Maintain self-awareness and self-regulation.
S	**Systems** ☐ Think systemically. ☐ Consider opposing perspectives. ☐ Manage complexities.
T	**Talents** ☐ Hire, retain, and deploy top talent. ☐ Build organizational capacity. ☐ Develop leadership at all levels.

leader, on the other hand, must weigh more radical alternatives to business as usual. While Old School strolls toward tomorrow, NCFOL races to create a bold new future.

Seeing the BOLDEST Leaders in Action

Let's look more closely at each of the competencies listed in Figure 6-1.

Crossing Boundaries

Building coalitions for change has never posed a bigger challenge (Figure 6-2). Convening all relevant stakeholders takes leaders out of isolation. BOLDEST leaders must reach across many boundaries to forge relationships and alliances in order to accomplish the seemingly impossible. In their own organizations, they must tear down functional silos and bring people together to solve big, complex challenges. When leaders lack sufficient knowledge about key issues such as supply chain traceability, cultural nuances in emerging markets, and energy alternatives, they must tap the expertise of specialists in everything from trash to biophysics. Steve Nygren did just that when he built coalitions for change by forming relationships with neighbors, farmers, builders, scientists, legislators, CEOs, NGOs, and environmental experts.

UK-based World Travel & Tourism Council (WTTC) offers a striking example of BOLDEST leadership in action. WTTC serves as a forum for the executives of the world's leading travel and tourism companies who

Figure 6-2. Boundaries.

B	Boundaries
	❏ Build coalitions across borders.
	❏ Influence key stakeholders.
	❏ Break down functional silos.

wish to address strategic industry priorities. Industry partners such as The Coca-Cola Company, Google, Toshiba, and several large consulting firms provide support and expertise. As one of the world's largest industries, travel and tourism employs 260 million people worldwide and generates 9 percent of the world's GDP. The WTTC advocates partnerships between the public and private sectors to bring long-term prosperity and growth by balancing profitability with people, culture, and the environment.

In 2013, David Scowsill, the President and CEO of the WTTC, closed the organization's 13th WTTC Global Summit in Abu Dhabi with a rousing speech that addressed the challenges facing the industry. By 2050, he said, the worldwide middle class will consist of 3 billion people working at good jobs and eager to travel. The WTTC views this potential future growth as a wake-up call to the private and public sectors to join together and create sustainable, long-term strategies for the next 10, 25, and even 50 years. In keeping with the theme of the 2013 Summit, A Time for Leadership, Scowsill urged the 1,000 delegates to step up and lead: "The art of leadership is to create a vision, to embrace that vision, and drive it to completion. As leaders in our industry, we must continue to work together … and to elevate the cause of Freedom to Travel, to influence policies for growth and boldly plan for a Tourism for Tomorrow."

The challenges to create that visionary future will require cooperation and collaboration by companies and governments across all global boundaries. Organizations such as the WTTC, the Consumer Goods Forum, the World Economic Forum, the World Business Council for Sustainable Development, and the World Resources Institute unite industry leaders with competitors, NGOs, regulators, researchers, and community leaders. These coalitions can more fully examine emerging trends and address issues around sustainability, health, regulatory changes, operational excellence, and people development.

One company's efforts can also make a big difference. Walmart's Sustainability 360 plan pursues multiple strategies to engage its more than 2 million employees, 100,000 suppliers, and hundreds of millions of customers around the world. Its Sustainable Value Network for waste management alone connects more than 800 people globally inside and outside the company and has resulted in the company diverting 89 percent of its U.S. waste from landfills.

Seizing Opportunities

Organizations need both executors and innovators. In most companies, senior leaders must concentrate on execution, getting the desired short-term results (Figure 6-3). They won their positions because they have proven that they get the job done. Today, however, leaders must do more than hit their numbers. They must possess the confidence and imagination to see possibilities much further away than the current bottom line. Visionary leaders redefine the problems speeding toward their organizations as opportunities for finding innovation and promoting optimism. BOLDEST leaders see what others do not see, creating and sharing compelling visions of the future that ignite passion and inspire people to action. Throughout this book, we've seen this ability demonstrated by visionary leaders, such as Unilever's Paul Polman, The Body Shop's Anita Roddick, Grameen Bank's Muhammad Yunus, and Serenbe's Steve Nygren.

Figure 6-3. Opportunities.

O	Opportunities
	□ See around the bend.
	□ Create compelling visions.
	□ Promote optimism.

When Ray Anderson began sharing his vision for turning Interface, a conventional 21-year-old carpet company, into an ecological leader, many thought he had lost his mind. One of his company's senior leaders became visibly upset at a company event, telling others that he couldn't stand to watch his hero jump off a cliff with this crazy environmental idea. Jim Hartzfeld told me how Anderson responded at the next meeting with his leaders. "I hear some of you think I've gone around the bend. Well I have! It's my job to see around the bend. That's what leaders do. Someone has to see what's out there." Crazy, and proud of it!

DIRTT CEO Mogens Smed also takes that label as a compliment. "I like people who are different." Under Smed's e-mail signature appears former BBC television presenter David Ickes's line: "The strong oaks of today were the nuts that held their ground." Like Anderson, Smed believes the world needs braver, more creative leaders. "Leaders need to create and sell the vision ... everyone has to work to a common vision, not individual departmental agendas."

That doesn't mean a visionary leader looks into a crystal-clear glass ball. Smed admits that "[in the beginning] we didn't have a clue what we were going to do. Conventional manufacturing in North America was dead. We thought, if we give clients what they want, do it quickly, with a sustainable solution, then we would have a winner." DIRTT's successful launch and growth, despite the Great Recession, began with a magnificent vision.

Leaders such as Smed, Anderson, Roddick, Polman, and Nygren know that you must do more than dream up a vision. People throughout the organization must see it and own it and let it drive everything they do as they learn and grow their way into the future.

Learning Continuously

Continuous learning has become essential in our fast-changing world (Figure 6-4). Everyone in the organization, from senior leaders to front-line workers, must quickly absorb complex information every day. Keeping up with and surpassing the competition, devising innovative strategies and corporate cultures, delighting customers, and controlling every other success variable all depend on daily education from formal training programs and university courses to self-study initiatives. It also means keeping a finger on the pulse of change, learning on the fly, and inviting those who offer conventional learning approaches to find innovative alternatives. Formal or informal, education is the mother of innovation.

Figure 6-4. Learning.

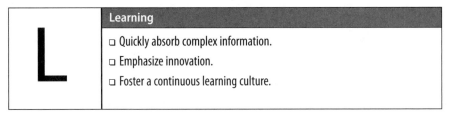

	Learning
L	❏ Quickly absorb complex information.
	❏ Emphasize innovation.
	❏ Foster a continuous learning culture.

Beyond their own development, bold leaders foster a culture of continuous learning at all levels. MIT senior lecturer Peter Senge popularized the concept of the learning organization in his 1990 book, *The Fifth Discipline: The Art & Practice of the Learning Organization*,[1] which *Harvard Business Review* named as one of the seminal management books published in the past 75 years. Senge believes decentralizing leadership in organizations increases the ability of all people to work together effectively toward common goals. Such so-called flat organizations facilitate learning at all levels because they tap into the commitment and ability of people to gain new knowledge in order to improve their performance and meet or surpass the organization's goals. BOLDEST leaders provide the tools everyone needs to engage in a culture of continuous learning. And they go beyond their own organization's boundaries to promote learning among their customers, suppliers, strategic partners, government regulators, and even their most aggressive competitors.

Learning can come from the usual sources, but it can also come from unlikely places. When Walmart's CEO Lee Scott set about creating a more sustainable way of doing business, he didn't study rival Kmart. He contacted sustainability leaders Interface, Herman Miller, and Patagonia to learn about their leading-edge practices. At first, Patagonia's CEO Yvon Chouinard didn't take Scott seriously. After all, Walmart was about 1,300 times the size of Patagonia and didn't exactly enjoy a reputation for saving the planet. Nonetheless, Patagonia shared with Walmart its knowledge about greening the supply chain and worked with the company to develop a sustainability index for its products, a scorecard for rating each product in terms of its social and environmental impact. Patagonia has helped Walmart learn to gauge the amount of water used in the manufacture of clothing and whether suppliers rely on pesticides or engage in other environmentally unfriendly practices. Patagonia benefits from this learning arrangement because Walmart's efforts help raise overall industry standards. Other organizations such as Nike, Gap, REI (Recreational Equipment Inc.), and North Face also learn from Patagonia's nearly three decades of fervent environmental advocacy. By doing so, they evolve their businesses in ways that allow them to remain profitable while putting themselves on a sure path to a more responsible future by setting standards before the government does.

Delivering Results

Leaders of organizations of all sizes, sectors, and locations must create a better tomorrow while delivering profitable results today (Figure 6-5). It takes courage to lead change, and it takes patience, focus, perseverance, and tenacity to turn the vision into reality. Reactivity won't cut it; leaders must be highly proactive. Achieving the organization's vision and strategy requires holding people accountable and aligning goals across the business. Coca-Cola Enterprises widely commits to "Deliver for Today; Inspire for Tomorrow" with a corporate responsibility commitment stating, "We will deliver for today, growing a low-carbon, zero-waste business, and inspire change for a more sustainable tomorrow." Novelis, the largest provider of aluminum in the world, has set a goal of obtaining 80 percent of the metal from recycled sources by 2020. The company's Chief Sustainability Officer, John Gardner, told me that Novelis is "investing massively in growth, almost all of which is sustainability based." At the same time that the company aims to reduce its energy and water use, cut its GHG emissions by half, and eliminate all landfill waste, it also seeks to double its earnings. Strong, responsible growth comes from leaders who know how to merge innovation with operational excellence. Novelis' efforts will be covered in greater detail in Chapter 8.

Figure 6-5. Deliverables.

D	**Deliverables**
	❑ Deliver today and create tomorrow.
	❑ Hold people accountable.
	❑ Produce both profit and purpose.

Unilever CEO Paul Polman has welcomed the challenge to build a sustainable company because he believes that strategy will spur the company's long-term growth and profitability. As leader of one of the largest global suppliers of consumer goods, Polman adamantly refuses to forfeit the future for the sake of short-term quarterly results. "The great challenge of the twenty-first century is to provide good standards of living for seven billion people without depleting the earth's resources or running up massive levels of public debt,"[2] he insists. "To achieve this, government and businesses alike will need to find new models of growth that are in both environmental and economic balance." As mentioned in Chapter 2, Unilever's 2010 Sustainable Living Plan aims to double its business, cut its environmental footprint in half, improve the health and well-being of more than a billion people, and source only sustainable agricultural raw materials.

At the other end of the size spectrum, Ted Turner and George McKerrow Jr. partnered to found Ted's Montana Grill with the initial goal of saving the American bison from extinction. Although their idea may sound counterintuitive, they felt ranchers like Turner himself would raise these animals, once slaughtered to the point of near extinction, if they saw a way to make money from a herd. It came down to simple economics: If you increase demand for the meat, you can increase the population of bison. Ted's Montana Grill restaurants serve hand-raised and free-range bison and other delicacies, all prepared from scratch. They shun microwaves and Styrofoam and use only a miniscule amount of plastic.

Diners read menus printed on recycled paper, sip from paper straws, and carry away doggie bags and takeout containers made from cornstarch. Bamboo floors and low-voltage lighting create an inviting ambience. Some locations obtain their energy from solar power. The chain also sells used vegetable oil as biofuel. Ted's Montana Grill's folksy motto says it all: "Eat great and do good." As of 2012, Ted's Montana Grill had grown to $104 million in annual revenue with 44 locations in 16 states and an ambitious goal to double the size of the company by the year 2021.[3]

Managing Emotions

Research by Daniel Goleman, Richard Boyatzis, Fabio Sala, and others has shed light on the fact that we do not thrive by our wits alone (Figure 6-6). Emotions matter as much as brainpower. Boyatzis and Sala built on the findings of other researchers to categorize Emotional Intelligence competencies in four clusters (Figure 6-7): self-awareness, self-management, social awareness, and relationship management.[4]

Figure 6-6. Emotions.

E	Emotions
	□ Lead with integrity and self-confidence.
	□ Display empathy and social skills.
	□ Maintain self-awareness and self-regulation.

Long-term success in life requires a high degree of emotional intelligence. An Einstein will not succeed in an organization if he does not play well with others. Yes, leaders need a certain amount of intellectual firepower to achieve their peak potential, but they will not get there by brains alone. You also need a fair amount of emotional competence. Leaders who display the first two strengths in Figure 6-7, self-awareness and self-management, operate with integrity and self-confidence. They know both their best and worst selves and strive to regulate their behavior and emotions. Those who do well with the last two, social awareness and rela-

Figure 6-7. Emotional Intelligence Competencies.

Self-Awareness	Maintains a strong sense of strengths, weaknesses, emotions, preferences, and self-worth.
Self-Management	Takes initiative, accepts accountability, keeps emotions under control, and remains adaptable and trustworthy.
Social Awareness	Acts with understanding of others and shows empathy toward their needs, concerns, and issues.
Relationship Management	Inspires and influences others to change through communication, relationship and team building, conflict management, and collaboration.

tionship management, demonstrate the empathy and other skills essential for effecting social interaction, influencing others, and building strong teams. BOLDEST leaders cultivate traits in all four categories in themselves and everyone else in their organizations.

You've read about Patagonia's founder, Yvon Chouinard, and many similarly skilled leaders throughout the book. Patagonia's sustainability journey began in 1988 when, during the first three days of a Boston store opening, employees complained about headaches and stomach pains. The company immediately closed the store and brought in an environmental engineer, who discovered that the store's ventilation system was recycling bad air and poisoning employees. Some companies would have merely adapted the ventilation system to bring in outside air. Chouinard's integrity demanded more. He needed to know the root cause of the poisoning. It turned out that the spring line, filled with lots of cotton, contained formaldehyde, a chemical used in the fabrication of wrinkle-resistant clothing. Chouinard and his team kept asking questions that ultimately led to a commitment to clean up their entire supply chain. Back in 1988, you could not rely on books or websites to learn about alternative fibers and toxic dyes, so Chouinard and his people had to learn on their own.

Chouinard could not rest easy just making money; he needed to create change. That meant stepping up and speaking out. This belief drove the third part of the company's mission statement: "to use business to inspire and implement solutions to the environmental crisis." Chouinard doesn't wait for customers to ask for something. He wants to welcome his customers to the future, not follow them there. When he decided that Patagonia would drop industrially grown cotton in favor of the organic alternative, he gave the company 18 months to make the change, even though doing so put 25 percent of his business at risk if people failed to come up with the right solution. Chouinard serves as a catalyst for change with an inner compass set for integrity and transparency. He never shies away from challenging his people to do more and to do better. Not only does Chouinard lead with strong emotional intelligence, he has created an emotionally intelligent company, unafraid to tip the sacred cows of business and challenge bigger companies to change their ways.

Every business is a relationship business. Every day, we sign virtual contracts with other people, from our friends and family to our colleagues at work, be they our superiors, our teammates, or our direct reports. We do it with every stakeholder who comes into contact with our organization: customers, suppliers, regulators, and competitors. No written code of conduct, no handshake, and no printed contract can ensure a great relationship any more than a marriage certificate can guarantee a life of wedded bliss.

Thinking Systemically

In this complex, interdependent world, each action casts a stone into a pond, sending ripples to every shore both inside and outside the organization. Leaders must rise above the trees to see the forest. Everything they and their people do functions like a gear in a larger system. Top performers think and operate systemically by managing complexities, recognizing patterns, and making connections (Figure 6-8). They consider opposing ideas simultaneously to gain different perspectives and surface innovative solutions. They see problems and opportunities earlier than

Figure 6-8. Systems.

S	Systems
	☐ Think systemically.
	☐ Consider opposing perspectives.
	☐ Manage complexities.

others, and they think differently about ways to seize those opportunities and solve those problems.

Lindsay Levin founded the social enterprise Leaders' Quest in 2001 to help leaders discover a greater role for business in the world, one combining profit and purpose. Leaders' Quest provides experiential learning programs (called Quests) that take people to places they ordinarily would not visit, where they meet extraordinary leaders, from grassroots organizers in poor communities to CEOs of global companies. Levin, who wrote the book *Invisible Giants*,[5] shared an interesting story in a 2013 British Airways magazine article:

> As companies grow into new markets and outsource core business functions, executives are increasingly called on to work across time zones, languages and cultures. There's constant pressure to respond to changing political realities, manage disparate global supply chains and face up to complex issues. Meanwhile, the decisions we make on a daily basis can impact the lives of people halfway across the world we've never even met.

> This truth was brought home to me on a trip to Kenya a few years back. I was there with a group of international bankers, and one evening we found ourselves sitting under a tree, in conversation with some local farmers. Knowing that their visitors worked in finance, one of the farmers asked: "How is it that when the financial crisis came to Europe and America that some of us had our goats and shacks repossessed?" This felt surreal. Here we were, in a village in Africa, responding to questions about the global financial crisis. I couldn't

quite believe that the consequences of decisions taken in London, Frankfurt and New York could reverberate all the way out here. But they did.[6]

A greater appreciation of context leads to better decisions. Peter Senge promotes bringing systems thinking fully into the business world. Since many people cannot easily see how their little cog fits into the bigger wheel, you can follow Senge's advice and draw a little chart or diagram that shows how their piece of the system fits together with all the rest. However you do it, engaging all stakeholders, not just employees, with knowledge of how everything fits together broadens everyone's perspective.

Developing Talent

We need good leaders everywhere, not just in large organizations and not just at the top (Figure 6-9). No matter how compelling the vision or brilliant the strategy, it takes all hands on deck to fulfill the vision and implement the strategy. BOLDEST leaders spend a lot of their time creating more leadership capacity throughout the organization. Hiring, retaining, developing, and deploying the best talent available must become their top priority.

Figure 6-9. Talents.

T	**Talents**
	☐ Hire, retain, and deploy top talent.
	☐ Build organizational capacity.
	☐ Develop leadership at all levels.

Leaders at Proctor & Gamble (P&G) know they won't move up until they've developed someone to take their place. When P&G won the top ranking in *Chief Executive* magazine's "40 Best Companies for Leaders 2012," the company's CEO, Bob McDonald, told the magazine, "I see my role as the chief talent officer of the company. Leadership is the one factor that will ensure our success long after I am gone as CEO."[7]

Former World Bank Vice President Mieko Nishimizu called this a world of "inescapable mutuality." During a World Bank mission to Cairo, Egypt, she committed herself to fighting bad governance and mentoring good leaders. She valued the sometimes latent talents of people in all walks of life: farmers, impoverished women, village elders, former prostitutes turned social workers, NGO activists, business leaders, students, teachers, presidents, generals, and ministers.

Within the World Bank, Nishimizu nurtured the talent of people at all levels in the organization by emphasizing the sport of continuous learning previously discussed. In the open environment she created, she urged everyone from assistants and secretaries to engineers to take initiative and deploy their talent in high-performing teams. To ignite her people's passion, she often took staff members on missions where they could both learn about World Bank clients firsthand and further develop their own talent for helping. This innovative approach became known as the Village Immersion Program (VIP).

Given the fact that no human being ever attains perfection, even the BOLDEST leader needs to rely on the talent that other people bring to the organization. A coalition of talent marshals complementary strengths that multiply the organization's ability to work through the most difficult and complex issues it faces. Imagine a beautiful mosaic depicting a rich and varied landscape of fields and forests and rivers and mountains. All of the varied interlocking pieces create a more complete picture than even the most colorful single piece can ever portray. The most effective leaders don't just recruit the best and the brightest; they assemble a diversity of talent, creating the best possible mosaic.

Developing the BOLDEST Leaders

Paul Schempp, founder of Performance Matters Inc., and author of the book 5 *Steps to Expert*, wrote, "No one is born an expert." He describes how top performers progress from beginner to capable, competent, proficient, and finally expert. Experts know that the mastery of their craft or profession depends on three key factors: experience, knowledge, and skills.[8] Experience alone won't make you a better golfer unless you undertake a program of deliberate, systematic, and continual practice and improvement. Experts never stop learning, and that keeps them consistently at the top of their fields. Watch any professional golf tournament, and you'll see coaches and caddies helping top players perform to the best of their ability. No matter how many innate or acquired skills you bring to a match, you must steadily and deliberately practice and apply critical skills before you can hope to become a champion. Just as no one is born an expert, no one is born a leader. Even the most charismatic, intelligent people can and should continuously develop their ability to lead, whether they hold a formal title or not.

Challenging Perspectives

Think of the business world as a large globe with a hundred windows scattered over its surface. Each time you look into a different window, you gain a slightly different perspective on the globe's contents. Sadly, most of us peer through only a few different windows, preferring to live in the comfort zone they create.

A wonderful exception occurs if you take the sort of Leaders Quest mentioned earlier in this chapter. In 2012, it took 20 SAP leaders from India outside the comfort of their research labs and sales offices to parts of the country they wouldn't ordinarily visit. When the group went to Mumbai, they met with Jyoti Mhapsekar, a social entrepreneur who runs a community of waste-picker women in the city's largest rubbish dump. These impoverished women were learning microfinance, improving their literacy, composting waste, and turning trash into improved living conditions for themselves and their families.

Of this experience, one senior SAP leader said, "I feel this small" as he pinched together his thumb and index finger. "I'm educated, I have a good career. Look at what these people have created out of nothing. What could we be creating with all of our resources?"[9]

Headquartered in Waldorf, Germany, SAP grew from a technology start-up in 1972 (as Systemanalyse und Programmentwicklung, or Systems Analysis and Program Development) to become a world leader in developing enterprise software and software-related services. Rachel Parikh, Sustainability Director at SAP, believes that experiences such as Quests inspire leaders to think about new ways to fulfill the company's vision to help the world run better and improve people's lives. Mumbai's population of more than 20 million people makes it one of the most crowded urban centers in the world. Many government agencies and businesses in this urban metropolis rely on SAP software to collect, manage, and analyze data to improve disaster management, resource availability, and the delivery of vital services to Mumbai's citizens. Exposing SAP people to grassroots leaders working in the most impoverished areas of the city challenges their perspectives on what business can do, how they create value, and what leadership must look like in the twenty-first century.

Starting with Strengths

In their book, *Strengths-Based Leadership*, authors Tom Rath and Barry Conchie cite decades of Gallup research supporting the need to emphasize the improvement of strengths over the elimination of weaknesses. They found that the most effective leaders invest in their strengths and those of their people, surround themselves with the right people to maximize the strength of their team, and understand the needs of those they lead.[10]

During a recent meeting with entrepreneurs, I heard a lot of complaints about the difficulty of focusing on what's most important to their business because so many distractions pulled their minds away from key issues. One of them, an earnest young man named Dan, offered a different view. "I have the opposite concern. I have incredible focus, which means that I'm not addressing other aspects of my business." These divergent needs encouraged the group to come up with ideas on how to spend time doing what each person did best, while building teams that could cover other areas. Enhancing our strengths or reducing our weaknesses means making a change, and, as neuroscientists will tell you, change scares us at a visceral level, whether we realize it or not.

Richard Boyatzis, a distinguished professor at Case Western Reserve University,[11] has conducted extensive research on how our brain reacts to change. In his Intentional Change Theory, Boyatzis proposes that when we try to change or adapt, our human systems move toward either a positive or negative state. He refers to these as Positive Emotional Attractors (PEA) or Negative Emotional Attractors (NEA). Emphasizing a person's weaknesses arouses the NEA, pulling you into a state of stress and decreasing your ability to think, learn, and perceive. You feel anxious, nervous, and worried, and your immune system is lowered, leaving you susceptible to illness. Arousal of the PEA, however, gets you operating at your cognitive and physical best. Your brain becomes energized and can create the new neural tissue needed for learning. You become more open to new ideas, feelings, and the perspectives of others. Arousing the PEA also strengthens the immune system.

Consequently, when we create a vision of the future based on our strengths, we open up the possibility to become what Boyatzis calls our Ideal Self. In contrast, when we allow others to define our vision, we fall prey to our Ought Self. A mismatch between the two causes resistance to change.

As you work and lead, and as you develop those around you to become better workers and leaders, pay attention to actions that arouse the PEA. Then everyone will strive for rather than resist change. If you make sure you and your people follow their own dreams and not just those imposed on them by others, you will find everyone excited by the opportunity to develop their competencies and work hard to shape a brighter future for themselves and their organization.

Cheng (not his real name), a senior manager at the technology firm Quazar (not the real name either), had built a reputation as a brilliant strategist, quick learner, and big thinker. However, people also found him aloof, uncommunicative, and rather cold and unemotional.

Unfortunately, these traits made it hard for Cheng to develop strong relationships with his peers and his staff. Unless he could fix that problem, he would see his career hit a brick wall. Cheng's boss suggested he work with Dr. Lipkin, a psychologist who specializes in leadership. Working with Dr. Lipkin, Cheng learned how to apply his conceptual strengths to the agendas and needs of his peers and staff. Gradually he learned to empathize more fully with other people's perspectives and to enter into more open conversations about the breakthroughs the team needed to achieve. As his relationships with others strengthened, Cheng's boss felt comfortable giving him more challenging assignments and eventually a major promotion. Drawing on his strengths rather than simply concentrating on his weaknesses helped Cheng improve his weaker areas much more quickly.

Coaching Elite Performance

Professor Boyatzis applies his Intentional Change Theory to coaching. What he calls coaching for compliance arouses the NEA, igniting stress, anxiety, and defensiveness and decreasing the ability to learn and make decisions. Better results come from coaching with compassion, which arouses the PEA and helps people tap into their Ideal Self. Scientific research shows that emphasizing hope for the future causes the human mind and body to function optimally, setting the stage for profound change. Furthermore, coaching with compassion arouses the PEA for the coach as well as it does for the person on the receiving end.[12]

It takes skill and experience and training to become a great coach. Many organizations save time and effort by hiring outside coaches like Dr. Lipkin to help individuals and teams perform at heightened levels. Others develop coaching and mentoring skills in their own leaders.

Sheila (not her real name), a highly effective and experienced middle manager at Brautigan's Eyeware (not the real company name), fretted that she had reached a glass ceiling. Her boss, Brautigan's COO, Ben told her she needed to display a greater executive presence. That suggestion made her laugh to herself. Very few of the male leaders above her displayed any more presence than a tree stump. She couldn't do anything about that, but she could do something about the way she projected herself at work. Taking the initiative to hire her own personal coach, she hired Dr. Lipkin to help her build her self-confidence and feel more comfortable with asserting herself during management meetings. When Dr. Lipkin showed her a videotape of their initial session, Sheila could see how her body language telegraphed insecurity: She kept crossing and uncrossing her legs, avoiding eye contact, and sitting back defensively in her chair. "Wow! I can't believe I look like such a mouse."

On the plus side, Dr. Lipkin pointed out Sheila's positive traits, ones she would use to make a stronger presence, among them her ability to grasp and communicate complex issues, summarize key insights, and think strategically. Working with her coach to project a more assured demeanor in meetings, Sheila eventually learned to send more powerfully confident signals with her posture, hand gestures, voice, and eye movements. She no longer leaned back; she leaned into a discussion. A new power wardrobe didn't hurt at all. As she presented her new self to her superiors and peers, she saw that glass ceiling turn into an elevator to the top floor.

Learning Through Experience

Whether you call it on-the-job training or on-the-job learning, most people quickly learn to swim when they find themselves splashing in the deep end of the pool. Some of the best learning programs stretch people to acquire and develop the needed skills. My friend, Davina Brown, went through a seven-month-long, full-time French language immersion program as part of her leadership development with Parks Canada. Merely taking conventional courses and listening to language tapes while commuting to work would not produce the same outcome as being required to speak French all day, every day. This sort of experiential learning can prove invaluable when you need to learn something quickly.

In September 2007, Starwood Hotel and Resorts Inc. hired Frits van Paasschen as its new CEO and President. The Chairman of the company's board, Bruce W. Duncan, cited van Paasschen's "intellectual fire-power" as a key reason the Board selected him over some 60 other can-didates.[13] Before joining Starwood, van Paasschen (pronounced "van pas-sion") had served in senior leadership positions with Disney and Nike and as CEO of Coors Brewing.

Van Paasschen goes for a serious run every day and often compares that exercise to his leadership style. He believes leaders must run faster and further, setting ever more ambitious goals, conquering personal fears, and continuously setting new records. Such leaders stay on a track of continuous learning, all-out listening, and well-calculated risk-taking.

Interestingly, he proved his commitment to learning by doing some-thing few leaders would even contemplate. In 2011, he temporarily relo-cated the company's headquarters from Stamford, Connecticut, to China, then again to Dubai in 2013. With more than 80 percent of Starwood's growth coming from emerging markets, he wanted Starwood's leaders to learn about their global customers by rubbing shoulders with them. They'd never learn as much just sitting in their offices back home. As van Paasschen said in a 2011 *Wall Street Journal* article, "I have a belief that in order to understand a market from a consumer point of view, you have to buy the proverbial groceries there."[14] Turning his com-pany into a virtual school has helped van Paasschen steer the company through recession and into global growth. Shortly after the 2011 reloca-tion, the company experienced greater growth within China, with more hotel openings there and with more Chinese travelers staying in Starwood hotels around the world.

Applying The New Corporate Facts of Life

We'll use a slightly different NCFOL Leadership Barometer to rate the strength of individuals and your entire organization with respect to the BOLDEST leadership competencies (Figure 6-10). It will help you design developmental programs for yourself and every other key leader on whose efforts the future depends.

Figure 6-10. BOLDEST Barometer Leadership.

Rating Key:

H–High: A true strength. I/we demonstrate excellence in this competency area.
M–Medium: Competent. I/we are effective in this competency area, but could do more to excel.
L–Low: A weakness. I/we are less than effective in this competency area.

	BOLDEST Leadership	Organization	You
B	**Boundaries**		
	☐ Build coalitions across borders. ☐ Influence key stakeholders. ☐ Break down functional silos.		
O	**Opportunities**		
	☐ See around the bend. ☐ Create compelling visions. ☐ Promote optimism.		
L	**Learning**		
	☐ Quickly absorb complex information. ☐ Emphasize innovation. ☐ Foster a continuous learning culture.		
D	**Deliverables**		
	☐ Deliver today and create tomorrow. ☐ Hold people accountable. ☐ Produce both profit and purpose.		
E	**Emotions**		
	☐ Lead with integrity and self-confidence. ☐ Display empathy and social skills. ☐ Maintain self-awareness and self-regulation.		
S	**Systems**		
	☐ Think systemically. ☐ Consider opposing perspectives. ☐ Manage complexities.		
T	**Talents**		
	☐ Hire, retain, and deploy top talent. ☐ Build organizational capacity. ☐ Develop leadership at all levels.		

CHAPTER 7

Engage to Excel

Humankind has not woven the web of life. We are but one
thread within it. Whatever we do to the web, we do to
ourselves. All things are bound together. All things connect.

—CHIEF SEATTLE, 1854

COMPANIES ADOPT SUSTAINABLE PRACTICES for many reasons, ranging from saving money to improving brand image and fulfilling customer requests. These all apply to the hotel industry. A typical room at a hotel uses as much energy as the average American home, making energy the second largest operating cost for a major hotel chain, second only to staffing costs. Maury Zimring, Director, Corporate Responsibility and Environmental Sustainability for InterContinental Hotels Group (IHG), told me that as large corporations have committed themselves to more sustainable practices, today's potential corporate customers ask about much more than the vague generalities included in the corporate responsibility plans of the past. "Customers now ask very specific questions such as: What's the carbon footprint of an average hotel room stay? What's your water footprint? What's your waste conversion?" Because companies can pick and choose from a myriad of options for events and regular corporate travel, they increasingly select those whose practices align with their own sustainability strategies.

For years, hotels have found ways to cut costs while operating more efficiently with water and energy conservation, but today's efforts go much further, with more sophisticated techniques that apply to every aspect of a hotel: its buildings, grounds, laundry, restaurants, golf courses, spas, housekeeping, guest services, and technology systems. This requires more internal and external stakeholder engagement than ever before. It also poses a particular challenge to the hospitality industry because many companies don't own all of the hotel properties that fall under their brand umbrella. IHG, for instance, is a global organization with nine hotel brands, including InterContinental, Crowne Plaza, Holiday Inn, and Staybridge Suites.[1] As of the end of the first quarter of 2013, IHG operated more than 3,900 franchised sites globally and managed another 678 in 100 countries around the world. Given the nature of its organization, IHG must motivate people through engagement rather than mandate.

IHG's Responsible Business practices underpin all of its strategic priorities. People throughout its entire operation collaborate to become more environmentally and socially responsible in ways that will benefit their businesses without compromising the guest experience. It requires a strong business case for change and specific advice on what to do and how to do it. To meet this challenge, the company developed a comprehensive Web-based sustainability tool called IHG Green Engage, which is designed to stimulate ideas, track progress, and benchmark against other properties. IHG Green Engage provides a roadmap and a wealth of ideas for every aspect of hotel operations, from selecting a suitable building site, to choosing energy-efficient systems and responsible cleaning materials, to training staff in sustainable practices. Each suggestion includes the return on investment, the amount of carbon reduction, and the impact on the guest experience.

"IHG Green Engage has been the catalyst for driving sustainability across the enterprise," Zimring says. The tool shows operators how to become more sustainable, save money, and increase efficiency at four levels. Level One recommends steps every hotel can take to save resources and create a so-called green team. Level Two emphasizes a return on investment (ROI) within one year. Level Three stresses ROI for between one and three years. And Level Four highlights best practices that may achieve ROI within seven years.

Paul Snyder, VP of Corporate Responsibility, Environmental Responsibility and Public Affairs for IHG, told me that, as of July 2011, 900 properties had signed up and that, less than two years later, nearly 2,300 properties, or a full half of the IHG estate, had enrolled. "It's the most successful subscription platform in the company," Snyder says. As a result, IHG's hotels save money, conserve resources, and engage employees more effectively than ever before while still delivering a great guest experience.

With IHG Green Engage, hotel green teams input data into the tool and create action plans on topics such as water, energy, and waste. To promote accountability, Green Engage tracks and reports progress and shows how any given property's efforts compares to others. At the outset, each hotel's green team identifies an IHG Green Engage champion outside the leadership team. This provides people at lower levels in the organization a great opportunity to enhance their team leadership and communication skills. One IHG property in Boston named a housekeeping supervisor as its champion. The supervisor works with the team to set goals, track results, and evaluate what to do next. This experience has helped her build relationships across the hotel as well as with people at IHG corporate headquarters. She proudly includes "Green Champion" in her title.

In 2012, IHG augmented the tool with case studies for each action item. In this way, a property can share its stories, detailing what it did, how it did it, what challenges it faced, what worked and didn't work, and who specifically made it a success. As Maury Zimring points out, "This allows experiences to be shared from one property to another. General Managers contact each other to learn more. It also provides recognition for those involved."

Launched in 2009, the IHG Green Engage platform aimed at a three-year goal for reducing energy across IHG properties from between

6 and 10 percent. By 2012, IHG had beaten that goal, reducing energy consumption by 11.7 percent and lowering the company's carbon footprint by 19 percent per occupied room between 2010 and 2011. This translates to reduced costs, lower carbon emission rates, greater profitability, an enhanced brand image, and more engaged employees throughout the hotel chain.[2]

Valuing Stakeholder Engagement

As we've seen throughout this book, every stakeholder plays a role in a company's future success. Companies affect their lives; they affect the success of their companies. That makes stakeholder engagement an extremely important activity, one that creates an ongoing dialogue about issues that concern all parties.

Figure 7-1 depicts stakeholder relationships at a typical company. For most organizations, employees, customers, and shareholders often require the strongest bond, as indicated by the shorter connection lines. Your own stakeholder map could differ quite a bit from this one. For instance, if you decided to collaborate more closely with NGOs, competitors, and government regulators to create industry-wide change, you

Figure 7-1. Stakeholder Relationships.

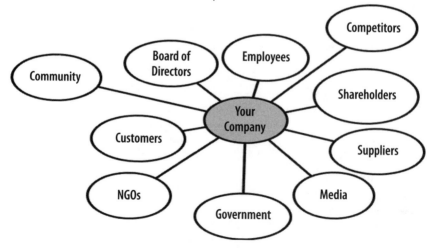

would draw them closer to the center. These stakeholders not only connect with your company, they often connect with each other. For example, your customers and employees connect with their communities through your company, and people from all three groups could own stock in your firm.

You can build and maintain relationships with stakeholders in a variety of ways. One-way communications, such as e-mail blasts, may send an important message, but they do not engage people in the sort of dialogue you need to grow a relationship. Rather, you need to adopt methods that pull people into your circle where you can engage them in a meaningful dialogue. The Stakeholder Engagement Continuum (Figure 7-2) ranges from ignoring to empowering. On the left side of the continuum, either no communication or nonengaging one-way communication takes place. On the right side, engaging, two-way communication occurs. The left side at best just provides information from the organization to stakeholders; the right side draws them into a circle of collaboration.

Figure 7-2. Stakeholder Engagement Continuum.

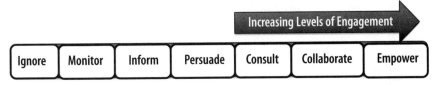

Relationships and levels of engagement vary due to the unique characteristics of different stakeholders and situations. Sometimes you just want to monitor a particular stakeholder group to guard against surprises. This often applies to government agencies contemplating new regulations or advocacy groups about to expose a problem in your supply chain. Other situations call for simply providing information or educating people, perhaps with a brochure or newsletter announcing certain initiatives. At the highest levels of engagement, you want to partner and collaborate with stakeholders, even empowering them to make decisions or take action. This frequently occurs with suppliers. In any event, before empowering stakeholders, you need to make sure you have defined the results you expect; for instance, "We will work with suppliers to ensure fair, ethical, and safe labor practices throughout the supply chain." Stakeholder engagement should address major issues where:

- ► The concerns of the company and the stakeholder overlap.
- ► The impact of a strategy, goal, or issue causes concern.
- ► You want to generate more options or solutions.
- ► Working collaboratively with others can help improve your knowledge.
- ► You can influence the outcome to some degree.
- ► Others can exercise some influence on the outcome.
- ► Some decisions on this issue remain undecided.

Engaging Internal Stakeholders

Companies, governments, NGOs, and others realize that success increasingly requires greater collaboration both inside and outside their organizations. Let's first look at the business case for engaging your internal stakeholders.

No company can implement even the most compelling strategy without the involvement of its employees. An engaged workforce makes things happen because engaged people love to work in an environment that continuously encourages them to learn and grow and express their utmost creativity, all leading to the best possible results. Leading-edge research has consistently validated the positive impact of employee engagement on business results. A 2012 Aon Corporation "Trends in Global Employee Engagement" report revealed a strong correlation between employee engagement and financial performance, even in unstable economic times. Companies with high levels of engagement outperformed the overall stock market index and posted total shareholder returns 22 percent higher than the 2010 average. Organizations with low engagement levels produced total shareholder returns 28 percent below average.[3]

Gallup's employee engagement index monitors workers' responses to 12 questions, all closely linked to performance results such as customer service, quality, productivity, retention, safety, health, and profit. In 2011, Gallup reported that 71 percent of American workers felt "not engaged" or "actively disengaged" in their work. Employees who lack engagement emotionally disconnect from their companies and generally fail to meet performance expectations. Disengaged employees put forth minimal effort, arrive late, and go home early. They lack energy and passion. In the worst case, they disrupt the workplace, undermining coworkers or bad-mouthing the company. Some even commit outright acts of sabotage.

Employee engagement matters even more during periods of economic uncertainty. Companies with highly engaged people enjoy a competitive edge in talent management and business results. They attract the best people and get the most from them. Maintaining high employee engagement not only helps companies survive during short-term economic volatility, it also strengthens long-term business performance by positioning the company for growth as market conditions improve.

Engaged employees choose to work harder for better results. Every person, in every job and on any given day, makes decisions, consciously or subconsciously, about how much physical or mental effort they'll devote to their work. Engaged employees come up with better ideas, more thoroughly delight customers, produce higher-quality products, relate more closely with teammates, and rack up better results. Highly engaged employees always go beyond mere compliance with organizational expectations. They strive to *exceed* expectations.

In a striking example of the power of engagement, high-end office furniture designer Herman Miller announced achievement of its goal of relying 100 percent on green energy on Earth Day, April 22, 2010, ten years earlier than targeted.[4] The company accomplished this feat primarily through the cost- and energy-saving suggestions from its employees. When Herman Miller set their sights on that goal, they had developed no concrete plans for getting there. Company leaders, however, expected to draw on the fact that adopting profitable sustainable business practices had become a deeply ingrained value in Herman Miller's culture. Its culture had always emphasized people using their heads to solve problems. "Things That Matter" at Herman Miller include curiosity and exploration, engagement, relationships, performance, design, inclusiveness, and transparency. Why not let its people apply those traits to the green energy goal? They quickly responded to the challenge and conquered it much sooner than expected. As former CEO Max DuPree once said, "Each of us is needed. Each of us has a gift to bring." That belief not only unites all employees, it also forms a foundation for their relationships with their community. By "community," Herman Miller means "A Better World," a value that attracts both talent and customers.

Does money motivate and engage people? Not so much. Deep commitment involves not just our brains (rational motivators) but also our hearts (emotional motivators). Rational commitment keeps us working because logic says we need that paycheck. But money doesn't make us happy. Doing something important, making someone else happy, or accomplishing a goal that we fervently believe in keeps us applying our utmost creativity to our work.

Extensive research into what causes employee engagement has revealed several key drivers:

- Career opportunities and development
- Recognition
- Organizational reputation and values
- Leadership
- A relationship with one's manager
- Innovation
- People and employment practices
- Believing that the organization values people's opinions and ideas
- Organizational mission and purpose

No company does all of this all the time. Each organization needs to develop its own unique mix. Coca-Cola Enterprises (CCE) surveys employees every two years to identify what drives engagement, and then leaders take specific steps to improve levels of engagement throughout the company. Pamela Kimmet, CCE's Senior Vice President of Human Resources, lists the company's current top three drivers of employee engagement as leadership, sustainability, and learning and development.

Identifying and hiring strong leaders and managers establishes the foundation for influencing all other engagement drivers and business performance. CCE leadership programs start with first-line managers and work their way up through the most senior executives. In addition to formal training programs, the company stresses that its leaders at all levels practice what they preach in their everyday actions and decisions. CCE's talent review process emphasizes engagement capabilities with questions such as, "Does this person create followership? Is she an effective communicator? How does he interface with his peers?" Measuring engagement leadership at CCE goes beyond simply asking whether people like their leaders.

Employees also commit themselves to the company's doctrine of Corporate Responsibility and Sustainability (CRS). They take immense pride in CCE's track record with respect to environmental issues. Frequent communications from every senior leader confirm the company's commitment to sustainable practices throughout its operations.

As the largest Western European bottling company for Coca-Cola products, CCE can make a real difference when it conserves water use, packaging, and energy. Each year, CCE holds CRS in Action Week, during which all employees around the world participate in events and activities with a positive social or environmental impact. The idea, which originated with a CCE employee, grew from a single-day to a full-week event. The company's zero-waste goal also arose from the efforts of one plant that decided to aim for zero waste. The efforts of employees in this plant caught the attention of CCE leaders, who promptly took it company-wide.

Pamela Kimmet refers to learning and development as "career growth and opportunity." "To be the best beverage company, you create a winning environment with opportunities for career growth and make investments in technology," she says. People need to know how to use the most up-to-date tools. CCE emphasizes the opportunity to learn even before it hires a new person. Its so-called thirst recruitment campaign also begins the engagement process by posing such questions as, "Do you have a thirst to make a contribution?" "Do you have a thirst to be in a high-impact job?"

Experienced managers know the benefits of managing by walking around (MBWA), a style popularized by Hewlett-Packard in the 1970s. CCE's John Brock regularly holds coffee meetings with employees at various levels to elicit ideas, to learn what's working and what's not, and to reinforce Coca-Cola Enterprises'priorities. These conversations not, only help employees see their connection to the bigger picture, they give Brock firsthand knowledge of what's really happening throughout the company.

Novo Nordisk's senior leaders in Clayton, North Carolina, spend every morning on the plant floor, moving as a group from one department to another to hear employee reports on their progress with respect to key performance indicators, discuss challenges, and engage people in contributing ideas and asking questions. Getting outside their functional silos gives managers insight into the way their department's activities affect every other department.

As an example of a clever way to promote employee engagement, SAP launched TwoGo in 2013. This mobile-enabled, cloud-based service takes carpooling to a new level and achieves two important goals. Carpooling reduces the commuters' carbon footprint, and it lets employees get to know one another in a social environment away from the office. An engineer learns about the challenges facing a salesperson, and a talent recruiter hears a senior manager talk about a crucial team project. The company hopes this engagement practice will lead to greater innovation as people at SAP think in fresh ways about their interconnectedness and how they can put their heads together to deal with forces of change confronting the company. TwoGo started as an internal SAP project and became an external product it sells to cities and other companies.

Engaging External Stakeholders

Engagement does not stop at the company's door; it sweeps into the lives of every external stakeholder as well: customers, suppliers, regulators, NGOs, investors, community leaders, and every single individual whose lives the company touches. CEO Brock believes that the broadest possible definition of stakeholders brings a valuable array of perspectives and ideas that the company can use to enhance efficiency and innovation. Fifteen years ago, CCE based its procurement decisions on price, service, and quality. However, input from a broad range of stakeholders over the years convinced executives they should seek suppliers who could also provide creative, exciting ideas on such important issues as bottle design, transportation, and water use. Suppliers who can't add value in terms of innovative, sustainable ideas and practices lose out to competitors who can.

Engaging external stakeholders can influence the core strategy, mission, and vision of an organization. Given the complexity of today's global and local challenges, no one entity can go it alone. Solutions to such big problems as economic uncertainty, food shortages, water scarcity, poverty, and the need for improved education and transportation require a concerted effort by many partners. United we succeed; divided we fail. In a practical sense, this means that companies must seek and welcome help to adapt their operations to address major risks and challenges while remaining profitable. Partnership-added social value goes hand in hand with greater shareholder value.

Brock admits that, in the past, a businessperson would usually dismiss working with NGOs as total heresy. Now he firmly believes that treating them as partners in progress enables his company to find responsible and profitable solutions to the sort of problems raised by environmental activists such as Greenpeace. In fact, Greenpeace now endorses Coca-Cola's vending machines and beverage cooling technology. The World Wildlife Fund (WWF) has also praised the firm's efforts to address the issues of water reclamation and deforestation.

Collaborating with external stakeholders to solve issues of mutual interest helps a company manage risk and protect its reputation. Successful negotiations create favorable headlines; raucous protests and demonstrations damage a company's reputation. Powerful NGOs like Greenpeace can create a headache, but they also influence consumer demand, government regulations, and community leaders. Treating them as friends rather than enemies can foster greater innovation if a company listens carefully to their demands and raises the bar when it comes to thinking about and ensuring the social and environmental well-being they promote. They may also sound a clear warning bell about any new forces of change coming the company's way. Like canaries in the coal mine, they live at the leading edge of many issues. Their signals can convince an organization to move from a reactive stance to a leadership position on a given issue. The best companies don't just follow directions, they help set the direction.

In the NCFOL world, companies don't engage stakeholders for purely altruistic reasons, they do it because they appreciate all the benefits that accrue, as shown in Figure 7-3.

Figure 7-3. Benefits of Engaging Stakeholders.

Internal Engagement	External Engagement
Aligns people with vision and strategy	Promotes achievement of strategy
Delivers better results with respect to:	Fosters buy-in and ownership
• Finances	Broadens perspectives and options
• Productivity	Strengthens relationships and trust
• Quality	Enhances brand image
• Safety	Turns adversaries into allies
• Innovation	Expands knowledge and expertise
• Employee retention	Fosters innovation and creativity
• Talent pool	Influences regulations
• Customer loyalty	Bridges cultural gaps
• Employee well-being	Avoids crises and conflicts
• Leadership succession	

Harnessing the Power of Participation

Stakeholder engagement accomplishes little if you do not connect it to specific business objectives. "We're all in this together, but for what purpose?" Once you make the connection—let's say, between stakeholders and the goal to produce healthier food products—you must monitor, assess, and improve progress toward the objective. This activity should become a key element in your strategic business planning process. In many cases, you can initiate a pilot program to test-drive your vehicle for establishing and strengthening stakeholder engagement. In the case of producing healthier food, you might invite a select group of your company's product managers, external dieticians, suppliers, and NGOs, perhaps representatives from the World Health Organization, to help find tasty and nutritious alternatives.

Establishing widespread stakeholder engagement will challenge leaders who have not honed the collaborative skills they need to pull people together both intellectually and emotionally in order to embrace the company's strategic objective. For instance, you would not talk to shareholders exactly the same way you would communicate with employees or government regulators. In the case of changing your food product mix, the shareholders worry about stock price, whereas employees fret over changes to their work processes, and government officials just want to make sure you do not violate food health regulations.

Two words should guide your efforts to engage stakeholders: respect and trust. Although such abstract concepts defy a formula, when it comes to respect or trust, people know it when they see it. Respecting people as peers, listening carefully to their concerns, assuring them that you will take their concerns to heart, and then trusting them to do the same with you goes a long way toward building alignment around a specific issue. You must take pains to make it clear that the well-being of each stakeholder group depends on the welfare of all other groups. Shareholders will not see the value of their investment increase if employees do not rally to develop nutritious food choices that appeal to consumers and satisfy health-care NGOs.

This all sounds good, right? No one can disagree with the importance of trust and respect and honesty and integrity and transparency. But how do you make all that happen? Earlier in this chapter, you read a few ideas for engaging employees. Now let's consider some creative methods you can use with both internal and external stakeholders.

Again, one size does not fit all, No two companies will use exactly the same tools, nor will a given company use the same tools with each and every stakeholder. Regardless of the ones you select, however, you must bear in mind the need to combine both formal and informal practices. Tailor the mix to achieve the specific outcomes you desire.

Contextual Stakeholder Engagement

Visit stakeholders in their own habitat. Nothing beats watching people as they go about their daily business. Observe how they behave, interact with others, and do their work. What makes them frown or smile or laugh or wince? What energizes them? What makes them nervous or restless? What worries them? Some companies place their own people on site with customers and suppliers. Others embed people throughout the supply chain to see firsthand what occurs every step of the way. Imagine how much intelligence you would gather about the health impacts of your food products and how many connections you could forge if you saw the effects on everyone with whom your company comes into contact.

Online Tools

Web-based programs provide ways for people to interact across timelines to share information, learn, and ask questions. For example, IHG Green Engage not only makes ideas available to all of its hotels enrolled in the program, it also captures ideas from people using the tool. Such an interactive two-way street allows users to report their experiences, good and bad, as they struggle to meet a particular challenge. IHG's hotel operators use it to learn from their peers as they implement new practices for energy efficiency, water conservation, or purchasing locally grown food. More generic options include such free online tools as the one offered by Boston, Massachusetts–based Practically Green (www.practicallygreen.com). The service not only helps people evaluate their current lifestyle choices, it also provides ideas for green and healthy living. Companies can also retain Practically Green to build a customized version for their employees or other stakeholders with whom they can run contests, share ideas, and monitor stakeholder engagement in their sustainability commitments.

Social Media

Social media continue to evolve as organizations find ways to engage employees, customers, and community members through Twitter, Facebook, LinkedIn, etc. Again, these tools create an information highway that runs both from the company to the stakeholder and from the stakeholder to the company. Data gathered from the flow of information helps companies better understand their stakeholders'concerns. Some companies have also relied on crowd sourcing to obtain input on strategies, products, services, and levels of engagement.

Appreciative Inquiry

The Appreciative Inquiry process gets people talking in an effort to elicit their deepest feelings and determine what really matters most to them. Carefully formulated questions (*inquiry*) elicit stories and examples of an organization's strengths and assets (*appreciative*) and ideas for creating a desired future. Focusing on strengths and channeling efforts toward a positive future engages people's imaginations. Contrast this with traditional problem-solving methods that focus on the problem and often result in defensiveness, finger-pointing, and denial. David Cooperrider developed Appreciative Inquiry (AI) as part of his doctoral research with the Cleveland Clinic in the late 1970s. Corporations, communities, governments, and schools have used AI all over the world. Dr. Cooperrider used AI at the United Nations to conduct its first Business as an Agent of World Benefit summit in 2004, which brought together 500 CEOs and civil society leaders to discuss ways for companies to "do well by doing good." The event surfaced thousands of ideas that could benefit both society and the bottom line.

World Café

World Café operates on the premise that a lot of great ideas pop up during breaks from business as usual. This simple, effective, flexible approach for engaging large groups in freewheeling dialogue starts by posing a penetrating question such as, "How can we develop healthier foods that will delight our customers?" During an initial 20-minute round of dialogue, small groups brainstorm ways to respond to the question. Each person can record ideas where others can see them, such as jotting them down on flip charts. At the end of the 20-minute session, people can vote with their feet by moving to another table, usually with one person remaining behind as that table's host. The second and subsequent groups add to the previous ideas. At some point, the discussion may drill down to a particular subtopic inspired by another penetrating question, "How can we develop food that helps prevent child malnutrition in impoverished areas?" You can also dedicate individual tables to discussion of specific subtopics.

My consulting team and I once designed a session using a combination of AI and World Café for a community-wide sustainability vision summit in the Atlanta metro area. The responses to questions posed during the AI interviews revealed a number of key issues the community needed to address in order for it to attain a more sustainable future. The group selected the top six topics for further discussion: transportation, health and wellness, education, economic development, senior housing, and buildings. People at different tables then wrestled with a crucial question about each of those topics; for example, "What would our city look like in the year 2020 if we had a highly sustainable transportation system?" After three rounds of people moving from table to table, a spokesperson reported each table's ideas to the group at large. After the meeting, a small cross-functional team collected the best of the ideas for integration into the city's strategic planning process and into its budget.

Project Teams

Cross-functional project teams provide opportunities for people to broaden their perspectives when they address key issues. Such teams often involve external stakeholders. A team environment offers a terrific venue for strengthening interpersonal and leadership skills while collaborating on creative solutions to challenging problems. The best teams not only bring together people from different functional areas, they include a broad demographic that includes senior and less experienced men and women from diverse cultural and professional backgrounds. Young recruits learn from veterans, new dogs teach old dogs some new tricks, and everyone gains insight from the different ways men and women often look at an issue. The youthful founders of Google and Facebook brought in more experienced talent as their companies matured. More established companies could do the reverse.

Connect the Creative with the Influential

A 2010 IBM survey of 1,500 CEOs ranked creativity as the most valuable management skill, even above operations and marketing. Most executives, however, have paid less attention to that skill than to the more concrete skills you need to analyze data and make operations run more efficiently. As author Craig Hickman pointed out in his book, *Mind of a Manager/Soul of a Leader*, management involves practicality, leadership demands ingenuity. A leader who feels a need for greater creativity can access it by bonding with creative people inside and outside the organization. When influential people (leaders and managers) work or play side by side with creative types (artists, musicians, designers, and writers), both gain a new perspective. Leaders provide resources to develop the ideas of the creative folks, and the creative folks pump fresh ideas into the heads of executives to help them break out of the status quo. If you're an accountant, you might hang out with an artist in the graphics department; if you're a Web designer, you might invite an engineer to lunch.

Developing a Stakeholder Engagement Process

You want to design a stakeholder engagement process that draws everyone into your company's circle of relationships. I recommend a six-step process (Figure 7-4), which has gotten great results for a lot of organizations.

Figure 7-4. The Six-Step Stakeholder Engagement Process.

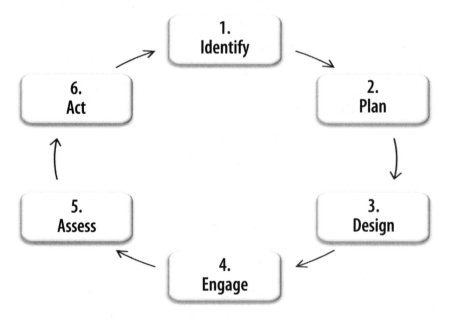

©2013 Strategic Imperatives Inc.

Step 1: Identify

In Step 1, you define the issue, identify the relevant stakeholders, and consider both the opportunities and the risks for engagement.

Let's consider an example with a university we'll call Atlanta Institute of Technology.[5] AIT received a grant from a prominent alumnus to create a plan to connect the sustainability efforts of the state's universities, colleges, and technical colleges in a way that would better prepare graduates to collaborate at various levels across disciplines. Stakeholders related to this issue include administrators and faculty from Georgia's universities, colleges and technical colleges, students, graduates, companies who hire graduates, community organizations such as city and state economic development boards, and chambers of commerce.

Before installing any initiatives to bring together all groups, you want to learn more about the issue. You form a steering committee with representatives from several institutions of higher learning, businesses and industries, and community economic development organizations. You call the initiative BEST (Business and Education for a Sustainable Tomorrow). The BEST steering committee suggests sending a survey to Georgia businesses to learn what capabilities employers consider important for graduates to possess with respect to advancing sustainability. Responses from nearly 250 companies provide valuable insights into both issues.

The BEST committee considers the opportunities for involving the broader group of stakeholders. How will engaging each one spur innovative ideas? How might working together influence relationships over the short and long terms? The committee recognizes that input from businesses across industries would clarify corporate needs and shed light on what schools can do to make graduates more prepared. What new programs should schools install? What community expertise could chambers of commerce and economic development groups bring to the table?

Every relationship with a stakeholder comes with risks for engaging and not engaging them. What unintended consequences can you anticipate? Do any conflicts exist between groups? What harm might it cause if we did not include a particular group? Who could feel ignored or slighted? How might we turn any naysayers into allies? Every engagement initiative should include a risk management element. The BEST committee considers the possibility that colleges and technical colleges might think universities view them as inferior, lower-level institutions. Smaller companies might feel intimidated by larger firms. Business leaders may shy away from participating alongside competitors. The steering committee decides to emphasize the value of all voices, large and small, as a key to finding excellent solutions. Positioning sustainability as a uniting force could also bring different players together for a higher purpose and to find solutions they can't accomplish on their own.

Step 2: Plan

At this stage of the process, you set the objectives and scope for engagement and prioritize stakeholders according to their relative significance in accomplishing goals and strengthening relationships. Wise planning sets the stage for successful, efficient engagement. You also identify initial ways to contact stakeholders and methods you might use to measure success.

The BEST committee sets one clear objective: "Create a plan to connect sustainability programs at all the universities, colleges, and technical colleges within Georgia so that graduates from each institution can more effectively collaborate on teams across functions and levels of an organization."

With this objective in mind, the BEST committee prioritizes stakeholders. Although it wants to include a wide spectrum of participants representing a broad diversity of backgrounds, programs, and regions within the state, it also realizes that the initiative absolutely must include certain groups. This brings academic institutions with highly respected sustainability programs to the forefront. Key players in agriculture, manufacturing, clean technologies, biotechnology, health care, logistics, transportation, and services also merit inclusion, as do economic development associations and chambers of commerce from both rural and heavily populated areas. Finally, the Green Chamber of Commerce, a nonprofit organization promoting sustainable business growth for companies in the southeast region of the United States, brings its strong focus on sustainable business to the mix.

With these stakeholders in mind, the BEST committee decides to hold an initial workshop in Athens, Georgia, focused on business and industry because it will need to understand their needs before proposing solutions.

Agreeing on how to measure success took some effort because the initiative's charter stops at proposing recommendations. Nevertheless, the BEST committee decides to measure progress by setting milestones for engaging stakeholders, formulating potential solutions, and developing the final proposal. The final BEST proposal would include measures for successful implementation of the plan.

Step 3: Design

At this stage, you establish principles for engagement, make initial stakeholder contact, and determine the best ways to involve diverse groups. You also agree on mutual objectives, set expectations, and design the engagement.

The BEST committee defines core principles for engagement as collaboration, transparency, learning, and respect. It agrees on initial objectives to meet the needs of all of the key groups. It wants to make clear that the charter at this point mandates the development of a plan. Creating academic programs or partnerships would follow but does not occur during this initial phase.

BEST retains a facilitator to help design the Athens workshop. This initial session focuses on revealing the needs of the business sector. A few other stakeholder groups will attend this meeting. While invitations garner a good response, the committee reaches out directly and personally to a few important stakeholders, including two companies and one technical college, to convince them that they really should attend the workshop.

Step 4: Engage

At this point, each engagement effort should progress through three distinct phases: preparation, implementation, and follow-up.

Once you have designed the method you will use to engage stakeholders, you must set the stage for its implementation, arranging logistics, issuing invitations, sending out materials, training facilitators, gathering background information on those who will attend, and so on.

When you actually conduct the engagement, all your preparation should make it run smoothly, but always expect some surprises. Keep the agenda flexible, address conflicts that arise, and take time to explore creative ideas that surface during the session. Allow for breaks and downtime and even playful interludes that give people time to reflect, recharge their batteries, and loosen up their thinking.

For the Athens workshop, the planning team issues invitations that include the objectives and a few questions for each participant to consider before attending the session. For the meeting itself, they adopt an Appreciative Inquiry format that will help participants tap into their past successes and present possible future scenarios. They also plan to conduct a World Café exercise.

During the workshop, a plant manager from a manufacturing company says college grads bring solid technical skills to their jobs but frequently lack strong people skills. "Employees at all levels, from our divisional vice president through managers and frontline supervisors, engineers, technicians, and assemblers, need to be able to work together to see the whole picture," the plant manager says. A health-care executive chimes in, saying, "Our groups are all led by managers. We would like to see teams start on their own to solve problems."

An executive from a telecommunications company talks about the company's self-directed work teams who live and work at sites around the world and who use the latest mobile and cloud-based conferencing tools for team interactions. This becomes a table topic during the World Café portion of the agenda, allowing people to share ideas on ways students could gain a real sense for how it would feel to work in such an environment.

Although the schools learn a lot about the skills companies would like to see in the graduates they hire, workshop participants do not offer many concrete ideas on what types of education programs could help build these skills. This will require deeper and broader thinking.

Before closing a session, you should promise to follow up with all participants. Also determine what steps the group might take next to achieve the objectives. Focus on action items, encouraging individuals to commit to doing something by a certain date.

Despite obtaining only a few innovative suggestions for changing curriculum, the BEST committee has learned much about employer needs. It plans to publish a summary of the key points raised during the session. Several of the more vocal company executives agree to join a subcommittee with academics and economic development stakeholders to come up with ideas for collaborating on jointly sponsored learning projects. The health-care executive for a prominent children's hospital will lead a team that hopes to find ways students and businesspeople could work together on community projects such as reducing childhood obesity.

Step 5: Assess

At this juncture of the process, you want to assess the outcomes of each and every engagement activity. Of course, you will compare what actually happened to what you expected to happen when you originally designed the process. Make sure you list what went well and what went wrong, adding notes about specific ways you could improve subsequent efforts.

While BEST's session with business leaders surfaced some great ideas and provided clear insights on industry needs, you were hoping for more creative, out-of-the-box thinking for education approaches. As a result, BEST's facilitators plan a different format for the next two sessions that should prompt more visionary thinking for a future collaborative education model.

Step 6: Act

At this final stage, you decide what you will actually do with ideas that emerged from the engagement process. Thoughts, learning, and outcomes from the engagement will make no difference to how you conduct your business if you do not actually make some concrete changes in the way you operate. The same applies to the stakeholders. What steps can they take to help achieve mutual objectives?

BEST's leaders take immediate steps to implement some of the action items that arose during the session, setting up subcommittees with a blend of academics, business leaders, graduates, and chamber representatives. A specific committee will organize the next two sessions. The lead facilitator contacts IDEA, a design firm experienced in developing engaging learning experiences, to join the team. A second team sets off to research unique collaborative learning programs on sustainability throughout the world. The third team explores the ways technology could enhance teamwork across different regions and countries.

Renewing Your Bonds

You cannot engage your circle of stakeholders and then forget about them. Good stakeholder relationships, like happy marriages, require constant care and attention. Even then, a sudden shift in the business landscape can severely damage or even destroy a relationship. For example, shoe company Timberland has actively promoted environmental protection in many ways, such as planting a million trees in China, hosting community regreening events, and even adopting a tree as its logo. The firm participates in cross-brand collaborations with NGOs to solve industry issues, powers its facilities with renewable energy, and even calculates the carbon footprint for each pair of shoes it makes.

Imagine the look on the face of Timberland's CEO, Jeff Swartz, when he came to work on June 1, 2009, to find himself ambushed by 65,000 angry e-mails from activists demanding that the company stop their deforestation practices in the Amazon. Swartz did not know that any of Timberland's suppliers were violating any agreements with his company that strictly prohibits deforestation. Greenpeace, the NGO behind the e-mail protest campaign, could have simply picked up the phone to reach an executive at Timberland because the organization had long ago formed a relationship with the company. However, in this NCFOL world of instant media messaging, a phone call would not have generated such big international fanfare. Greenpeace's grandstanding tactic to accuse first and engage later helps the NGO recruit new members and collect membership fees. While Timberland, Greenpeace, and other stakeholders ultimately formed an alliance to address the deforestation issue, the shoe company had some damage control to do, realizing that it must remain keenly vigilant lest some other stakeholder with whom it has built a mutually beneficial relationship goes on the attack.

Applying The New Corporate Facts of Life

What steps have you taken to engage internal and external stakeholders with respect to The New Corporate Facts of Life? Using the NCFOL Barometer (Figure 7-5), determine where you are building strong connections and where you might do more to strengthen relationships. After working your way through the NCFOL Barometer, list your critical stakeholders, and jot down ideas about more fully engaging them.

Figure 7-5. The New Corporate Facts of Life Stakeholder Engagement Barometer.

Rating Key:

H–High: We excel at engagement in this aspect.
M–Medium: We engage some stakeholders some of the time but could do more.
L–Low: We're not actively engaging stakeholders on this aspect.

NCFOL	Engaging Stakeholders Through the NCFOL	H	M	L
Disruptive Innovation	❏ We stimulate creative thinking within our organization. ❏ We encourage people to offer new ideas. ❏ We invite external stakeholders to propose innovations.			
Economic Instability	❏ We foster engagement during good times and bad. ❏ We ask our employees to contribute financial ideas. ❏ We seek external expertise for wider economic perspectives.			
Societal Upheaval	❏ We form relationships with people in all communities where we operate. ❏ We seek solutions that benefit society and our business. ❏ We ensure that all suppliers use ethical business practices.			
Stakeholder Power	❏ We engage our people at all levels early and often. ❏ We regularly seek the input of external stakeholders. ❏ We take a broad, inclusive view of all stakeholders.			
Environmental Degradation	❏ We seek experts to help us grasp environmental issues. ❏ We reward employees for submitting environmental ideas. ❏ We work with regulators on environmental legislation.			
Globalization	❏ We involve key stakeholders in our global value chain. ❏ We strive to understand other cultures and norms. ❏ We promote cultural diversity within our organization.			
Population Shifts	❏ We promote intergenerational workplace interaction. ❏ We bond with people in emerging markets. ❏ We collaborate to find solutions to population growth.			

CHAPTER 8

Design a Resilient
Organization

*Architecture does not create extraordinary organizations by
collecting extraordinary people; it does so by enabling very
ordinary people to perform in extraordinary ways.*

—JOHN KAY, ECONOMIST AND AUTHOR

STARBUCKS IS RESILIENT BY DESIGN. Back in January 2008, when Chairman
Howard Schultz contemplated his return as the company's CEO, he knew
he would need to navigate the company through a perfect economic
storm: a global financial crisis, a burst domestic housing bubble, high
unemployment, and a stock price that had plunged to less than half its
previous high. In a February 2007 memo to then CEO Jim Donald,
Schultz questioned previous corporate decisions that he believed had
watered down the Starbucks brand and made its outlets seem like part of
a chain operation rather than neighborhood coffeehouses. Schultz felt that
the company had sacrificed some of its soul to achieve efficiencies of scale
and concluded that the coffee giant needed to "get back to the core and
make the changes necessary to evoke the heritage, the tradition and the
passion that we all have for the true Starbucks experience."[1]

To accomplish that goal, Schultz worked to align the company with its
core strategy and values with a transformation he called a "holistic restora-
tion." The organization would always sell coffee, but it would do so while
both serving a higher purpose and maintaining a healthy bottom line. For
Starbucks to recapture its mission as a company engaged in "the moment

of connection business," Schultz knew he needed to figure out how to "inspire and nurture the human spirit" across more than 50 countries.

Schultz's transformation agenda included seven key points: (1) Be the undisputed coffee authority; (2) engage and inspire its employees; (3) ignite emotional attachment with customers; (4) expand global presence (while making each store the heart of its neighborhood); (5) be a leader in ethical sourcing and environmental impact; (6) create innovative growth platforms worthy of the product; and (7) adhere to a sustainable economic model.

Schultz refused to listen to any suggestions that contradicted Starbucks' values and heritage. In 2008, he proved his commitment by going ahead with a conference of its 10,000 store managers, despite the cost and destination (New Orleans, then only recently ravaged by Hurricane Katrina). The company's leaders spent the first day engaged in community service projects: planting trees, building playgrounds, painting a stadium, creating murals at 25 public schools, and cleaning city streets. This boots-on-the-ground commitment helped rekindle the Starbucks values and guiding spirit within each participant before they convened to talk business.

Nevertheless, in the wake of its dismal fiscal 2008 earnings report, a November 2008 *CNN Money* article referred to Starbucks as "a broken growth stock." To the investment community, Schultz's transformation agenda seemed little more than a desperate spin tactic. After all, the company's fourth-quarter net income had sunk 97 percent, the company had closed 600 stores in the United States, and its stock price had fallen 52 percent year-to-date.[2]

But the skeptics underestimated Starbucks' resiliency. A mere three years later, despite a still depressed economy and soaring coffee prices, the company reported its best financial results ever, with a record number of stores and rapid global expansion. In 2011, *Fortune* magazine honored Schultz's achievements as a corporate capitalist and a public activist by naming him the top Businessperson of the Year.

Note the words *capitalist* and *activist*. Schultz's success underscored the fact that you can make money by doing the right thing. As he said in Starbucks' 2012 Global Corporate Responsibility Report, "Not only is standing for something beyond making a profit the right thing to do, it is the way business must be conducted in the 21st century."

Continuing to grow globally while preserving its values depends on the three pillars of Starbucks' Shared Planet initiative: ethical sourcing, environmental stewardship, and community involvement. Honoring those tenets means taking such steps as using ecofriendly and locally sourced materials in its stores and displaying the work of local artists on the walls, all while remaining faithful to the company's brand identity. Starbucks' alignment continues throughout its supply chain as it strives to ensure that suppliers grow coffee beans with responsible agricultural practices, fair labor conditions, and the conservation of natural resources.

Today, successful companies like Starbucks consider the New Corporate Facts of Life while they enhance growth and profitability. And, like Starbucks, the healthiest, most enduring ones remain resilient in the face of change. That means combining *agility* with *consistency*. Resilient organizations consistently focus on and align with a coherent set of values and a sound business strategy while remaining flexible enough to adapt to whatever surprises may pop up on their radar screens. Also like Starbucks, they design their companies to harness today's powerful economic, social, and environmental forces in a way that serves all stakeholders by engaging employees, thrilling customers, outpacing the competition, satisfying shareholders, serving communities, and strengthening the bottom line. They do this by design. Without the right organization design, even your most brilliant business strategy will ultimately sink. With a resilient one, you can weather any storm.

Designing a Resilient Organization

When most people think about organization design, they picture charts full of boxes with arrows showing lines of responsibility. True organization design encompasses much more than a company's structure. It means

*aligning structure, processes, management, and people practices with busi-
ness strategy.*

Weathering today's volatile business conditions and societal issues
requires unprecedented nimbleness. Companies must not only see the
winds of change coming their way, they must react to them swiftly and
effectively. But you can't do this willy-nilly. You must do it by design.
Resilient organizations always keep scanning the horizon for the next
competitive threat or disruptive innovation.

Even when unexpected lightning strikes, they can efficiently and
effectively deal with the challenge. We're not talking about crisis management; we're talking about built-in capabilities that can prevent disaster or that, if disaster strikes, enable the firm to move forward without
falling apart. Enduring organizations build resilience into their DNA.
They naturally evolve and transform themselves in both large and small
ways to navigate all the fast-breaking storms and turbulent weather that
typify today's business landscape. Their DNA enables them to adhere to
all of the basic principles we have discussed in this book. Nothing rattles
them. Nothing blows them permanently off course.

How do people in your organization handle uncertainly and surprise?
It's only natural for those conditions to arouse fear. Resilient organizations adapt to change, minimize fear, and motivate innovation; rigid,
bureaucratic organizations change too slowly and allow fear to run ram-
pant and stifle radical innovation. While people working for companies
that accept the latter approach scurry to hide under their desks, hoping
and praying that the storm won't cost them their jobs, those working for
the former can take a hit, get back up, and keep on going.

The world of software development provides an instructive example.
Traditionally designed technology companies use a so-called waterfall
process whereby one team defines the product, the next builds a mock-
up, and yet another builds it to meet specifications. Those who have
adopted a more avant-garde agile product design assign one team to work
together through the whole development process, an approach that
enables them to adapt and adjust more quickly than a traditional design

would ever allow. The same agility must apply throughout all aspects of a business, where tweaks, adjustments, and course corrections must be made on the fly.

Aligning the Organization's Design with Your Strategy

A company's strategy provides the roadmap for achieving the vision and maintaining competitive advantage. The key organization design elements (*structure, integration systems and processes,* and *people practices*) support the company's strategic direction.

Structure sets the framework for the organization by determining where power and authority resides, the relationships between roles and functions, and the hierarchy. Defining the responsibilities for functional units and how they relate to one another ensures that the right people do the most important work as efficiently and effectively as possible.

Some barriers to collaboration exist in even a well-designed organization. In this hyperconnected world, the design must rely on *integration systems and processes* to link people and work inside and outside the company. Networks and relationships should promote collaboration with customers, NGOs, regulators, and communities. They should facilitate innovation, wider sharing of information, and trust. Cross-functional teams can promote learning, along with problem-solving and early-warning systems. Virtual teams can work together at a distance 24/7/365. Policies set standards across the organization, while systems collect and report data that can inform good decision making.

People practices help each employee see how his or her work fits into the big picture. Honesty, respect, transparency, and accountability govern every individual's role in achieving the organization's strategy. Learning systems build knowledge, skills, and necessary capabilities. People practices include traditional human resource services such as recruitment and training, but they also incorporate initiatives that enable *very ordinary people to perform in extraordinary ways.*

Internally, the organization design influences the behaviors of employees and shapes the culture. Externally, it influences relationships with key stakeholders. Fully assembled, the design influences the performance of the organization. Success will hinge on developing the right organizational capabilities, all of which spring from the structures, integration systems and processes, and people practices you put in place to foster certain behaviors.

For Starbucks to get to the point where it used only ethically sourced coffee, the company needed to work with its vast global supply chain to ensure that it followed environmentally and socially responsible practices. To build the capabilities needed to implement all of Starbucks' Shared Planet initiatives, the company appointed a new senior-level chief community officer in 2012 to lead a number of relevant corporate teams, including those responsible for community outreach, partner resources, government relations, diversity, and global responsibility. These teams today concentrate on coming up with creative ideas for finding the opportunities in every problem, and on acting quickly to implement solutions that would drive toward achieving the company's goal. No chart on the wall or software program or job description can make that happen. Only people can.

Paradoxes abound in our NCFOL world. Adopt sustainable practices *and* make more money. Remain loyal to bedrock values and constantly change. Structure your work *and* make unstructured decisions. A well-designed organization manages all the inevitable paradoxes. For instance, consistency comes through reporting relationships, policies, procedures, and systems, but innovative collaboration works out solutions in a free-wheeling, creative fashion.

An organizational leader, whether the CEO of a company or leader of a five-person project team, performs few tasks more important than designing the way people work together to get results. To do it well, you need to think through all the implications and unintended consequences of your design decisions. Imagine designing a plane. If you use a flawed design, you won't stay airborne for long. Bad design will send any strategy into a tailspin. Good design will result in a cutting-edge aircraft that a well-trained crew and an efficient flight pattern can take swiftly and safely to its destination.

Designing an Organization for Sustainable Success

Aluminum manufacturer Novelis serves as a great case study of how to design a resilient organization because the company's transformational strategy has compelled it to change many of its 100-year-old industry practices.

As the world's largest manufacturer of rolled aluminum, Novelis was producing about 19 percent of the world's supply in 2012. Its customers in the automotive and beverage industries, as well as high-end makers of electronics and building materials, use rolled aluminum in a wide range of products. In 2012, the Atlanta-based company operated in 11 countries across four continents and generated $11 billion in revenue as a wholly owned subsidiary of Hidalco Industries Limited, one of Asia's largest producers of aluminum and copper. Hidalco, in turn, serves as the flagship company of the Aditya Birla Group, a $40 billion multinational conglomerate with operations in 36 countries. Imagine engineering a radical transformation inside such a sprawling giant.

When leaders at Novelis envision the world of 2020, they see a planet with nearly 8 billion inhabitants, an ever expanding urban population, and a rising middle class, many of them living in developing nations. Strategic thinkers at Novelis believe that this ballooning consumer segment will demand affordable green products produced by responsible companies. Those products will include many millions of tons of aluminum with the vast majority of it retrieved, recycled, and reused to manufacture new products. These trends strongly shape the company's strategic direction to transform the industry into a sustainable business equipped to compete in the twenty-first century. To do that, Novelis must find a way to grow while conserving limited resources and minimizing

environmental harm. Phil Martens, President and CEO of Novelis, suc-
cinctly summed up the company's commitment to sustainability when he
said, "It's where our attention, our resources, our investments, and our
brand are headed."

To appreciate how this strategy affects the company's business
model, it helps to understand a bit about the life cycle of aluminum.
Novelis purchases new metal or recycles old metal to make the aluminum sheets it sells to its customers for use in automobiles, beverage
cans, electronic devices, and countless other products. Even with significant efforts to recycle used aluminum, many of these products still end
up in landfills. This not only causes environmental issues, it depletes a
valuable and limited resource. Novelis would love to do more to solve
these problems.

Unlike other recycled materials such as paper and plastic, aluminum
can be recycled over and over at the same level of quality. Using recycled
aluminum satisfies two critical priorities. First, it reduces the need to
mine primary aluminum from the earth. Mining for metals creates environmental issues. In the case of aluminum, miners extract a soft ore
called bauxite, which, when refined into aluminum, consumes a tremendous amount of energy and water. Second, recycled aluminum emits only
5 percent of the greenhouse gases created during the production of primary aluminum. Obviously, improved recycling represents both an envi-
ronment-protecting and profit-enhancing opportunity for Novelis.
However, that transformation means changing the way the company conducts business during every stage of aluminum's life cycle and in its operations around the world.

In 2011, Novelis added an ambitious set of sustainability goals to its
overall strategy. Environmental targets include obtaining 80 percent of its
aluminum from recycled metal while dramatically reducing its energy
consumption, greenhouse gas emissions, water use, and landfill waste. Its
people goals aim to reach zero injuries, to engage more fully with the
communities where they operate, and to ensure that all employees and
suppliers adhere to the company's codes of conduct. Novelis has com-

mitted itself to sustaining its profitability as well the environment. It seeks, in fact, to double its 2011 profits by fiscal year 2016.

Becoming more sustainable means the company must dramatically rethink every aspect of its basic business model. Doing so requires significant innovation to reimagine products, design new technology, and redesign manufacturing processes. All of this, of course, demands that the company acquire and/or develop some specific capabilities. Those capabilities include:

- ➤ Promoting innovation in all roles, products, and processes and creating alignment and excitement across the company to drive change.

- ➤ Collaborating internally and externally to influence consumer behavior to recycle and to become thought partners with customers and other stakeholders.

- ➤ Redefining current production and reclamation methods to increase efficiency, reduce resource use and redesign, and manage the supply chain.

Novelis continuously examines and realigns its structure, integration systems and processes, and people practices to build these critical capabilities and to remain resilient in order to achieve its strategic goals. With the correct capabilities in place, a company like Novelis can continue the organization design process with 10 critical NCFOL success factors in mind.

Ten Strategies for Designing a Resilient Organization

Ten strategies determine success in designing a resilient organization (Figure 8-1). To illustrate how a company can address these strategies as it moves forward with an organization design built for speed and resiliency in a world where the NCFOL often demand a major transformation, we'll take a closer look at how Novelis has done it and is continuing to do it. If a large old-style manufacturing company can recreate itself, so can you.

Figure 8-1. Ten Strategies for Designing a Resilient Organization.

1. Design an organization to manage anticipated and unanticipated challenges.

Structure

2. Put in place a future-oriented structure that builds on your organization's current strengths.

3. Create an all-encompassing structure for systemic change.

4. Distribute accountability and authority throughout the organization.

Integration Systems and Processes

5. Link functions with networks to get things done.

6. Engage internal and external stakeholders to address major issues.

7. Amass financial, social, and natural capital.

People Practices

8. Foster leadership at every level.

9. Create a stimulating work environment that promotes diverse thinking.

10. Attract, develop, deploy, and retain the best people.

©2013 Strategic Imperatives Inc.

Strategy 1: Design an Organization to Manage Anticipated and Unanticipated Challenges

Resilient organizations prepare themselves for what they can and cannot see down the road. When Novelis set about developing its comprehensive strategy, the company identified and prioritized the sustainability trends and issues most important to itself and its key stakeholders. It forecasted that these sustainability drivers would increase global demand for flat rolled aluminum products to more than double 2010 levels by 2020. To grow and solidify its position as the industry leader, it decided that it needed to innovate more sustainable practices. That meant investing $1.7 billion in expanding production and recycling capacity and in research and development that would lead to a dramatically reduced environmental footprint, while simultaneously growing and increasing profits.

Resilient companies constantly monitor the market for potential risks and opportunities. Novelis' groundbreaking strategy depends on keeping its finger on the pulse of change, discovering best practices, creating next practices, and making sure it doesn't grow complacent with its success. To help with all that, the company set up a Sustainability Advisory Council. The Council consists of sustainability thought leaders and experts from outside the company and senior-level Novelis executives, including its CEO, Chief Sustainability Officer, and Chief Commercial and Strategy Officer. This collection of stakeholders provides expertise, advice, and critical analysis with respect to the organization's sustainability goals. It also supplies information on evolving stakeholder expectations and the sustainability efforts of other companies.

I first became aware of Novelis through one of the Council members, Matt Arnold, Head of Environmental Affairs at JP Morgan Chase, who applauded the company's aggressive goals and industry-changing practices. Another Council member, Stuart Hart, the S.C. Johnson Chair in Sustainable Global Enterprise at Cornell University and author of the book *Capitalism at the Crossroads*, agrees: "Novelis has set in motion an audacious strategy to reinvent the entire aluminum industry—to effectively become 'aboveground miners.' "[3]

Strategy 2: Put in Place a Future-Oriented Structure That Builds on Your Organization's Current Strengths

Transforming any industry from a postindustrial model to one that reflects the NCFOL takes more than a few minor adjustments. For Novelis, it means investing in infrastructure and innovation, which involves building new recycling facilities that use state-of-the-art technologies. Sustainable expansion means prioritizing investments for the future while building on the strengths of the past and present.

For instance, Novelis' new recycling center in Nachterstedt, Germany, takes advantage of an existing site and an infrastructure already in place for water, energy, and other resources as well as the experience of its existing employees and a good local talent pool to attract others. The largest recycling facility in the world, this geographically centered operation can draw from scrap sources throughout Eastern and Western Europe, supplying Novelis with ample quantities of used metal collected in one place. This approach saves energy, reduces logistics costs, provides jobs, and stimulates the local economy.

This raises a crucial point. Future-focused organization design emphasizes preparing for future flight over making minor corrections to an existing flight plan. That's why you must pay close attention to global trends when deciding where to invest in your company's structure. For Novelis, Asia has risen as a top priority because two-thirds of the projected growth for aluminum over the next decade will come from that region. Growth in emerging markets such as China, India, Brazil, and parts of Southeast Asia adds an emerging middle class eager for products that require aluminum—automobiles, appliances, electronic devices, and packaged foods. To meet the growing demand for aluminum, Novelis is expanding its global production and recycling capacity by building an auto sheet plant in Changzhou, China, and a new recycling center and additional rolling capacity in Yeongju, South Korea. In Brazil, the company has opened five scrap collection centers to connect with small scrap yards and thus increase the supply of material for recycling. Novelis also opened its first collection center in Asia in 2013, located in Vietnam.

Strategy 3: Create an All-Encompassing Structure for Systemic Change

The NCFOL usher in the need to unite people and organizations in a way that will benefit business while solving major societal issues. This means crawling out of the restrictive functional silos of isolated sustainable solutions into the fresh air of systemic solutions. Isolated solutions attack problems one tree at a time; systemic solutions take the whole forest into account. Resilient structures adapt to and even embrace instability by building bridges instead of boundaries. Novelis calls an essential part of its business transformation *One Novelis*. The label conjures up the forest. It captures the company's vision of a globally integrated organization. Operating in many countries with customers and supply chains that span the globe forces it to deal with a huge amount of complexity. The organization must consider many factors in enlarging its global presence, including proximity to other existing plants, its customers, raw materials, and qualified talent pools.

In 2011, Novelis moved its North American headquarters from Cleveland to Atlanta, location of the company's world headquarters. The new facility's LEED® Gold-Certified building reflects its environmental commitment, and the open office environment encourages collaboration and interaction and feels more like a twenty-first-century high-tech firm than a twentieth-century manufacturer. In 2012, Novelis opened a new state-of-the-art global research and technology (R&T) center, also in the Atlanta area. Locating the R&T center close to headquarters allows researchers to interact closely with the company's key teams, including global commercial, manufacturing excellence, engineering, environment, health, and safety (EHS), leadership, and strategy.

Another approach to creating connections between traditionally separate boxes involves integrating sustainability functions throughout business units and regions around the world. Some of these functions report to two different executives. For instance, at Novelis, the Director of Business Development and Marketing for the Recycled Can business reports to both the Vice President of Sustainability and the Senior Vice President of Commercial because the business development director must enjoy direct access to everyone whose decisions affect something like can recycling. Qualifications for this job include the ability to deal with ambiguity, to generate energy and direction around a new project or idea, and to thrive in a highly collaborative, team-oriented workplace. Being able to work across boundaries effectively brings us to the next design strategy.

Strategy 4: Distribute Accountability and Authority Throughout the Organization

Novelis CEO Phil Martens knew that the company needed to add a new sustainability function to its basic structure. In 2011, Martens tapped John Gardner, Vice President for Human Resources and Communication for Novelis Europe, to become the company's first Chief Sustainability Officer (CSO). The CSO reports directly to the CEO and serves on the Novelis Executive Committee. That move sent a strong message about the company's commitment to its sustainability strategy: We're not tacking on a sustainability plan; we are making commitment a part of our corporate DNA.

Rather than growing a huge separate empire around this strategic imperative, Novelis installed a core team reporting to the CSO, as well as sustainability catalysts and integrators and other positions that report to other business leaders. This structure reinforces the firm's belief that everyone shares accountability for sustainability, not just those in the sustainability department. Integrated and embedded across global operations are related functions working closely with the CSO, such as recycling and environmental health and safety. Every business unit pursues sustainability-related goals and pushes authority and decisions down to the appropriate level. Its expanded global recycling group works with community organizations. Its plants find ways to reduce energy and water use while ramping up recycling capacity and ensuring safe operations. Its human resources department develops training, performance management, and rewards programs. Its research and development teams seek new and innovative processes for production and reclamation.

Every organization structure contains certain flaws that can turn into landmines if you do not address them in the design process. Consider the disruption to business Toyota suffered after the Japanese tsunami and nuclear power plant disaster. Toyota had become so efficient that it lacked sufficient inventory to meet demand. In hindsight, the automaker would have benefitted from a little less efficiency and a little more redundancy and had stored extra inventory outside Japan.

Whereas formal structures often set up boundaries and define restricted roles, integration systems and processes connect functions and people across boundaries. Well-designed integration systems and processes harness the organization's strengths and minimize the adverse impact of its weaknesses. In 2012, Novelis added a new role of Chief Technical Officer to oversee, streamline, and integrate across operations such as engineering, research and development, and environment, health, and safety (EHS). The One Novelis perspective means aligning the company's culture, customer interactions, processes, and systems to ensure a consistent approach across all of the company's operations. This leads us to the fifth strategy for designing a resilient organization.

Strategy 5: Link Functions with Networks To Get Things Done

Formal organization charts depict people in boxes connected to each other with solid and dotted lines. This establishes a consistent framework. Yet work really gets done through flexible webs of networks that connect people with various systems and processes. Figure 8-2 displays both elements found in resilient organizations: a formal structure for consistency and informal networks for flexibility.

Networks facilitate agility and the ability to handle complexity. Note that in the network diagram, certain nodes appear larger than others. That's because these nodes connect to more people and functions, serving as major hubs for communication and teamwork. All of this interconnectivity fosters knowledge sharing and innovation, but it also invites vulnerability. Removing or changing a highly connected node can disrupt the whole network. Leaders should understand the informal power sources in their organizations and study how employees really connect to one another and how information actually flows through the organization.

Figure 8-2. Formal and Informal Organization Networks.

A Formal Organization Structure

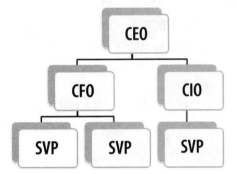

How Work Really Gets Done

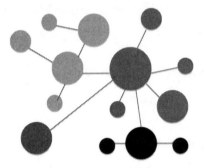

Who serves on key project teams? Which functions support others? Whom do people approach for guidance and advice? Who influences others to change (or not to change)?

While some nodes grow organically through relationships and expertise, some come about because the organization foresees the need for certain connections that require new processes and systems. At Novelis, the company has deliberately woven sustainability into a wide range of policies and systems and processes. Sustainability targets accompany financial and operational goals, and they appear on the scorecard the company uses to track performance with respect to its strategic objectives.

The deliberate design of roles, systems, and processes supports critical relationships and workflow across functions. For instance, a person in a recycling role in a Novelis facility connects internally across plant operations, with research and technology, the sustainability function, and external programs such as Every Can Counts in the United Kingdom and the Curbside Value Partnership in the United States, two programs aimed at expanding the company's collection infrastructure.

Strategy 6: Engage Internal and External Stakeholders to Address Major Issues

An international study jointly commissioned by Google and the Future Foundation found an 81 percent positive correlation between collaboration and innovation.[4] Transforming to a sustainable business model brings people together to collaborate across boundaries, inside and outside the organization. Internal functions (such as facilities, marketing, product development, manufacturing, and human resources) work with external partners (such as energy and building experts, NGOs, communities, universities, and industry associations) in an effort to keep improving and transforming industries. Technologies, reporting, processes, policies, and standards help guide their efforts, track their results, and analyze the impact of their decisions.

Integration systems and processes extend beyond a company's operations to align and connect work up and down the value chain. Novelis' practices provide transparency and traceability throughout aluminum's life cycle and in every nook and cranny of the organization. These processes include diligently preventing, monitoring, and addressing corruption, human and labor rights issues, environmental impacts, and the health and safety practices of suppliers. To define standards that suppliers must meet, the company launched a new Supplier Code of Conduct in 2013 and conducts periodic audits to ensure compliance.

Closing the life cycle loop for aluminum requires downstream processes that connect Novelis to its customers and other external stakeholders. A common sustainability agenda drives stakeholder engagement and transforms the company's relationship with customers from transactional suppliers to thought partners. For instance, Novelis collaborates with its automotive customers to improve fuel efficiency and reduce emissions. It also works with its beverage customers to change the design of the traditional aluminum can in ways that will allow those customers to package their consumer products with up to 100 percent recycled metal. This design makes it possible for the cans to be recycled over and over again.

The company's Novelis Neighbor program helps its locations engage with communities in three areas closely tied to its vision, "To make the world lighter, brighter and better."

1. **Brighter Futures:** Investing in education to develop more scientists, engineers, and technologists.
2. **Lighter Living:** Extending its safety-first value into communities.
3. **Better Environment:** Supporting environmental initiatives such as recycling.

One way the Novelis Neighbor program helps communities is to raise funds for good causes. In 2010, the company held its first Employee World Cup with the express goal of engaging its people in team competitions to benefit local charities selected by each company team. Its fourth event in 2013, a two-day soccer and volleyball competition held at Soccerworld in Dortmund, Germany, brought together 38 teams from all of its regions and raised over $100,000. Several months of competition, practice, and community outreach prior to this popular event promotes the One Novelis culture and the company's values of *integrity, commitment, seamlessness,* and *speed.*

Strategy 7: Amass Financial, Social, and Natural Capital

New demands for information on a company's social and natural capital are forcing changes in corporate accounting practices that once focused almost exclusively on financial capital. A company's traditional profit and loss statement doesn't show all the costs and benefits associated with its activities. When a business like Novelis depletes natural capital such as minerals, water, and trees, it accrues both costs and benefits. The same applies to social capital because business activities create measurable costs and benefits with respect to human beings and their communities. You may strain local resources, but you add jobs to the local economy. London-based professional services firm Trucost helps organizations put a price tag on, and understand the environmental implications of, their use of natural capital. For instance, Trucost has determined that if a business priced water to reflect its availability, that cost would wipe out more than a quarter of a major global corporation's profits.

Peter Bakker, former CEO of transport company TNT, sees a "radical transformation of capitalism in view of better balancing the financial, natural, and social dimensions of capitalism as the only way to future-proof our economies."[5] Bakker currently serves as the President of the World Business Council for Sustainable Development (WBCSD), comprised of CEOs from more than 200 companies around the globe who have committed to seeking business solutions that will contribute to a more sustainable world. WBCSD's collaborations with other organizations, such as the Prince's Accounting for Sustainability Project (a cause championed by Britain's Prince Charles) and the International Integrated Reporting Council, promote the idea that businesses report on sustainability performance and risks. Prince Charles advocates change "to help ensure that we are not battling to meet 21st century challenges with, at best, 20th century decision-making and reporting systems."[6]

Demands for greater transparency with respect to natural and social capital also require companies to disclose a wealth of new information to both internal and external stakeholders. These reports reveal trends for each area of the business and help link functions together. Just one problematic operation can send ripples throughout the entire organization. Chop down trees without a reforestation program in Brazil, and your whole company will eventually pay for the consequences. The same will happen if your suppliers in Bangladesh operate unsafe factories.

Given the, at times, bewildering amount of data a company might track, it makes sense to focus on the sustainability issues that create the greatest value or pose the greatest risks. Novelis measures and reports on key data tied to its target goals, including recycling rates, energy and water use, health and safety issues, community outreach programs, and feedback on employee performance. All this data, which appears on the company's scorecard, shows business unit results, and it all ties to performance management systems and pay practices, such as incentive plans. Novelis publishes an annual sustainability report based on the Global Reporting Initiative (GRI) methodology. The GRI, a well-respected sustainability tool, prompts companies to report results on key areas, such as strategy and analysis, and on environmental, social, and economic performance. Having signed the United Nations Global Compact (UNGC), Novelis also reports on its progress toward upholding the Compact's principles on human rights, labor standards, environmental protection, and anticorruption. Major risks and impacts, such as potential resource shortages or price increases, appear in the company's annual report.

At Novelis, the company's structure and tools (scorecards, key performance indicators, and reports) drive behavior, consistency, compliance, and continuous improvement. But tools and structure alone cannot motivate people to create futuristic models that support transformation to a sustainable business model. To achieve ambitious sustainability goals, a company must influence the very core of how employees work, make decisions, interact with others, and nourish a culture that fully embraces sustainable practices. As discussed in Chapter 5, creating and nurturing this sort of culture requires strong leadership throughout the organization.

Strategy 8: Foster Leadership at Every Level

The journey toward an aggressive sustainability strategy begins with cultivating the right leaders at all levels of the organization. If the board of directors doesn't fully embrace sustainability, they may select a CEO who only pays lip service to it. Real progress demands more than a cosmetic effort. No matter how much green lipstick you put on a brown pig, you still end up with a brown pig. Novelis made a fortuitous decision when it hired Phil Martens, a former Ford executive, in 2009. Martens's experience at Ford had convinced him of the importance of sustainability as a key business driver. Novelis' CSO, John Gardner, describes Martens as "fantastically supportive" of the sustainability strategy. However, the company's commitment doesn't stop in the CEO's office; it cascades throughout the company to include all senior executives, each of whom must deliver on some aspect of the sustainability plan.

Leadership extends even further as people lead initiatives and project teams in an effort to find new ways to improve operations and develop better practices. The company's career page on its website starts with a bold statement: "Shape a New Sustainable World." A career ad for a technical job describes someone who can "promote employee involvement to enhance quality, generate new ideas/methodologies to foster a team atmosphere." Messages to employees concerning the company's sustainability efforts regularly appear on "What You Can Do" updates that help link every person's actions to the company's ambitious targets.

In an effort to become a world-class developer of strong leaders, Novelis has created six levels of leadership development programs, each one geared to its particular participants' experience. The company constantly studies what other great companies, such as GE, do to develop talented leaders. In 2012, it expanded the curriculum for four of its leadership programs to include a hands-on community engagement component. The company wants to make employees leaders not only within the walls of Novelis but in the towns and cities where it operates.

Novelis also holds leadership summits at least once a year. These conferences always include topics related to sustainability. Novelis' Code of Conduct for the board of directors and senior managers, in addition to a similar Code of Conduct for all employees, also reinforces the company's ethical principles and core values. Every leader accepts responsibility to create the right work environment, which leads to the next success factor.

Strategy 9: Create a Stimulating Work Environment That Promotes Diverse Thinking

Sadly, only about 20 percent of employees in today's workforce believe their companies provide the opportunity for them to do what they do best each and every day. Too many organizations shut down critical thinking and force a go-along-to-get-along attitude. Yet it's the out-of-the-box thinker, the maverick, or the positive deviant who often comes up with the bright ideas that make a company more efficient, more sustainable, and more profitable.

Like many other forward-thinking companies, Novelis has found that embracing sustainable business practices excites and motivates creative thinking. Its people at every point in the aluminum life cycle play a role in creating a sustainable design, innovating best practices, and maintaining manufacturing excellence. Without them, the company could not possibly reinvent a century-old industry. Through employee ideas, Novelis has discovered new and better ways to collect and recycle scrap materials and increased outreach to communities and customers on postconsumer recycling programs. Engaged employees, as seen earlier in this book, make all the difference in (and for) the world.

Novelis strives to nurture a culture in which every employee across its global operations feels invested in helping it achieve its goals and in which they get the support and development they need to produce great results and gain deep satisfaction from their work. Greater use of cross-functional teams and partnerships with customers and communities provide employees with deeply satisfying opportunities to learn, contribute, and open their perspectives to new, exciting possibilities for their own and their company's future.

Strategy 10: Attract, Develop, Deploy, and Retain the Best People

All executives talk about the importance of talent. The teams with the most talented players will win championships, but the smart ones know that it takes more than a bunch of superstars to bring home the trophy. You must provide the right training and coaching for them to work harmoniously *as a team.*

Novelis manages its employment brand as diligently as it does every other aspect of its business. The company's dedication to sustainable practices has elevated its image in the minds of exactly the sort of prospective employees the company most fervently wants to hire. People want to work for organizations that lead the way, do the right thing, and care about their employees. That's why Novelis seeks to hire people that not only bring the right experience and technical backgrounds to the party but who, even more importantly, can work collaboratively with others to find creative solutions. Without strong teamwork, the company cannot transform itself, much less an entire industry.

Looking to the future, Novelis recognizes the shortage of an extremely valuable resource: engineers. The Mercer 2012 Attraction and Retention Survey, among others, has identified positions in research and development, science, and engineering as the so-called hot jobs in North America. The demand for those skills far outstrips the present supply. Novelis' aggressive global expansion plan requires people who possess the technical and interpersonal skills to lead and manage complex projects and find innovative solutions. To that end, the company has designed a three-stage process to attract the best engineers:

► **Stage 1:** Introduce more students to engineering at younger ages by encouraging young people to take STEM (science, technology, engineering, and math) classes and to major in those subjects. In one effort to advance this cause, Novelis has begun a partnership with FIRST Robotics, supporting teams and innovation competitions in every region where the company operates.

► **Stage 2:** Engage more students who have chosen to pursue an engineering career. Novelis builds strong relationships with top universities and technical schools. For instance, the company provides internships and scholarships through its alliance with

Georgia Tech, located near Novelis' world headquarters and the company's research and technology center. Such partnerships, designed to create a pipeline of future engineers who might someday work for the company, span the globe.

▶ **Stage 3:** Invest in the engineers who already work for Novelis. The company offers a two-year engineering development program to entry-level engineers that afford them an opportunity to learn on the job and participate in five separate week-long learning programs where they can gain knowledge about Novelis' business and technical processes. Most importantly, the sessions give them a chance to interact with and build relationships with their engineering colleagues in other regions. Novelis also offers multiple career paths to its engineers, including one that enables employees to become technical experts and another that helps them grow into technology leadership roles.

Applying The New Corporate Facts of Life

No single organization design approach will work for every business. But every organization can benefit from a resilient one that is flexible enough to adapt to change, while remaining aligned with its vision, values, and strategy. If you keep the ten strategies in mind as you design and redesign your own organization, you will solve many of the problems that plague companies that are struggling to prosper in an NCFOL environment with outdated organization designs. Like athletes intent on designing their bodies to turn in gold medal performances, NCFOL companies design themselves to keep fit, trim, and flexible.

To determine your own company's design fitness, you can complete the NCFOL Barometer for Organization Design (Figure 8-3). Any areas that you rate as either medium or low should receive immediate and ongoing attention.

Figure 8-3. The NCFOL Barometer: Organization Design.

Rating Key:

H–High: : Our organization design pays strong attention to this success factor.
M–Medium: We pay some attention to this success factor.
L–Low: We pay little attention to this success factor.

	H	M	L
1. Design an organization to manage anticipated and unanticipated challenges.			
Structure			
2. Put in place a future-oriented structure that builds on your organization's current strengths.			
3. Create an all-encompassing structure for systemic change.			
4. Distribute accountability and authority throughout the organization.			
Integration Systems and Processes			
5. Link functions with networks to get things done.			
6. Engage internal and external stakeholders to address major issues.			
7. Amass financial, social, and natural capital.			
People Practices			
8. Foster leadership at every level.			
9. Create a stimulating work environment that promotes diverse thinking.			
10. Attract, develop, deploy, and retain the best people.			

©2013 Strategic Imperatives Inc.

Lessons for
the Road

Live as if you were to die tomorrow.
Learn as if you were to live forever.

—MAHATMA GANDHI

I AM SITTING AT THE SAME DESK where I thought so hard about what to write in the Introduction to this book. What can I say? That I hope you've enjoyed the book and will profit from it as you continue your own journey toward a prosperous future? I'd rather tell a story.

Sometimes the letter carrier brings the happiest news. One day a few years ago, he delivered a beautifully embossed envelope. I guess I shouldn't have felt all that surprised by the card inside. After all, I had attended an event that had prompted this invitation (more about that in a moment). But I still felt quite a thrill of anticipation when I read:

His Royal Highness The Prince of Wales requests the pleasure of the company of Miss Diana Rivenburgh at the Cambridge Programme for Sustainability Leadership Alumni Reunion to be held at St. James's Palace on Thursday, 9th June 2011.

Well, when a prince invites you to a ball, what do you do? You cancel every other engagement, pack your best gown (or suit), book a flight, and

217

try to contain your excitement as a jumbo jet whisks you across the pond. During the flight, I fired up my Kindle and flipped through Prince Charles's recently published book, *Harmony: A New Way of Looking at our World.* In it, he puts forth a call for people to reconnect our businesses, our communities, our farms, and our lives with nature.

After landing safely in England, I did what any good international visitor does. I got sick as a dog with food poisoning. After an uncomfortable day and night trying to will myself back to some semblance of good health, I took a cab to St. James Palace, praying I would not repeat my performance as a 12-year-old girl when I went to church with a stomach virus and—but that's another story.

That day at the conference, His Royal Highness The Prince of Wales (HRH for short) joined a distinguished group of presenters speaking to a diverse group of leaders from around the world on various topics related to sustainability. I sat among executives from Nestlé, Unilever, Coca-Cola, Shell, Skanska, DuPont, Novo Nordisk, and Arup; educators from the University of Cambridge, the University of Michigan, and other top schools; thought leaders from the World Resources Institute and Forum for the Future; and directors of many major NGOs, among them Friends of the Earth and the Clinton Climate Initiative. I felt a bit like a lowly Cinderella at the Royal Ball. But as I listened to all these luminaries talking about a subject so dear to my heart that I had made it my life's work, I realized that we had much in common with each other.

The mission statement for the Cambridge Programme for Sustainability Leadership that HRH had helped establish in 1994 reflects my own passion: "To deepen leaders' understanding of the social, environmental and economic context in which they operate and help them to respond in ways that benefit their organizations and society as a whole." Of course!

Still, my growing comfort level (and settling stomach) did not prepare me for a personal chat with HRH during the seminar's lunch reception. In his earlier remarks, he had steadfastly asserted that the United States needed to step up and assume a stronger leadership role in the struggle to combat climate change and promote sustainable development. We ended up discussing the sad fact that political disagreements had thwarted the much-needed, sensible discussion of so many issues vital to the survival of the human race. A damaged environment, communities ravaged by poverty and illness, and a world fractured by distrust and anger would hurt all humans, all countries, and all of the companies that provide jobs and wages for the citizens of the world. I shared my view that the combined efforts of the United States government and the governments of all the nations on earth combined could not do as much to solve the world's most pressing problems as the business enterprises whose futures depend on the right solutions. Just before HRH departed at the polite insistence of his royal handlers, he smiled and said he would contact his friend Mike Duke, CEO of Walmart, to urge him to do more to promote sustainable agriculture. "Knock me over with a feather," I thought, "the glass slipper actually fits. I got a prince to make me a promise!"

As I have found with other tales involving princes, I could see a few underlying lessons in this story. Four, in particular, have kept cropping up during my unending quest to help companies adopt a new business model built around The New Corporate Facts of Life.

Lesson 1: You Can Meet the People You Need to Meet

Be a connector and get connected. One introduction can open a thousand doors. Strands of the same web connect all of the people on the planet. I met HRH through a series of events that started with one person in Atlanta, Georgia. Jorge Fernandez, Vice President for Global Commerce at the Metro Atlanta Chamber of Commerce, always connects me with the right people in the right places at the right times. When I once asked him, "Who should I meet in Singapore?" he shot back, smiling, "I'll introduce you to the U.S. ambassador there."

That's how I later came to meet HRH. I serve on the Atlanta Chamber's Global Commerce Committee, as well as its Environmental Policy and Sustainability Committee. Jorge and I often chat about attracting global companies to consider Atlanta as a location for their U.S. operations by promoting the city's sustainability efforts and strategies. It all comes down to linking sustainable growth to the bottom line and a high quality of life.

In 2010, Jorge introduced me to Karen Flanders-Reid, a former director of sustainability for Coca-Cola and currently working for the University of Cambridge Programme for Sustainability Leadership. Ding! That introduction eventually resulted in an invitation to join a consortium working to bring The Prince of Wales's Business and Sustainability Programme (BSP) to Atlanta. Through this group, I met leaders from many organizations committed to sustainable business, among them Coca-Cola, InterContinental Hotels Group, Haverty's Furniture, and the consulting firm PwC. I also connected with people from the University of Cambridge and with His Majesty's British Consul General, Annabelle Malins.

In May 2011, I attended the BSP held in Serenbe, about 30 minutes from the Atlanta airport, where I met Steve and Marie Nygren and discovered the sustainable community we explored in Chapter 6. My network expanded to include thought leaders and corporate executives intent on transforming the way companies do business. Participants in the program included leaders from Aflac, LaFarge, Boeing, Coca-Cola, PwC, Weston Foods, and Arup, to name a few, plus directors of NGOs, a college president, and a government official. One of the corporate participants, Denise Quarles, went on to become the Director of Sustainability for the City of Atlanta.

Attending the BSP placed me in an elite group of more than 4,000 leaders around the world who have attended senior executive seminars hosted by the University of Cambridge Programme for Sustainability Leadership (CPSL) across more than 40 countries. Each year, CPSL hosts an alumni reunion that brings together people from around the globe to learn more about the latest research from leading academic experts and business innovators, such as Jeffrey Immelt, CEO of GE, and Peter Voser, CEO of Royal Dutch Shell.

Many of the leaders I've met through the BSP have shared their ideas as I wrote this book. One of the faculty members, Matt Arnold, now a managing director and head of the Office of Environmental Affairs for JP Morgan Chase, later introduced me to John Gardner at Novelis, the company profiled in Chapter 8. And so the journey of a billion connections continues, one connection at a time.

Lesson 2: You Can Learn What You Need to Know

The week-long BSP taught me as much as a mini-MBA. I soaked up information like a sponge and forged new connections as if my life depended on making new friends. I also furiously scribbled notes about specific ways I could use all I was learning to help my clients. I, in turn, shared my knowledge and resources with others.

Such faculty members as Jonathon Porritt, founder director of Forum for the Future, Polly Courtice of the University of Cambridge, Kirsty Jenkinson from the World Resources Institute, and Professor Tom Gladwin from the University of Michigan created an outstanding learning experience for us all. And it did not take place in an ivory tower removed from the real world. It was a total down-to-earth, boots-on-the-ground experience where thought leadership shook hands with the real world and executives shared their sustainable, profitable business models. Michael Kobori, VP Supply Chain Social & Environmental Sustainability for Levi Strauss & Co., told us how his company had slashed 30 percent off the costs of goods through energy and water conservation. Twenty years earlier, the company had led its industry by establishing health, safety, and environmental supply chain standards. Later that week, on May 11, 2011, John Anderson, President and CEO of Levi

Strauss, publicly announced updated terms of engagement for the company's global supply chains to raise the bar even higher. It made me want to rush out and buy a new pair of Levis!

I learned to look at every activity as a potential school, every new contact as a potential teacher. And I tried to return the favor. I joined organizations such as the Women's Network for a Sustainable Future and participated in public-private sustainability initiatives with Georgia Tech, Emory University, and Sustainable Atlanta. They taught me, and I'd like to think I taught them. I read a lot of books, and I wrote a book myself. May the circle be unbroken.

Lesson 3: You Can Turn Every Problem into an Opportunity

During the BSP event in Serenbe, I encountered Jeff Seabright, Vice President for Environment and Water for Coca-Cola, who shared a story of the company's transformation. In 2004, the company's board of directors asked Neville Isdell, a 40-year veteran of the company, to return from retirement to help Coke get back its fizz. The company had been struggling ever since the death of CEO Roberto Goizueta in 1997. In a seven-year period, two CEOs had come and gone, and Coke's total return to shareholders had fallen far behind that of arch-rival PepsiCo. Employee morale had gone underwater. Shortly after he took the helm of this floundering ship, Isdell assembled the firm's top 150 executives to create a Manifesto for Growth that would include a sustainable growth model encompassing the 5 Ps: people, partners, profit, portfolio, and planet. Two short years later, the company had applied the tenets of this manifesto to transform every aspect of operations. Sales soared, staff turnover plummeted, employees became more engaged, and shareholder value rose dramatically.

I suppose by this point I don't need to say it again because I've said it so many times throughout this book, but I can't help myself:

Effective leaders do not see problems; they see opportunities for innovative, sustainable, and profitable solutions.

Lesson 4: You Can Lead from Where You Stand

Dr. Robert Franklin, the President of Morehouse College in Atlanta at that time, also attended the 2011 BSP. Morehouse College, founded in 1867, is the only historically all-male, black college in the United States, matriculating such notable leaders as Nobel laureate Dr. Martin Luther King Jr., filmmakers Samuel L. Jackson and Spike Lee, and Maynard Jackson, Atlanta's first African American mayor. Dr. Franklin told us that when Martin Luther King Jr. attended Morehouse, the school's president suggested to the young man that he make his anger redemptive and to allow his oppressors to find redemption as well. This advice reflects the institution's mission "to develop men with disciplined minds who will lead lives of leadership and service." It all began just two years after the end of the Civil War, when Atlanta's community leaders compiled a list of 37 men, some of them recently freed slaves, who would make up the first class at what later became Morehouse College. These so-called Morehouse Men learned to overcome obstacles, to strive to eradicate racism and oppression, and to make a difference in the world. I have found that the best business leaders pursue that same mission.

We can all do the same. We can lead from where we stand. We can lead without an official title or a big budget. We can start small, learn quickly, and bring others along the path to success.

If change doesn't happen in our organizations or our communities, we can't blame it on too few resources, the lack of mentors and partners, too little information and knowledge, or a closed door. Failure to change would come only as a lack of leadership. To paraphrase comic strip character Pogo's famous line, "We have met the solution, and the solution is us."

Or as Gandhi put it: "Be the change you wish to see in the world."

Notes

Introduction

1. David Cooperrider, founder of the Master's in Positive Organization Development program at Case Western Reserve University, developed the Appreciative Inquiry model of large-scale change used at the United Nations and at companies, communities, and governments around the world.

2. Chris Laszlo is associate professor at Case Western Reserve University, author of several books, including *Sustainable Value and Embedding Sustainability*, and founder of consulting firm Sustainable Value.

3. Richard Boyatzis, author of many articles and books on leadership and emotional intelligence, including as coauthor of the books *Primal Leadership* and *Resonant Leadership*.

4. Coping with Drought and Water Scarcity, a report to the U.S. Army Corp of Engineers by the Chronicles Group, is based on a panel discussion at the Center for Strategic and International Studies on June 17, 2010.

Chapter 1

1. Robert Costanza, Maureen Hart, Stephen Posner, and John Talberth, "Beyond GDP: The Need for New Measures of Progress," Boston University: The Frederick S. Pardee Center for the Study of the Longer-Range Future Report, The Pardee Papers, Number 4, January 2009.

2. Benefit Corporation Information Center description, available at http://benefitcorp.net/

3. Susan Kim and Erin McLaughlin. "Bank Transfer Day: Marches Planned on Banks Nationwide." November 5, 2011, available at http://abcnews.go.com/Business/bank-transfer-day-marches-planned-banks-nationwide/story?id=1488, September 29, 2012

4. Dan Currell and Tracy Davis Bradley, "Greased Palms, Giant Headaches, Harvard Business Review (September 2012): 21–23.

5. Jill Tucker, "Marin Schoolkids Want Crayola to Go Green," *San Francisco Chronicle*, SF Gate, May 30, 2012.

Chapter 2

1. In *The Fifth Discipline Fieldbook*, by Peter Senge et al., Rick Ross uses a similar process referred to as The Ladder of Inference.

2. Adam Kahane, *Transformative Scenario Planning: Working Together to Change the Future*, Kindle ed. (Berrett-Koehler, 2012).

Chapter 3

1. Robin White and Ray C. Anderson, *Confessions of a Radical Industrialist* (Blackstone Audio, 2010).

2. White and Anderson.

3. Interface, "Our Progress: Footprint" (2012), available at http://www.interfaceglobal.com/Sustainability/Our-Progress.aspx

4. Peter Lacy, Tim Cooper, Rob Hayward, and Lisa Neuberger, "A New Era of Sustainability: UN Global Compact-Accenture CEO Study 2010" (United Nations Global Impact, June 2010).

5. "Six Growing Tends in Corporate Sustainability: An Ernst & Young Survey in Cooperation with GreenBiz Group" (2012), available at http://www.greenbiz.com/sites/default/files/1112-1315117_CCaSS_SixTrends _FQ0029_lo%20res%20revised%203.7.2012.pdf

6. Homi Kharas, "The Emerging Middle Class In Developing Countries," OECD Development Centre Working Paper No. 285, Paris, France (January 2010).

7. "Growing Beyond: Innovating for the Next Three Billion: The Rise of the Global Middle Class—and How to Capitalize on It," Ernst & Young Global Ltd. (2011).

Chapter 4

1. UPS and Advanced BioHealing case study video transcript, available at http://www.ups.com/content/us/en/bussol/browse/industries/healthcare-case-studies.html

Chapter 5

1. See Novo Nordisk's "Blueprint for Change" programs, available at http://www.novonordisk.com/sustainability/how-we-manage/blueprints.asp

2. Excerpted from interviews with Novo Nordisk employees (2011).

3. Denison Consulting, "Impact on Performance 1995–2010" (2012), available at http://www.denisonconsulting.com/resource-library/impact-performance-1995-2010

4. Katie Thomas and Michael S. Schmidt, "Glaxo Agrees to Pay $3 Billion in Fraud Settlement," *New York Times*, July 2, 2012. http://www.nytimes.com/2012/07/03/business/glaxosmithkline-agrees-to-pay-3-billion-in-fraud-settlement.html?pagewanted=all

5. Iean Groeger, "Big Pharma's Big Fines," *ProPublica*, July 3, 2012, available at http://www.propublica.org/special/big-pharmas-big-fines (The article cites the Department of Justice as the original source.)

6. The Novo Nordisk Way Essentials, Novo Nordisk company Web site, available at http://www.novonordisk.com/about_us/novo_nordisk_way/nnway_essentials.asp

7. Interview with Laura Lee Bocade, DIRTT Environmental Solutions, Savannah, Georgia (July 2, 2012).

8. Novo Nordisk video on Facilitation, available at http://video.novonordisk.com/4465685/4855300/69cfbf2113a4b8f52278b7d8f7361866/video_medium/site/global-facilitation-making-video.mp4

9. Clarke examples are from interviews with John Lyell Clarke III and *Engaging the Whole for Transformative Change*, a video presentation given by John Lyell

Clarke III, President and CEO of Clarke, at the 2012 Sustainable Brands conference, available at http://www.sustainablebrands.com/digital_learning/ event-video/engaging-whole-transformative-change

Chapter 6

1. Peter Senge, *The Fifth Discipline: The Art & Practice of the Learning Organization* (Crown Business, 1994).

2. Paul Polman, Unilever Message from CEO, available at https://www.unileverusa.com/sustainable-living/ourapproach/messageceo/

3. Terry Unger, "Ted's Montana Grill CEO: In a 100-Yard Dash, I Give People a 99-Yard Leash," *Atlanta Journal Constitution*, Business Beat, October 20, 2012, available at http://blogs.ajc.com/business-beat/2012/10/20/teds-montana-grill-ceo-ëin-a-100-yard-dash-i-give-people-a-99-yard-leash'/?cxntfid=blogs_business_beat

4. Eric H. Kessler and James Russell Bailey (Eds.), *Handbook of Organizational and Managerial Wisdom* (Sage, 2007).

5. Lindsay Levin, *Invisible Giants: Changing the World One Step at a Time* (Vala Publishing, 2013).

6. Lindsay Levin, "Impact of Your Business," *British Airways Business Life*, April 2013, available at http://www.invisible-giants.com/coverage/in-ba-business-life/#sthash.R6m47oam.dpuf

7. J. P. Donlon, "40 Best Companies for Leaders 2012: How Top Companies Excel in Leadership Development," *Chief Executive*, January 12, 2012, available at http://chiefexecutive.net/40-best-companies-for-leaders-2012-how-top-companies-excel-in-leadership-development

8. Paul G. Schempp, 5 *Steps to Expert: How to Go from Business Novice to Elite Performer* (Davies-Black, 2008).

9. Rachel Parikh, "A Life-Changing Trip: Impact of SAP's First Quest (Parts 1 and 2), February 23, 2013, available at http://www.leadersquest.org/blog/a-life-changing-trip/ http://www.leadersquest.org/blog/a-life-changing-trip-the-impact-of-saps-first-quest-to-india-part-2/

10. Tom Rath and Barry Conchie, *Strengths-Based Leadership: Great Leaders, Teams and Why People Follow* (Gallup Press, 2009).

11. Richard E. Boyatzis, PhD, professor, Departments of Organizational Behavior,

Psychology, and Cognitive Science and the H.R. Horvitz Chair of Family Business, Case Western Reserve University.

12. Richard E. Boyatzis, Melvin Smith, and Ellen Van Oosten, "Coaching for Change," *People Matters* (June 2010): 69–71.

13. Barbara DeLollis, "CEO Profile: Starwood, Van Paasschen Both on the Move," *USA Today*, 2007, available at abcnews.go.com

14. Alexandra Berzon, "Starwood CEO Moves to China to Grow Brand," *Wall Street Journal*, June 6, 2011, available at http://online.wsj.com/article/SB10001424052702304563104576363771868768 108.html

Chapter 7

1. IHG has nine hotel brands in total: InterContinental® Hotels & Resorts, Hotel Indigo®, Crowne Plaza® Hotels & Resorts, Holiday Inn® Hotels and Resorts, Holiday Inn Express®, Staybridge Suites®, Candlewood Suites®, EVEN™ Hotels, and HUALUXE™ Hotels & Resorts.

2. Interviews with Paul Snyder, VP of Corporate Responsibility, Environmental Sustainability and Public Affairs; Maury Zimring, Director, Corporate Responsibility and Environmental Sustainability for IHG. The IHG Green Engage website is http://www.ihgplc.com/index.asp?pageid=742

3. Aon Hewitt, "2012 Trends in Global Employee Engagement," Aon Corporation, available at www.aonhewitt.com

4. "Herman Miller Achieves 100 Percent Green Electrical Energy," April 22, 2010, available at http://www.hermanmiller.com/about-us/press/press-releases/all/herman-miller-achieves-100-percent-green-electrical-energy-use.html

5. The Atlanta Institute of Technology example is based on an actual experience, but the names and details have been modified to protect the confidentiality of the institution and others involved in this project.

Chapter 8

1. Howard Schultz memo to CEO Jim Donald with the subject line, "The Commoditization of the Starbucks Experience" (February 14, 2007).

2. Patricia Sellers, "Starbucks' Schultz Needs to Get Real," *CNN Money*, November 11, 2008, available at http://postcards.blogs.fortune.cnn.com/2008/11/11/starbucks-schultz-needs-to-get-real/#sthash.etTgAZs8.dpuf

3. The first Novelis Sustainability Council, founded in fiscal year 2012, included the following external members selected to serve for three years: Matt Arnold, Head of Environmental Affairs, JP Morgan Chase; Stuart Hart, S.C. Johnson Chair in Sustainable Global Enterprise, Cornell University; Jeffrey Keefer, former Executive Vice President, DuPont; Miguel Milano, board member Instituto LIFE, Fundação O Boticário de Proteção a Natureza; and Jonathon Porritt, founder, Forum for the Future.

4. Jeff Davis, "Google: Innovation at the Pace of 100%," p. 2, available at www.arzika.com/Davis.pdf

5. Peter Bakker, President of World Business Council for Sustainable Development, "It All Begins and Ends with Measurement," March 5, 2013, available at http://president.wbcsd.org/

6. His Royal Highness, Prince Charles, The Prince's Accounting for Sustainability Project, available at http://www.accountingforsustainability.org/

References and Resources

Chapter 1

Anthony, Scott D. "The New Corporate Garage." *Harvard Business Review* (September 2012).

Apple. "iPhone 5 Pre-Orders Top Two Million in First 24 Hours." Apple Press Info (September 17, 2012), http://www.apple.com/pr/library/2012/09/17iPhone-5-Pre-Orders-Top-Two-Million-in-First-24-Hours.html

B Corps, http://www.bcorporation.net, http://www.bcorporation.net/patagonia

Bertelli, Patrizio. "Prada's CEO on Staying Independent in a Consolidating Industry." *Harvard Business Review* (September 2012): 39–41.

Block, Ben. "U.N. Raises 'Low' Population Projection for 2050." Worldwatch Institute (October 10, 2012), http://www.worldwatch.org/node/6038

Brock, John, Chairman and CEO of Coca-Cola Enterprises. Author's interview (May 18, 2011).

Brock, John. Insights on Leadership meeting at the Metro Atlanta Chamber of Commerce (October 9, 2012).

Carbon Disclosure Project (CDP). S&P 500 report (September 19, 2011), https://www.cdproject.net/en-US/Pages/SP500.aspx

Clinton, Bill. "Creating Value in an Economic Crisis." *Harvard Business Review* (September 2009): 70–71.

Clinton, Bill. "The Case for Optimism." *Time* (October 1, 2012).

Costanza, Robert, Maureen Hart, Stephen Posner, and John Talberth. "Beyond GDP: The Need for New Measures of Progress." Boston University: The

Frederick S. Pardee Center for the Study of the Longer-Range Future Report, The Pardee Papers, Number 4 (January 2009).

Court, David, and Laxman Narasimhan. McKinsey Quarterly. "Capturing the World's Emerging Middle Class." *Forbes* (July 22, 2010), http://www.forbes.com/2010/07/22/emerging-markets-globalization-marketing-leadership-citizenship-mckinsey.html

Currell, Dan, and Tracy Davis Bradley. "Greased Palms, Giant Headaches." *Harvard Business Review* (September 2012).

D'Aveni, Richard A. "When Consumers Win, Who Loses?" *Harvard Business Review* (September 2012): 36.

Dias, Washington. "The 22-Year-Old Who Led the Charge Against Bank of America." *Time* (November 7, 2011), http://www.time.com/time/nation/article/0,8599,2098715,00.html

Dubsky, Eoin. "Puma Leaps Ahead of Nike and Adidas in Detox Challenge." Greenpeace International (July 26, 2011), http://www.greenpeace.org/international/en/news/Blogs/makingwaves/puma-leaps-ahead-of-nike-and-adidas-in-detox-/blog/35881/

Fox, Emily Jane. "Wal-Mart, Gap Sign Bangladesh Safety Agreement." *CNN Money* (July 10, 2013), http://money.cnn.com/2013/07/10/news/companies/walmart-bangladesh-agreement/

GE and StrategyOne. "GE Global Innovation Barometer." Global Research Report (January 2012).

Gillies, Richard. "A Year of Progress and Change." M&S (September 29, 2012), http://www.marksandspencer.com/plana

Global Footprint Network. "Earth Overshoot Day" (September 25, 2009).

Global Impact Investing Network. "Impact Investing" (2009–2012), http://www.thegiin.org/cgi-bin/iowa/resources/about/index.html

Graham, Fiona. "M-Pesa: Kenya's Mobile Wallet Revolution." *BBC News* (November 22, 2010).

Hopkins, R. B. "What's Your Company's Sustainability Filter?" *MIT Sloan Management Review* (January 18, 2011).

Idea Watch Vision Statement. "Can Start-Ups Help Turn the Tide?" *Harvard Business Review* (September 2012).

Ideas Lab, "Global Innovation Barometer 2013," April 2013, http://www.ge.com/innovationbarometer/

Investopedia. "Businesses That Started During a Recession," July 20, 2013, http://www.investopedia.com/slide-show/recession-businesses/?article=1

Joint Roadmap, Version 2. Zero Discharge of Hazardous Chemicals Programme (June 2013).

Jones, Richard. "Finding Sources of Brand Value: Developing a Stakeholder Model of Brand Equity." *International Retail and Marketing Review*, 4, no. 2 (2008): 43–63.

Kyte, Rachel. "Mobile Phone Access Reaches Three Quarters of Planet's Population." *The World Bank, News & Views* (July 17, 2012).

Marks & Spencer. "About" (2011), http://plana.marksandspenser.com/about

Nidumolu, Ram, C. K. Prahalad, and M. R. Rangaswami. "Why Sustainability Is Now the Key Driver of Innovation." *Harvard Business Review* (September 2009).

Peterson, G.P., President of Georgia Institute of Technology. Author's interview (March 7, 2011).

Pool, Hannah. "Question Time with Hannah Pool." *The Guardian* (July 30, 2008), http://www.guardian.co.uk/business/2008/jul/31/5

Reuters. "German Court Removes Hurdle to Euro Zone Bailout" (September 12, 2012).

Scott, Lee, Wal-Mart. "21st Century Leadership" (October 24, 2005).

Shrinivasan, Rukmini. "Mobile Use up Six Fold Since 2000." *The Times of India* (July 18, 2012).

Siemens. "Sustainable Cities," http://www.usa.siemens.com/sustainable-cities/

Starbucks. "Responsibility," http://www.starbucks.com/responsibility

Trimble, Chris. "Reverse Innovation and the Emerging-Market Growth Imperative." *Ivey Business Journal* (March/April 2012).

Troianovski, Anton. "Health: Child's Play: Food Makers Hook Kids on Mobile Games." *Wall Street Journal* (September 18, 2012).

UNCTAD. "ICTs, Enterprises and Poverty Alleviation." Information Economy Report (2010).

UNEP Year Book 2012. "Closing and Decommissioning Nuclear Power Reactors" (2012): 36.

United States Environmental Protection Agency, Office of Transportation and Air Quality. "EPA and NHTSA Set Standards to Reduce Greenhouse Gases and Improve Fuel Economy for Model Years 2017–2025 Cars and Light Trucks." EPA-420-F-12-051 (August 2012).

Unruh, Gregory, and Richard Ettenson. "Winning in the Green Frenzy." *Harvard Business Review* (November 2010): 111–112.

Walmart. "Environmental Sustainability," http://corporate.walmart.com/global-responsibility/environment-sustainability

World Wildlife Foundation, Global Footprint Network and ZSL Living Conservation. "Living Planet Report" (2012), http://wwf.panda.org/about_our_earth/all_publications/living_planet_report/2012_lpr/

Chapter 2

Lipkin, Nicole. *What Keeps Leaders Up at Night*. New York: AMACOM, 2013.

Losad, Marcial, and Emily Heaphy, "The Role of Positivity and Connectivity in the Performance of Business Teams," *American Behavioral Scientist*, 2004.

MIT Sloan Management Review and The Boston Consulting Group. "Sustainability Nears a Tipping Point." Research Report. (Winter 2012).

Thurm, Ralph. "Towards Zero-Impact Growth: Strategies of Leading Companies in 10 Industries." Study by Deloitte Innovation B.V. (2012).

Unilever. "Sustainable Living," http://www.unilever.com/sustainable-living/ourapproach/messageceo/index.aspx

Yunus, Muhammad. *Building Social Business: The New Kind of Capitalism that Serves Humanity's Most Pressing Needs*. New York: Public Affairs, 2010.

Chapter 3

Caterpillar. "Vision, Mission, Strategy," http://www.caterpillar.com/sustainability/vision-mission-strategy

Hankey, Jennifer. "Toxic Flame Retardants in Children's Products-Children's Plush Toys." Organic Baby University (June 12, 2011), http://organicbabyuniversity.com/blog/2011/06/toxic-flame-retardants-in-your-home-part-2-childrens-plush-toys/

Hawkin, Paul. *The Ecology of Commerce*. New York: HarperCollins, 1993.

Kouzes, James M., and Barry Z. Posner. "To Lead, Create a Shared Vision." *Harvard Business Review* (January 2009).

Makower, Joel, and the editors of GreenBiz.com. "State of Green Business 2013, GreenBiz Group and Trucost" (2013).

Oliberté Limited, http://www.bcorporation.net/community/directory/oliberte

Roddick, Dame Anita. "The Body Shop, About Us," http://www.thebodyshop.com/services/aboutus_anita-roddick.aspx

Schomer, Stephanie. "The 100 Most Creative People in Business 2012." Fast Company, http://www.fastcompany.com/most-creative-people/2012/tal-dehtiar

TheCityUK. "Next Generation Vision," http://www.nextgenerationvision.co.uk/

Toor, Amar Toor. "Japan to Reduce Rare Earth Consumption in Response to China's Export Controls." engadget.com (February 8, 2012), http://www.engadget.com/2012/02/08/japan-china-rare-earths-consumption/

Toyota Motor Corporation. "Toyota Global Vision," http://www.toyota-global.com/company/vision_philosophy/toyota_global_vision_2020.html

Virgin Group. "About Virgin," http://www.virgin.com/about-us

Chapter 4

Carbon Disclosure Project. "Climate Disclosure Leadership Index 2012 and 2011."

Information was also obtained from "UPS Corporate Sustainability Report 2011," "UPS Materiality Matrix 2012," and the UPS Web site, www.ups.com

Interbrand. "Third Annual Best Global Green Brands Report" (June 12, 2013).

The following UPS leaders provided the author with information and examples for this chapter: Kurt Kuehn, Scott Wicker, Ross McCullough, Michael Johnson, Patrice André, Paul Nieminen, Dean Foust, and Karen Kreager.

United States Environmental Protection Agency, Center for Corporate Climate Leadership. "2012 Climate Leadership Award Winners," http://www.epa.gov/climateleadership/awards/2012winners.html

Chapter 5

Clarke, John Lyell, CEO of Clarke. Author's interview.

Cox, Diane, Novo Nordisk. Author's interviews.

Denison, Daniel, Robert Hooijberg, Nancy Lane, and Colleen Lief. *Culture Change in Global Organizations*. San Francisco: Jossey-Bass, 2012.

Kimball, Charlie. "Taking the American Dream to Victory Lane," http://www.charliekimball.com/about.php

Smed, Mogens Smed, Tracy Baker, and Laura Lee Bocade. Author's interviews with DIRTT executives (May 2013).

Chapter 6

Boyatzis, Richard E., Anthony Jack, Regina Cesaro, Masud Khawaja, and Angela Passarelli. "Coaching with Compassion: An fMRI Study of Coaching to the Positive or Negative Emotional Attractor." Case Western Reserve University (January 13, 2010).

Boyatzis, Richard, and Annie McKee. *Resonant Leadership*. Boston: Harvard Business School Press, 2005.

Chouinard, Yvon. "The Company as Activist." Greenbiz.com, Greenbiz Forum Presenters Yvon Chouinard and Joel Makower (March 1, 2013), http://www.greenbiz.com/video/2013/03/01/patagonia-responsible-company

Chouinard, Yvon, Jib Ellison, and Rick Ridgeway. "The Sustainable Economy." *Harvard Business Review* (October 2011).

Nishimizu, Micko, World Bank, http://www.sophiabank.co.jp/english/about/partners/nishimizu.html

Nygren, Steve, Serenbe. Author's interview. (2013).

Rivenburgh, Diana. "Leadership for a Sustainable World: Combining Profit and Purpose" (2008).

Rivenburgh, Diana. "Strategic Imperatives Inc., BOLDEST Leadership Competency Model" (2013).

World Travel and Tourism Council 13th Global Summit in Abu Dhabi, http://www.wttc.org/news-media/news-archive/2013/wttc-issues-wake-call-private-and-public-sector-work-closely-tog/

Chapter 7

Blacksmith, Nikki, and Jim Harter. "Majority of American Workers Not Engaged in Their Jobs: Highly Educated and Middle-Aged Employees Among the Least Likely to Be Engaged," http://www.gallup.com/poll/150383/majority-american-workers-not-engaged-jobs.aspx

Brock, John, CEO of Coca-Cola Enterprises. Author's interview (May 18, 2011).

Contextual Stakeholder Engagement,
http://www.usabilitynet.org/tools/contextualinquiry.htm and
http://www.usabilitynet.org/tools/userobservation.htm

Cooperrider, David L., and Michelle McQuaid. "The Positive Arc of Systemic Strengths: How Appreciative Inquiry and Sustainable Designing Can Bring Out the Best in Human Systems." *Journal of Corporate Citizenship* 46 (Summer 2012). © Greenleaf Publishing 2013.

Kimmet, Pamela, SVP of Human Resources for Coca-Cola Enterprises. Author's interview, 2013.

Nussbaum, Bruce, "How to Find and Amplify Creativity." *Harvard Business Review* (March 7, 2013),
http://blogs.hbr.org/cs/2013/03/how_to_find_and_amplify_creati.html

Practically Green, www.practicallygreen.com

Swartz, Jeff. "Timberland's CEO on Standing Up to 65,000 Angry Activists." *Harvard Business Review* (September 2010).

World Café, http://www.theworldcafe.com/about.html

Chapter 8

Gardner, John, Chief Sustainability Officer (author's interview, 2013). Information about Novelis also obtained from the company's 2011 and 2012 Sustainability Reports.

McKinsey Quarterly. "Starbucks' Quest for Healthy Growth: An Interview with Howard Schultz" (March 2011).

Rivenburgh, Diana. "Ten Strategies for Designing a Resilient Organization." Strategic Imperatives Inc. (2013).

Starbucks. "2012 Global Responsibility Report."

Index